the
best vegetarian
recipes

the
best vegetarian
recipes

FROM GREENS TO GRAINS,
FROM SOUPS TO SALADS:
200 BOLD-FLAVORED RECIPES

Martha Rose Shulman

WILLIAM MORROW
75 YEARS OF PUBLISHING
An Imprint of HarperCollins*Publishers*

FOR LIAM

FIRST EDITION

DESIGNED BY LEAH CARLSON-STANISIC

Printed on acid-free paper

Library of Congress Cataloging-in-Publication Data

Shulman, Martha Rose.
    The best vegetarian recipes : from greens to grains, from soups to salads : 200 bold-flavored recipes / by Martha Rose Shulman.—1st ed.
        p.   cm.
    Includes index.
    ISBN 0-688-16827-2
    1. Vegetarian cookery.   I. Title.
TX837 .S467697 2001
641.5'636—dc21

                                                                00-065350

        01   02   03   04   05   QW   10 9 8 7 6 5 4 3 2 1

contents

Acknowledgments

Sometimes books begin as one thing and halfway through the process evolve into something else. That's what happened here, and I am grateful to my editor, Harriet Bell, for steering this project into the book that it has become. Thanks also to Andrea Chesman for thoughtful copyediting suggestions.

As always, thanks to my agent, Molly Friedrich.

And of course, thanks to Bill again, for liking just about everything I cook.

Introduction

I began my career as a vegetarian cook more than twenty-five years ago, when vegetarianism was considered to be a counterculture fad. Vegetarianism has come a very long way since those days, as our food and flavor horizons have broadened and our appreciation for unadulterated seasonal produce has deepened. Many people think nothing of going without meat for a few days, though they wouldn't call themselves vegetarians. I don't define myself as a vegetarian anymore; but at heart, it's the way I prefer to eat, and the way my family and I eat at home most of the time.

This is a book for occasional and full-time vegetarians who are looking for the best vegetarian recipes—vivid-tasting dishes that require little fuss, that you can rely on both for everyday dining and for entertaining. Many of them can be thrown together using nothing more than the ingredients in a well-stocked pantry, such as pasta, rice, or chickpeas; canned tomatoes, olive oil, garlic, and herbs.

What makes a good recipe? When I pose that question I think of a time in my life when I was learning to cook. I learned from recipes. We ate well at home, although differently than I eat now—it was a meat-centered diet—and the dishes I first learned to make were those I was used to eating for dinner. I would tell my mother what I wanted to cook, and she would direct me to the recipe in the cookbook she used for that particular dish. I would follow the recipes step by step, and they always worked. A good recipe, then, is one that both a beginner and a seasoned cook can follow with consistent results. And those results must be enticing, pleasing to the palate, with familiar yet evocative flavors.

Of course, the ingredients have to be good to begin with, or no recipe, no matter how well written or brilliantly conceived, will give you the best results. Fortunately, there is now a nationwide demand for high-quality ingredients. The recipes here will allow you to take advantage of all the marvelous resources for food that we have today—farmers' markets, whole foods stores, supermarkets with huge produce selections, Internet grocery services for those who find it difficult to get to a market, and specialty food catalogs and Internet sites.

The Lingering Myths of Vegetarianism

Even though vegetarian eating has become much more mainstream over the years, and many people who are not vegetarians appreciate the joys and benefits of a vegetarian diet, it still remains mysterious to some people. Their concerns are not much different than they were twenty-five years ago: They wonder about getting enough protein, not getting too many carbohydrates, and time requirements.

- PROTEIN • Getting enough protein is really not a problem for vegetarians if the diet is a varied one that includes beans, whole grains, dairy, and/or soy products. Proteins are made up of amino acids, eight of which can be obtained only from food. These are the "essential amino acids." High-protein foods such as meat, fish, eggs, soy, and dairy products have high amounts of all eight amino acids and are known as "complete proteins." Plant foods, such as grains and legumes, are good sources of some of the essential amino acids but lack others. We obtain the absent amino acids from bacteria in our own digestive tracts and by combining foods that have amino acids that complement one another. This can be done in the course of a day, or at a given meal. Nature has been very accommodating with the distribution of these proteins; foods that naturally pair together for gastronomic reasons (beans and grains, tofu and rice, grains or pasta and dairy products) also complement one another in the protein department. Examples of dishes in this book that provide complete plant protein are Rice Pilaf with Chickpeas; Couscous with Chickpeas, Greens, and Fennel; Polenta with Tomato Sauce, Sage, and Beans; and all of those containing tofu. Eggs and dairy products provide a valuable source of high-quality protein as well, and you'll find plenty of those dishes here.

- CARBOHYDRATES • Some of the most popular and successful diets that have come along in the past decade have been low-carb diets. I believe that overall calorie consumption is the most important aspect of weight control. And since one of the easiest ways to keep calories down is to keep fat consumption low, a moderately low-fat vegetarian diet is a sensible way to go.

If you have found, however, that you have had success with weight control by eating a low-carbohydrate diet, you can still enjoy a vegetarian diet. In place of pasta, concentrate on the egg and dairy recipes, the salads and vegetable soups, the vegetable and the tofu recipes. Choose whole grains such as bulgur, millet, and barley over white rice, couscous, and potatoes. When you do eat rice, choose basmati, which is the least starchy of the rices, and avoid risottos.

- TIME REQUIREMENTS • Feeding yourself and your family well requires a certain amount of time, but so does shopping for prepared food. Certainly it's not an unreasonable amount, and vegetarian cooking doesn't have to be any more time-consuming than other cooking. Many dishes in this book are quickly made; some of the pasta sauces, for example, can be assembled in the time it takes for water to come to a boil. Canned beans can often replace dried; quick-cooking grains, such as bulgur, couscous, and quinoa, require very little effort; tofu marinades require no cooking at all; and omelets take just minutes to prepare.

As in all cooking, the more organized you are, and the more experience you gain in the kitchen, the more efficient you will be. Having a well-stocked pantry is essential to eating well and doing so easily, for vegetarians as well as meat-eaters. With basic ingredients on hand and the recipes that follow, you may need to market only once a week, but you will eat well every day.

Putting Together a Vegetarian Meal

Menus can be daunting for any cook, and particularly for a beginning vegetarian cook. My menu philosophy for everyday family meals is to focus a meal around one dish, and fill out the menu from there. If the dish I have in mind is pasta, it's easy: All I need is a salad and some bread. The same goes for most soups. But, say, I want to make a gratin with the lovely greens and tomatoes I bought at the market. This by itself may not be enough to constitute a meal: I can't accept the vision of it sitting alone on a plate. So I'll cook some grains or a potato dish, or corn in season, to serve on the side. If it's summer and I've come home with a basket of corn, tomatoes, and green beans, I may make a green bean and tomato stew and serve it with the corn; or if I don't serve the stew with the corn, I'll serve it over pasta. The pantry really helps when it comes to putting together menus, because by accompanying a light vegetable dish with grains, noodles, or beans, I've got a main-dish plate. One-dish meals are much more the norm in vegetarian cooking than in traditional meat cookery: A couscous topped with stew, a pasta or risotto or minestrone, a stir-fry with rice or a hot-pot with noodles constitutes dinner. I usually follow a main dish, no matter what it is, with a salad. But a salad can also precede the main dish, or it can be the meal.

For entertaining, I like to serve filling, hearty, showy favorites like risottos, stews served over couscous or noodles, and pastas, preceded or followed by a salad, depending on whether I've made something else as a first course. I might make a frittata or a tart as an appetizer to serve with drinks, or serve croutons topped with a spread. I consider the overall composition of the meal and color. I don't want all the dishes to be "busy" and complex, and I want the ethnic composition to be consistent, or at least complementary. If the main dish is one with muted colors, I try to garnish it with something bright, or serve a bright dish alongside. I also avoid repeating pronounced flavors in every course: If there is a lot of garlic in the hors d'oeuvre and the main dish, I won't put garlic in the salad dressing. If I'm serving a tart or omelet as an hors d'oeuvre or first course, my main dish will not be based on eggs or cheese. My menus for entertaining always include dessert, whereas for everyday dining they don't. My mother taught me long ago that guests might not remember anything else they ate at a dinner party, but they always, "especially the men," remember the dessert.

The Well-Stocked Pantry

A healthy pantry extends from the cupboard to the refrigerator to the freezer. You don't need tons of space, but you need a cabinet or two large enough to hold a selection of cans; some bags of pasta, rice, grains, and beans; and bottles of vinegar, oil, soy sauce, and spices. If your kitchen is a tiny apartment kitchen and the space isn't there, use a shelf in the linen closet or coat closet.

CANNED, BOTTLED, AND PACKAGED GOODS

Canned tomatoes in juice (both 28-ounce and 14-ounce size) • Prepared pasta sauce • Canned beans, such as chickpeas, white beans, and black beans • Canned or bottled roasted peppers • Bottled salsa (red or green) • Canned vegetable broth

NONPERISHABLE STAPLES

Italian pasta: several shapes and sizes • Asian pastas such as buckwheat noodles (soba) and wheat noodles (somen) • Long-grained white rice • Basmati rice • Italian Arborio rice for risottos • Brown rice • Couscous • Bulgur • Wild rice • Millet •

Wheat berries • Pearl barley • Kasha (buckwheat groats) • Quinoa • Polenta • Lentils • Black beans • Chickpeas • Black-eyed peas • White beans • Pinto beans • Flour • Sugar

OILS, VINEGARS, FLAVORINGS, AND CONDIMENTS

Extra virgin olive oil • Canola oil* • Asian sesame oil* • Peanut oil* • Red wine vinegar or sherry vinegar, or both • Balsamic vinegar • Rice wine vinegar • Soy sauce • Asian chili paste* • Chipotles en Adobo • Capers* • Dijon mustard* • High-quality vegetable bouillon cubes • Dried mushrooms • Harissa* • Salt • Pure vanilla extract • Pure almond extract • Vanilla beans • Dried herbs and spices (bay leaves, oregano, thyme, rosemary, caraway, cayenne pepper, crushed red pepper flakes, chile powder, cinnamon, coriander seeds, cumin seeds, curry powder, whole nutmeg, black peppercorns)

WINES AND SPIRITS

Dry white wine* • Dry sherry* • Red wine (such as Merlot or Côtes du Rhône) • Triple Sec, Cointreau, or Grand Marnier • Kirsch

VEGETABLES AND FRUIT

Onions • Garlic • Potatoes • Lemons (a few) • Fresh fruit in season • Oranges

REFRIGERATOR

Gruyère • Parmesan (save the rinds for flavoring soups) • Goat cheese • Feta cheese • Imported brine-cured black olives • Fresh ginger • Tofu (firm Chinese-style): not essential if you're not a tofu eater • Eggs • Cottage cheese • Yogurt • Milk • 2 to 4 vegetables: good keepers such as broccoli, carrots, green beans, sugar snap peas, zucchini, winter squash, beets, bell peppers, cabbage, romaine lettuce

FREEZER

Frozen peas • Whole-grain bread • Corn tortillas • Homemade stock, if possible

*Refrigerate after opening

How to Follow a Recipe

Cooking schools teach cooks to prepare all ingredients ahead and arrange them in separate containers. This is called a *mise en place*. It's a good practice, particularly for beginning cooks. It makes it easier to be neat and precise as you cook, and you never get into a panic because everything is there in front of you.

As you become more experienced and confident, you'll find that you might not need to prep everything before, that you can actually be measuring out an ingredient or preparing another while the onions are cooking or the water is coming to the boil. As my colleague Deborah Madison points out in her excellent book, *Vegetarian Cooking for Everyone*, cooking is not a linear activity. For example, you begin boiling the pasta water first, although the pasta is the last thing you cook. But to understand the order and rhythm of cooking you need some experience.

1. *Read the recipe all the way through first.* This is essential, no matter how much experience you have. After all these years of cooking, I still regret it if I don't read a recipe through. You'll be able to visualize the dish, and you won't be hit with surprises while cooking the food.
2. Get out the ingredients called for. You don't necessarily have to prepare them all, but they should be nearby.
3. Get out the equipment that you'll need (steps 2 and 3 can be reversed).
4. Decide on serving dishes. Will you be serving directly from the pan or in separate serving dishes? Will you serve the plates in the kitchen or at the table?
5. Prepare ("prep") the ingredients as instructed, or at least decide what needs to be prepped first. Measure out seasonings or have them at the ready with dry measuring spoons.
6. Read through the recipe again, then proceed step by step as directed.

TASTING AND SEASONING

Following a recipe isn't all there is to cooking. If it were, everybody would be a good cook. *To succeed with a dish, you have to taste.* You are not finished with the dish until you have tasted and approved it. Keep a special spoon (not the cooking spoon) handy for tasting. Different cooks taste at different times. I usually taste toward the end of cooking, while others taste constantly throughout. What I am looking for is *flavor*. Think of the best dishes you've ever eaten. Their flavors were vivid. This is how you want your food to taste. If you don't feel that the flavors linger long enough on your palate, or that the ingredients are in sharp focus, ask yourself first if there's enough salt. It's very common for dishes to be undersalted.

Sometimes it's a bit more garlic that's needed, or maybe another pinch of herbs or a bit of acid, like a sprinkle of lemon juice or peel. Or does it need a bit more heat? Cayenne or more chile pepper? Remember that your clove of garlic may be smaller than mine, and the jalapeño I used to test a recipe might be hotter than yours. In the end, the flavors of your dish depend on your taste buds.

If you're not exactly sure what the recipe needs, ladle or spoon out a small amount into a small bowl. Add a little bit of what you think it needs; for example, sprinkle on a very small amount of salt or a drop of lemon juice, give the mixture a stir, and taste. You will know when you've hit it right.

Spreads, Dips, and CONDIMENTS

The recipes in this chapter are primarily dips and spreads that I serve most often as welcoming openers when friends come for dinner. Be it a dinner party or friends stopping by for drinks, or just one friend sharing a meal with us, I always try to have something ready to eat when people arrive at the door. It can be something simple, such as imported olives, a bowl of beautiful radishes, or roasted almonds, that requires no preparation at all, just a well-stocked pantry. But if I do have time, I'll make a lusty spread, such as Tapenade, Spicy Red Pepper Spread, Hummus, or White Bean Pâté, and serve it on toasted croutons, a thinly sliced baguette, or on country bread.

Also included here are an assortment of sauces, salsas, and dips. Robust sauces, such as Cilantro Sauce or Romesco Sauce, can transform the simplest meal of grilled vegetables, polenta, or grains into a feast, and they also make great toppings for tofu, bruschetta, or crostini.

For those who are looking for ways to work more soy foods into their diets, there are Tofu Green Goddess Dressing and Tofu Mayonnaise, both terrific, high-protein, low-fat substitutes for mayonnaise, and they make great dips as well as spreads.

Finally there are condiments to have on hand for use in dishes like Tunisian stews and pastas. Harissa, a North African chile paste, and Gremolata, a mixture of lemon zest, parsley, and garlic, will add a new dimension to a pasta or vegetable dish. And Yogurt Cheese is used in many ways. Like a spreadable cheese, it can be used for sandwiches or dips, but I use it also for frozen yogurt or a dessert topping and for some Mediterranean salads.

roasted red peppers

Roasted red peppers are wonderful to have on hand, to eat as a salad, or to add to salads, pastas, bruschetta, sandwiches, and other dishes. They can also be blended into a spread or sauce, as they are in the Spicy Red Pepper Spread on page 5. Whenever you find that you have some peppers lingering in the refrigerator, even if the skins are beginning to shrivel, you can roast them and make good use of them. Peppers that are roasted in the oven or grilled under a broiler or above a gas flame or on an actual grill are all often referred to as roasted peppers. Grilling them gives you that nice charred flavor, but roasting them in the oven is neater and yields more juice, which is great for sauces and for marinating the peppers. Broiling is the quickest.

4 medium red or yellow bell peppers
Coarse salt and freshly ground black pepper to taste

OPTIONAL
1 to 2 tablespoons extra virgin olive oil
1 tablespoon red wine vinegar or balsamic vinegar
Minced or pressed garlic to taste
2 tablespoons slivered fresh basil or thyme leaves

1. Preheat the oven to 400°F. Line a baking sheet or pan with foil.

2. Place the peppers on the foil and bake in the hot oven for 30 to 45 minutes, until the peppers are soft and the skin is brown and puffed. Using tongs, turn the peppers every 10 minutes.

3. Remove from the heat and transfer to a bowl. Cover the bowl with a plate and let sit for 30 minutes or longer.

4. Carefully remove the skins and seeds from the peppers, holding them over the bowl so you don't lose any of the liquid. Cut into wide or thin strips. Toss with salt and pepper in another bowl, and strain in the juice.

5. Add the olive oil, vinegar, and/or the garlic, if you are using these ingredients. Refrigerate until you are ready to serve. Serve chilled or at room temperature.

6. Toss with the basil, if you wish, shortly before serving.

Advance preparation: Roasted peppers will keep for at least 5 days in the refrigerator. Keep the peppers submerged in their own juice topped up with olive oil, which will help preserve the peppers.

- GRILLED PEPPERS • Grilling the peppers directly over a flame goes quickly if you only have one or two peppers and they have straight, smooth sides. Use gas burners or a gas or charcoal grill.

  Turn on the burner or prepare a medium fire in a grill. Place the peppers directly over the flame. Grill, turning the peppers with tongs or two long spoons, until uniformly charred. Remove from the heat and place in a bowl covered with a plate or in a plastic or paper bag until cool enough to handle. The pepper will continue to soften. Peel the pepper and rinse with cold water. Pat dry and cut in half over a bowl to catch any juice. Remove seeds and membranes, and slice as above.

- ROASTED PEPPERS, USING THE BROILER • Preheat the broiler. Line a baking sheet with foil. Place the peppers on the baking sheet and place under the broiler, 2 or 3 inches from the heat (at the highest setting). Broil, watching the peppers and turning often (every 2 to 4 minutes), until uniformly charred, as above. Remove from the heat and proceed as in the instructions for grilled peppers, above.

spicy red pepper spread

I adapted this spread from *The Melting Pot: Balkan Food and Cookery* by Maria Kaneva-Johnson and serve it spread on toasted croutons as a dinner-party starter. Guests always rave. Make it ahead if you can; it keeps well in the refrigerator. **MAKES ABOUT 1 CUP**

*2 pounds (6 medium or 4 large) fleshy red bell peppers,
    roasted (see page 3)
2 to 3 hot chiles, preferably red ones
2 tablespoons tomato paste
1¼ teaspoons salt, or more to taste
2 garlic cloves
¼ cup extra virgin olive oil*

1. Roast the chile peppers in the oven or grill along with the bell peppers. Use the directions for roasted red peppers (page 3), but check more frequently.

2. When the peppers have softened thoroughly and are cool enough to handle, peel and remove the seeds and membranes (wear plastic gloves to handle the chiles). Rinse and transfer to a food processor fitted with the steel blade.

3. Add the tomato paste and puree the peppers with the paste until smooth.

4. Combine the pepper mixture with ¼ cup water and 1 teaspoon of the salt in a heavy nonstick skillet and bring to a simmer over medium heat. Cook, stirring, for about 10 minutes. Meanwhile, place the garlic cloves in a mortar with ¼ teaspoon salt and pound to a paste. Stir the oil and garlic into the peppers and continue to simmer for another minute or two, until the sauce is quite thick.

5. Remove from the heat, cool, and refrigerate in a covered bowl or jar.

Advance preparation: This spread keeps for 2 weeks in the refrigerator.

tapenade

Tapenade is a Provençal olive paste that traditionally contains anchovies, capers, and herbs, as well as the rich black olives of the region. This vegetarian version, without the anchovies, is marvelously pungent. Use imported black olives; don't use canned California olives, which have a metallic taste that does not resemble the flavor of Mediterranean olives. An olive/cherry pitter will help to make this recipe a snap. You can also pit the olives by crushing them with the flat side of a knife and pulling out the pit. Serve the tapenade with croutons, or spread on baby cherry tomatoes and other baby vegetables. **MAKES ABOUT 1½ CUPS**

½ pound imported black olives
2 large garlic cloves
1½ tablespoons capers, drained and rinsed
1 teaspoon fresh thyme leaves or ½ teaspoon dried
1 teaspoon chopped fresh rosemary or ½ teaspoon crumbled dried
1 teaspoon Dijon mustard
2 tablespoons fresh lemon juice
2 tablespoons extra virgin olive oil
Lots of freshly ground black pepper
Chopped fresh herbs or sprigs

1. Pit the olives, using either an olive/cherry pitter or the flat side of a knife. (Lay the olive on a cutting board, lay the flat side of a chef's knife on the olive, and push down hard so that the olive splits. Then remove the pit.) Make sure you have discarded all the pits, and that there are none with the olives.

2. Turn on a food processor fitted with the steel blade and drop in the garlic. When it is chopped, turn off the machine and scrape down the sides. Add the olives, capers, thyme, rosemary, and mustard. Blend together until fairly smooth. Add the lemon juice, oil, and pepper. Continue to blend until you have a smooth paste.

3. Scrape into an attractive serving bowl and garnish with the herbs. Refrigerate until ready to serve.

Advance preparation: This keeps for 2 weeks in the refrigerator.

herbed goat cheese dip

The distinctive flavor of the goat cheese is what stands out here, even though most of the volume of the dip comes from the nonfat cottage cheese. Serve this dip with crudités, use it as a sandwich spread, or spread it over warm Buckwheat Crêpes (page 130). **MAKES ABOUT 1½ CUPS**

1 to 2 garlic cloves
½ pound nonfat cottage cheese (about 1 cup)
¼ pound mild, fresh goat cheese, such as Montrachet
¼ cup plain nonfat yogurt
½ cup chopped fresh herbs, such as parsley,
 chives, dill, tarragon, or basil
Salt and freshly ground black pepper to taste

1. Turn on the food processor and drop in the garlic. When the garlic is chopped and adhering to the sides of the bowl, stop the machine, scrape down the sides, and add the cottage cheese. Process until fairly smooth. Scrape down the sides and add the goat cheese and yogurt. Process until very smooth.

2. Transfer to a bowl and stir in the herbs. Taste and add salt and pepper as desired. Refrigerate until you are ready to serve.

Advance preparation: The dip can be made a day ahead, but the fresher it is, the better.

yogurt cheese

Yogurt, particularly nonfat yogurt, has a high water content and can be thickened by being drained in a cheesecloth-lined strainer over a bowl for a few hours. It will lose half of its water and become thick and spreadable, almost like fresh cheese in consistency. You can serve it plain, as a spread, dip, or topping; or season it with herbs and/or garlic, or with honey for desserts. **MAKES 1 CUP**

2 cups plain nonfat yogurt

Line a strainer with a double thickness of cheesecloth and set it over a bowl. Or you can use a large coffee filter in a Melita, as long as your Melita doesn't smell too much of coffee. Place the yogurt in the strainer or filter and refrigerate for at least 1 hour and preferably 4 hours or longer. Transfer to a covered container and refrigerate.

Note: You can also purchase a yogurt strainer (mine is a Progressive Yogurt Strainer) in some kitchen equipment stores.

Advance preparation: This will last through the sell-by date on your yogurt. It will continue to give up water in the container, which you can simply pour off.

hummus

I don't care how much hummus there is out there in the market, none will be as good as the hummus you make at home, following this recipe. Commercial hummus has more tahini—sesame paste—and more oil than this version, and the garlic and lemon are often not fresh, so it's never as vivid or fresh tasting as it should be. This takes just minutes to prepare if you use canned chickpeas. Serve it as a topping on bread, crostini, or crudités—it's especially nice on cucumber rounds—or keep it around for sandwiches. **MAKES ABOUT 2 CUPS**

2 garlic cloves, peeled
2 cups cooked or canned chickpeas,
    rinsed and drained
Salt to taste
½ teaspoon ground cumin
¼ cup fresh lemon juice
2 tablespoons extra virgin olive oil
3 to 4 tablespoons plain nonfat yogurt or
    broth from the beans
2 to 3 tablespoons sesame tahini

Turn on the food processor and drop in the garlic. When the garlic is chopped and adhering to the sides of the bowl, stop the food processor and scrape down. Add the chickpeas, salt, and cumin, and turn on the machine for about 30 seconds. Stop the machine, scrape down the sides, and start the machine again. With the machine running, add the lemon juice, olive oil, and 3 tablespoons yogurt or broth, and blend until smooth. Add the tahini and blend again. Taste and adjust salt. The hummus requires a fair amount. Thin out with more yogurt if desired. Transfer to a bowl and refrigerate until ready to serve.

Advance preparation: This keeps for 2 to 3 days in the refrigerator. It will become more pungent as it ages.

white bean pâté

This savory spread can be cut into slices for a first course, served as an hors d'oeuvre on croutons, or eaten for lunch in a sandwich. For best results, make the pâté a day or two ahead of serving. The delicate flavors will mature overnight in the refrigerator. It looks very pretty when made in a traditional pâté mold. **MAKES ABOUT 8 SERVINGS**

1 heaped cup dried navy beans or small white beans,
*   picked over and washed*
1 medium onion, chopped
5 large garlic cloves, 2 crushed, 3 minced
1 bay leaf
2 teaspoons salt, plus more to taste
1 tablespoon extra virgin olive oil
2 large eggs
2 tablespoons fresh lemon juice
½ cup fresh bread crumbs
Freshly ground black pepper
*   (about 10 twists of the mill)*
¼ teaspoon dried thyme

1. Soak the beans in water to cover for 6 hours or overnight.

2. Drain the beans and combine with 4 cups water in a saucepan or bean pot. Bring to a boil and skim off any foam that rises during the first few minutes. Add half the onion, the crushed garlic cloves, and the bay leaf. Cover, reduce the heat to low, and simmer for 1 hour. Add salt to taste (about 1 teaspoon) and continue to cook, until the beans are very tender, 30 to 60 minutes.

3. While the beans are cooking, heat the oil in a heavy nonstick skillet over medium heat. Add the remaining chopped onion. Cook, stirring, until tender, 3 to 5 minutes. Add the minced garlic and cook, stirring, until fragrant, about 1 minute. Remove from the heat and transfer to a medium bowl. Set aside.

4. When the beans are tender, remove from the heat. Drain through a colander placed over a bowl. Measure out ⅓ cup of the cooking liquid and set aside. Remove and discard the bay leaf. Oil a loaf pan or a 1-quart pâté mold and preheat the oven to 400°F.

5. Puree the beans in a food processor fitted with the steel blade until smooth. Scrape down the sides and add the eggs, lemon juice, and about 1 teaspoon salt. Turn on the machine and add the ⅓ cup cooking liquid from the beans. Process until completely smooth.

6. Scrape the beans into the bowl with the onion. Stir in the bread crumbs, pepper, and thyme. Pour or scrape into the oiled baking dish, cover tightly with foil or a lid, and place in the oven. Bake for 50 to 60 minutes, until the top is just beginning to color.

7. Allow to cool, then chill until you are ready to serve, or serve warm. This is best if it has a day to mature in the refrigerator.

Advance preparation: The pâté keeps for 4 days in the refrigerator and can be frozen for 2 to 3 months.

salsa fresca

There are hundreds of bottled salsas available, but nothing will taste as good as the salsa you make from fresh ripe tomatoes in season. Serve with tacos and quesadillas, with chips or refried beans. The vinegar or lime juice is necessary if the tomatoes have a dull flavor, which they will if they are out of season, but look for sweet juicy local ones. Lime juice has a more traditional Mexican flavor, but balsamic vinegar will add the sweetness that the tomatoes may lack. **MAKES ABOUT 2 CUPS**

¼ small red onion, minced and rinsed with cold water
1 pound fresh, ripe tomatoes, finely chopped
1 to 3 jalapeño or serrano chiles,
    minced (seed them for a milder salsa)
4 to 5 tablespoons chopped fresh cilantro
2 teaspoons fresh lime juice or
    balsamic vinegar (optional)
Salt and freshly ground black pepper to taste

1. Toss together all the ingredients.

2. Allow to stand at room temperature for 15 to 30 minutes before eating, if possible, so that the flavors will blend and ripen.

Advance preparation: The salsa is best served the day it's made, but you can make it a few hours ahead.

- SALSA WITH AVOCADO • To the above salsa, add 1 small avocado, diced small.

- SALSA WITH BLACK BEANS • To the above salsa (or the Salsa with Avocado), add one 15-ounce can black beans, drained and rinsed.

- SALSA WITH CORN • Steam the kernels from 1 ear fresh corn for 5 minutes (on or off the cob), then refresh with cold water, and add to the above salsa.

Working with Chiles

First of all, to avoid irritating your hands and any other part of your body you touch with your hands after handling fresh chiles, wear rubber gloves or surgical gloves (you can buy them at the pharmacy). If you are not seeding the chile—if you like things hot and the seeds contain lots of capsaicin, which is what makes hot peppers hot—then cut away the stem, quarter lengthwise, and mince, using a quick up-and-down sawing motion with your chef's knife. If you wish to remove the seeds, for a milder dish, quarter the chiles lengthwise and cut away the seed pod using a paring knife. To seed large jalapeños, hold the pepper by the stem and cut off the tip, about ⅛ inch from the bottom. Stand on a cutting board on the cut end and, holding the pepper by the stem, slice off the sides. You'll be left with the stem, seeds, and inner membranes to discard in one piece. Slice or mince the chile as directed.

cilantro sauce

The first time I tasted this, I was struck by the harmonious marriage of the intense, sweet dried fruit and the cilantro and other savory herbs—a delightful combination. **MAKES 2 CUPS**

2 ounces dried apricots (about ⅓ cup)
¼ cup shelled walnuts
4 garlic cloves
¼ cup fresh lemon juice
1 to 1½ teaspoons salt, or to taste
Freshly ground black pepper to taste
Pinch of cayenne
1½ cups chopped cilantro leaves (2 good-size bunches)
1 cup chopped fresh parsley
½ cup chopped mixed basil, tarragon, and dill
¼ cup walnut oil

1. Place the dried apricots in a bowl and pour in boiling water to cover (at least 1 cup). Let sit for at least 1 hour, more if possible, so that the soaking liquid will be sweet and flavorful. Drain over a measuring cup and retain ½ cup of the soaking water.

2. Put the walnuts in the bowl of a food processor fitted with the steel blade and turn on. With the machine running, drop in the garlic. As soon as the garlic adheres to the sides of the bowl, stop the machine and scrape down. Add the drained apricots, lemon juice, salt, pepper, and cayenne to the bowl and process to a puree. Add the cilantro, parsley, and mixed chopped herbs and puree, stopping the machine to scrape down the sides several times. Combine the walnut oil and soaking water from the apricots, and with the machine running, gradually add it to the puree. Process until smooth.

3. Transfer the puree to a bowl and let it sit for 1 hour. Taste and correct the salt.

Advance preparation: The sauce keeps for 2 to 3 days in the refrigerator. Bring to room temperature before using.

tofu mayonnaise

This low-fat, high-protein mayonnaise can be used in all the ways that regular mayonnaise is used—as a spread for sandwiches, a dressing for salads, or a dip for crudités. It can be made with regular tofu, but silken tofu will result in a smoother texture with no hint of chalkiness. The small amount of regular mayonnaise gives this sauce a mayonnaise flavor with a fraction of the calories. **MAKES ABOUT 1 CUP**

2 tablespoons fresh lemon juice
1 tablespoon vinegar
    (wine, sherry, cider, or rice wine vinegar)
1 garlic clove, minced
1 teaspoon Dijon mustard
2 tablespoons plain nonfat yogurt or buttermilk,
    plus additional for thinning
½ pound silken tofu
1 to 2 teaspoons dark soy sauce,
    such as tamari or Kikkoman
¼ teaspoon salt
2 tablespoons extra virgin olive oil
    or canola oil
2 tablespoons Hellmann's or
    Best Foods mayonnaise (optional)

Combine all the ingredients in a blender or food processor and blend until completely smooth. Thin with water or additional yogurt if desired.

Advance preparation: This keeps for 3 to 4 days in the refrigerator.

romesco sauce

This is a simplified, lighter version of authentic Spanish romesco sauce, which is made with both almonds and hazelnuts, and more olive oil. Grilled or broiled peppers and tomatoes replace some of the nuts and oil here, while still capturing the texture and spice. The pungent sauce is thick enough to spread on crostini or tofu but also can be stirred into a bowl of beans or rice, or dolloped onto polenta, or eaten with grilled or steamed vegetables.   **MAKES ABOUT 2 CUPS**

1 large red bell pepper
3 medium tomatoes or 4 plum (Roma) tomatoes (about ¾ pound)
2 large garlic cloves
¼ cup toasted almonds
2 thick slices (about 2 ounces) baguette or
    country-style bread, lightly toasted
1 to 2 teaspoons pure ground chile powder or
    red pepper flakes, to taste (pepper flakes are hotter)
1 tablespoon chopped fresh flat-leaf parsley
1 teaspoon paprika
1 to 1½ teaspoons salt, or to taste
Freshly ground black pepper to taste
2 tablespoons sherry vinegar
¼ cup extra virgin olive oil

1. Preheat the broiler and cover a baking sheet with foil.

2. Place the pepper on the baking sheet and grill under the broiler, 2 to 3 inches from the heat (at the highest setting), and turn every 3 minutes or so, until uniformly charred. Remove from the baking sheet and place in a plastic bag, twist the bag shut, and set aside to cool.

3. While waiting for the pepper to cool, place the tomatoes on the baking sheet and place under the broiler 2 to 3 inches from the heat (at the highest setting). Broil for 2 to 4 minutes, until charred on one side. Turn over and broil on the other side for 2 to 4 minutes, until charred. Remove from the heat, transfer to a bowl, and allow to cool.

4. When the pepper is cool enough to handle, remove the charred skin (you can do this under running water), cut the pepper in half lengthwise, and remove the core, seeds, and membranes. When the tomatoes are cool enough to handle, peel and core.

5. Turn on a food processor fitted with the steel blade and drop in the garlic cloves. When the garlic is chopped and adheres to the sides of the bowl, stop the machine and scrape down the sides. Add the almonds, bread, and chile powder and process to a paste. Scrape down the sides of the bowl and add the roasted pepper, tomatoes, parsley, paprika, salt, and pepper. Process until smooth. With the machine running, add the vinegar and olive oil in a slow stream. Process until well amalgamated.

6. Scrape the sauce into a bowl. Taste and adjust seasoning, adding salt or chile powder as desired. If possible, allow the sauce to stand for an hour at room temperature before using.

Advance preparation: The sauce keeps for several days in the refrigerator; the garlic will become more pungent over time.

Toasting Nuts

I usually buy almonds already toasted, but they are easy to toast in the oven. Nuts of all kinds toast quickly, so keep a vigilant eye on them.

Place the nuts on a baking sheet. Preheat the oven to 375°F. Place in the oven and roast 10 minutes, or until the nuts smell toasty and are beginning to brown. Remove from the heat and transfer at once to a bowl. If you leave them on the hot baking sheet they will continue to roast and may burn.

tofu green goddess dressing

Tarragon gives this creamy dressing its extraordinarily vibrant flavor. Use silken tofu for the best texture. Serve with asparagus or artichokes, as a sandwich spread, or thin and use as a dressing on green, spinach, or tomato salads. **MAKES 1¼ CUPS**

2 tablespoons fresh lemon juice
1 tablespoon vinegar (wine, sherry, cider, or rice wine vinegar)
1 teaspoon Dijon mustard
2 tablespoons plain nonfat yogurt or buttermilk, plus additional for thinning
½ pound silken tofu
1 to 2 teaspoons dark soy sauce, such as tamari or Kikkoman
¼ teaspoon salt
2 tablespoons extra virgin olive oil or canola oil
2 tablespoons Hellmann's or Best Foods mayonnaise (optional)
1 to 2 tablespoons chopped fresh tarragon
2 tablespoons chopped scallion, white and light green parts (optional)
¼ cup chopped fresh parsley or spinach

Combine all the ingredients in a blender or food processor and blend until completely smooth. Thin with water or additional yogurt if desired.

Advance preparation: The dressing keeps for 2 to 3 days in the refrigerator.

Salads

T_he recipes in this chapter_ are, for the most part, salads that can start or end a meal, or be eaten as a side dish. There are also main-dish salads, such as Black-Eyed Peas with Cumin Vinaigrette and Wheat Berry Salad. Whether they are part of a meal or the meal itself, what all of these dishes have in common is a fresh, vibrant character, the result of contrasting textures, the use of fresh herbs, and the choice of fresh produce in season tossed with just the right amount of tangy dressing. The range of ingredients you can use is endless. Most salads are based on lettuces, and today's markets offer you a wide choice. But other vegetables like cucumbers, carrots, bell peppers, and mushrooms shouldn't be overlooked, and cooked vegetables—potatoes, beets, broccoli—also wear dressings very well. More substantial salads can be made with beans, grains, and eggs.

As clothes make the man, a dressing can define a salad. It's important that the ingredients in your dressing be of the highest quality. Olive oil should be extra virgin, walnut oil should taste of walnuts. Explore other nutty oils, such as roasted peanut oil and Asian sesame oil, an ingredient used in Asian dishes. As for vinegars, I use sherry vinegar for most of my salads, but a good red wine vinegar can also be used. For some salads, Asian rice wine vinegar is appropriate. Balsamic vinegar is another ingredient I use in dressings, but I usually use it in combination with more acidic vinegars, so the dressing won't be too sweet. Lemon or lime juice replaces vinegar or is used in conjunction with it in some dressings for a tangy citrusy flavor that doesn't have the bite of vinegar.

The simplest ingredients can be transformed into a salad. If I have a can of chickpeas, some vinegar, olive oil, and garlic on hand, I have the makings for a salad. Red bell peppers, roasted or raw, broccoli, cucumbers, and romaine lettuce are all good keepers and can be transformed easily into salads. Stale bread is never thrown away, but sliced, rubbed with garlic cloves, and added to lettuces and other vegetables (especially tomatoes) to soak up the dressing and add pungency and crunch to the dish. Other leftovers in my refrigerator—cooked vegetables and grains, beans, and pasta—will see their way into a salad with a tart and luscious dressing long before they're ready to be thrown out.

Tips for Successful Salads

Use fresh herbs, such as tarragon, chives, basil, dill, or parsley, to season salads. • Wash and dry lettuces, greens, and herbs thoroughly. • Toss leafy salads with just enough dressing to coat the leaves just before serving. • Tear lettuces gently to avoid bruising. • Use scissors to cut up fresh herbs. • Add bright green vegetables and herbs to dressed salads shortly before serving, unless instructed otherwise.

Using Leftovers and Pantry Items in Salads

- Cooked and raw vegetables can be the basis for a salad (think of potato salads). Roasted peppers are a favorite; when you see them beginning to shrivel, roast them up. Some of the best salads from North Africa are made with cooked carrots, cooked zucchini, and cooked eggplant. A cooked vegetable tossed with a simple vinaigrette, or simply lemon juice, olive oil, garlic, and salt can be truly delicious. Grilled vegetables also make good salads.

  If you have bits and pieces of vegetables, such as peppers and cucumbers, in the refrigerator, or if you have herbs that you haven't used up, chop and combine them with grains—quick-cooking grains like couscous, bulgur, or rice—or with canned beans. And vice versa—if you have leftover grains or beans, toss them with a dressing.

- Combine foods of different textures. For example, if you are going to make a salad of leftover beans, include something crunchy, such as diced pepper or onion.

- For main-dish salads, add a high-protein item from the pantry, such as beans or hard-boiled eggs. Pantry items can garnish, fill out, or be the basis for a salad. The most useful are:

  - Canned roasted peppers • Olives (particularly imported brine-cured black olives) • Capers • Canned beans • Rice, bulgur, couscous, pasta • Parmesan cheese • Goat cheese • Walnuts, pecans, pine nuts • Chipotle chiles • Eggs • Potatoes • Bread (fresh or stale, for croutons)

Washing and Drying Lettuce

Lettuce, even the precut brands, is sandy, so it must be washed before you make a salad. It's the main task in salad making.

FOR HEADS OF LETTUCE

Fill the bottom part of a salad spinner, a large bowl, or half of a double sink with cold water. While you are running the water, break the leaves off the head and run each one under the water, turning them over once and rubbing the base of the leaf between your thumb and forefingers; the sand sticks in that curved bit at the base of the leaf. Place the leaves in the bowl or sinkful of water. Swish them around with your hands or, if your sink has a spray nozzle, run the spray into the water full blast to swish the leaves around and knock sand off the leaves. (This is one of the greatest uses for spray nozzles.) Put the top part of a salad spinner or colander over a bowl or over the other half of your sink. Lift the leaves out of the water with your hands and transfer to the colander or top of the spinner. Don't dump it out or the sand will go with it. Drain the sandy water out of the sink or bowl in which you swished around the salad leaves, and rinse away all the sand. Fill again with water, and submerge the lettuce again. Swish it around once more, lift from the water, and transfer again to the top of your spinner or to a colander set over a bowl or sink so water won't run all over your counter or floor. Spin dry, or if you don't have a spinner, put a clean, dry dish towel on your counter. After you've washed the lettuce, shake each leaf over the sink, and lay the lettuce on top of the towel in one layer. Place another towel on top and gently press down, or roll the bottom towel up so that you have a roll of lettuce between two towels.

PRECUT LETTUCE

These will be much less sandy, but the greens still need a swish. Fill your sink or bowl with cold water as above. You don't have to rinse the leaves under running water. Put in the lettuces and swish around, with your hands or with the spray nozzle. Lift from the water and drain. You don't have to repeat the rinsing process with most precut lettuce.

classic vinaigrette

A classic French vinaigrette can be made with extra virgin olive oil, vegetable oil, or a combination. I prefer olive oil, but if I am making a large amount of dressing, I often combine canola oil and olive oil. The formula I have always followed for oil to acid proportions is 3 parts oil to 1 part acid (vinegar or lemon/lime juice); for every tablespoon of vinegar or lemon juice, I use 3 tablespoons oil. These proportions are not set in stone, however. Some people prefer a stronger dressing, others like to show off their high-quality olive oil to better advantage. Use this recipe as a guideline, but feel free to vary amounts. Vinaigrette and the low-fat variations that follow are classic dressings for lettuce salads, both mild and pungent, and spinach salads. They also go beautifully with grain salads, potato salads, bean salads, carrot salads, and green bean salads. **MAKES ABOUT ½ CUP**

> *2 tablespoons wine, sherry, or*
> *Champagne vinegar*
> *Salt to taste*
> *1 teaspoon Dijon mustard*
> *1 very small garlic clove, minced*
> *⅓ cup extra virgin olive oil*
> *Freshly ground black pepper to taste*

Stir together the vinegar, salt, and mustard. Add the garlic, then whisk in the oil and add pepper. Keep at room temperature, or if not using within a few hours, refrigerate. Allow to come to room temperature before using.

- LEMON VINAIGRETTE • Substitute lemon juice for all or part of the vinegar.

- WALNUT VINAIGRETTE • Walnut oil is one of the most fragrant of oils, and you don't need much to make a very aromatic dressing. The dressing goes well with bitter chicories, such as radicchio, Belgian endive, frisée, curly endive, and escarole. It also makes a perfect dressing for wild rice and other grain salads. Substitute 2 to 3 tablespoons walnut oil for 2 to 3 tablespoons of the olive oil. For a low-fat version, substitute nonfat yogurt or low-fat buttermilk for the rest of the olive oil.

- BALSAMIC VINAIGRETTE • Add 1 to 3 tablespoons balsamic vinegar to the Classic Vinaigrette. Good with pungent greens like arugula.

Making Dressings Ahead

Advance preparation for salad dressings: Salad dressings that contain lemon juice hold less well than vinegar-based dressings, as the flavor of the lemon juice becomes harsher over time. Garlic will also become more pungent, though this is less obvious in a sharp vinegar-based, mustardy vinaigrette. As a rule of thumb, I try not to make lemon juice–based dressings more than a couple of hours ahead of serving. Vinegar-based dressings will keep for a week in the refrigerator, though the garlic becomes more pungent. See Vinaigrette for the Week, page 32, for a solution to this problem.

cumin vinaigrette

Cumin gives this vinaigrette a Mediterranean/Mexican flavor. It goes particularly well with substantial bean, egg, and grain salads, and it's also very nice with carrot salads, both cooked and raw. **MAKES ABOUT ½ CUP**

1 tablespoon fresh lemon juice
1 tablespoon red wine, sherry, or
*   Champagne vinegar*
1 small garlic clove, minced
⅛ to ¼ teaspoon salt
½ teaspoon ground cumin
½ teaspoon Dijon mustard
⅓ cup extra virgin olive oil
Freshly ground black pepper to taste

Mix together the lemon juice and vinegar with the garlic, salt, cumin, and Dijon mustard using a fork or a small whisk. Stir in the olive oil. Add pepper to taste.

• LOW-FAT CUMIN VINAIGRETTE • For a low-fat dressing, replace the ⅓ cup olive oil with 1 tablespoon olive oil and 4 tablespoons plain nonfat yogurt or 5 tablespoons low-fat buttermilk. Add 1 tablespoon water, more to taste, if using yogurt.

lime balsamic vinaigrette

This dressing, with its hint of sweetness, goes well with spicy, peppery greens, such as arugula and cress; bitter chicories, such as Belgian endive and escarole; sturdy greens, such as dandelion greens and beet greens; tomato salads; and grain salads. **MAKES ABOUT ⅓ CUP**

2 tablespoons fresh lime juice
2 teaspoons balsamic vinegar
Salt and freshly ground black pepper to taste
1 small garlic clove, minced (optional)
¼ teaspoon Dijon mustard
5 tablespoons olive oil

Combine the lime juice, vinegar, salt and pepper, garlic, and Dijon mustard. Whisk in the olive oil.

• LOW-FAT LIME BALSAMIC VINAIGRETTE • Replace the 5 tablespoons olive oil with 1 tablespoon olive oil and ¼ cup low-fat buttermilk or plain nonfat yogurt. Add 1 tablespoon water, if using yogurt.

Low-Fat Salad Dressings

If you are trying to reduce calories in your overall diet, use these low-fat dressings where yogurt or buttermilk stands in for most of the oil; you won't feel deprived. The yogurt-based dressings are tart, because whenever you reduce the fat in an acidic dish, the acid becomes more pronounced. A small amount of olive oil smooths out the flavor.

yogurt or buttermilk vinaigrette

MAKES ABOUT ½ CUP

2 tablespoons red wine, sherry, or Champagne vinegar,
or 1 tablespoon fresh lemon juice and
1 tablespoon vinegar
1 small garlic clove, minced or pressed
Salt to taste
1 teaspoon Dijon mustard
1 tablespoon extra virgin olive oil
4 tablespoons plain nonfat yogurt or 5 tablespoons low-fat buttermilk
Freshly ground black pepper to taste

Mix together the vinegar, garlic, salt, and Dijon mustard using a fork or a small whisk. Stir in the olive oil, yogurt, and 1 tablespoon water. (Do not add water if using buttermilk.) Add black pepper to taste. Thin with additional water as desired.

• LEMON YOGURT OR BUTTERMILK VINAIGRETTE • Omit the vinegar and use 2 tablespoons fresh lemon juice.

asian dressing

Serve this nutty, gingery dressing with Asian greens, such as mizuna, tatsoi, and baby bok choy, and with buckwheat noodles and other Asian noodle salads. **MAKES ABOUT ½ CUP**

1 tablespoon fresh lime juice
1 tablespoon rice wine vinegar or
balsamic vinegar
1 small garlic clove, minced or pressed
1 to 2 teaspoons finely minced fresh ginger
1 tablespoon soy sauce, such as tamari or Kikkoman
½ teaspoon Asian hot chile oil or pinch of
cayenne pepper (optional)
1 tablespoon Asian sesame oil
4 to 5 tablespoons low-fat buttermilk or
plain nonfat yogurt
Salt and freshly ground black pepper to taste

Stir together the lime juice, vinegar, garlic, ginger, soy sauce, and chile oil. Whisk in the sesame oil and buttermilk. Thin with water, if desired, and add salt and pepper to taste.

tomato vinaigrette

This vinaigrette should only be made with tomatoes in season. Serve it with pasta or over grains. **MAKES ABOUT ¾ CUP**

½ pound ripe tomatoes, peeled, seeded, and
*   very finely chopped or crushed in a food processor*
*   or mini food processor*
1 garlic clove, minced
1 tablespoon balsamic vinegar
1 tablespoon red wine or sherry vinegar
Salt and freshly ground black pepper to taste
2 tablespoons extra virgin olive oil
2 tablespoons chopped fresh basil

Stir together all the ingredients. Let sit for 10 to 15 minutes before using.

vinaigrette for the week

This recipe makes a week's supply for me and my husband, but we are only two, so it might not stretch as far for you if your family is bigger. The reason many vinaigrettes should not be made too far in advance is that the lemon juice, if called for, becomes quite acidic, and the garlic becomes very strong. I do away with the lemon juice here, using just vinegar, but I temper the wine vinegar with a bit of balsamic. The garlic is sliced, so that it flavors the dressing but doesn't go into the salad. To prevent the garlic from going into the salad, spear the slices onto a toothpick, or use a squirt bottle. I also make this more acidic than a vinaigrette should be. That way, if you want to use yogurt instead of oil for some of the fat, you can add it just before tossing the salad; or you can add additional oil. **MAKES ABOUT 1 CUP**

1 tablespoon balsamic vinegar
5 tablespoons sherry vinegar or red wine vinegar
Salt (preferably sea salt) to taste
1 tablespoon Dijon mustard
⅓ cup extra virgin olive oil
⅓ cup canola oil (or omit and use ⅔ cup extra virgin olive oil)
2 garlic cloves, cut into slices lengthwise
⅓ cup plain nonfat yogurt, or use an additional ⅓ cup olive oil

1. Whisk together the vinegars, salt, and mustard. Whisk in ⅓ cup olive oil and ⅓ cup canola oil (or ⅔ cup olive oil). If you are going to keep the dressing in a container without a squirt top, run a toothpick through the slices of garlic, keeping them separated on the toothpick so that the surfaces are exposed to the dressing. Add the garlic. Transfer to a container, preferably one with a squirt top. Refrigerate until you are ready to serve.

2. If you are serving all the dressing at once, whisk in the yogurt or the additional oil. If you are using only part of the dressing, as I do, shake the dressing well and measure out 3 tablespoons. Add 1 tablespoon olive oil or yogurt and whisk together well. If the yogurt makes the dressing too thick, thin with a little water. The proportions, then, for additional yogurt or olive oil are 1 part yogurt or olive oil to 3 parts dressing.

Advance preparation: The dressing keeps for a week in the refrigerator.

mixed greens with beets, goat cheese, and walnuts

I think of this as a winter salad, even though beets are in season year-round in southern California. I make it more often than any other salad, especially when I'm entertaining, during the fall and winter months. There are a number of wonderful flavors and textures working alongside each other here—sweet beets and pungent greens, soft goat cheese and crunchy walnuts, all doused with a nutty dressing. **MAKES 6 SERVINGS**

4 medium beets (red, golden, or a combination)
½ to ¾ pound salad greens, preferably a mixture of
    baby spring greens and arugula
⅓ cup walnut pieces, preferably from fresh shelled walnuts
1 ounce fresh, mild goat cheese, such as Montrachet,
    crumbled (about ¼ cup)
1 to 2 tablespoons chopped fresh herbs, such as chives,
    tarragon, or parsley (optional)

DRESSING
1 tablespoon balsamic vinegar
2 tablespoons sherry vinegar or red wine vinegar
Salt and freshly ground black pepper
1 small garlic clove, minced (optional)
½ to 1 teaspoon Dijon mustard
3 tablespoons walnut oil
4 tablespoons olive oil or plain nonfat yogurt

1. Preheat the oven to 425°F.

2. Cut away the beet leaves by slicing across the top end, about ½ inch above where the stems and root meet (save the leaves for another use). Scrub the beets under warm water with a vegetable brush. Place in a baking dish and add about ¼ inch of water. Cover and bake for 30 to 60 minutes, depending on the size of the beets. Medium-size beets take about 45 minutes, small ones 30 minutes, and large ones take 1 hour. Test for doneness by sticking a knife into a beet. It should slide in easily. Remove from the oven and allow to cool. When the beets are cool, it will be easy to slip their skins off. Skin and cut in half lengthwise, then slice the beets very thin, or cut into small wedges.

3. If the nuts are not very fresh and just shelled, roast them for 15 minutes in a 350°F oven, until just toasty. Transfer immediately to a plate or bowl.

4. Toss the beets with the salad greens, walnut pieces, goat cheese, and fresh herbs.

5. Make the dressing: Mix together the vinegars, salt and pepper, garlic, and mustard. Whisk in the oils. Taste; if you want the dressing to be a bit more acidic, add another teaspoon of sherry or wine vinegar. If the dressing was made with yogurt, thin with water.

6. Toss the salad with the dressing and serve.

Advance preparation: The cooked beets will keep for 3 to 4 days in the refrigerator. The dressing can be made several hours ahead of serving.

Preparing Herbs

Herbs, like lettuces, are also sandy, particularly the leafy ones, such as parsley and cilantro, that are sold in bunches. The sand lodges down in the stems and sticks to the leaves (although you might not see it).

PARSLEY, BASIL, TARRAGON, DILL

Stem, wash, and dry following the directions for lettuce. After you spin-dry the herbs, wrap in paper towels for a few minutes to blot any remaining water. Place in a wide jar or a glass measuring cup. Take a pair of kitchen scissors, point the tips straight down in the jar, and cut the herbs with the scissors.

CHIVES

Hold the bunch in your hand and run under cold water or plunge several times into a bowl of cold water. Shake over the sink, then roll up in paper towels, and let drain for a few minutes. Either snip with scissors or lay on a cutting board and cut across the bunch.

CILANTRO

Fill a bowl or the bottom of your salad spinner with water. Hold the bunch, leaves facing down, and plunge into and out of the water several times. Drain the water and rinse out the bowl. Repeat until sand no longer accumulates in the water. Shake the cilantro over the sink, then spin a couple of times in the salad spinner, emptying out the water from the bowl between spins. Then wrap in a few layers of kitchen towel and let it sit for a few minutes. To cut, with the cilantro still in a bunch, lay on a cutting board and, using a sharp chef's knife, cut across the leafy end of the bunch so that you are cutting slivers off the leaves. Don't worry if little bits of stem are mixed in.

THYME

Rinse, dry, and pull the little leaves from the stem by running the stem between your finger and thumb, from the top to the bottom.

ROSEMARY

Rinse, dry, and pull the leaves from the stems, from top to bottom. Chop on a cutting board or in a jar or glass with scissors.

If you mince herbs on a board, use quick strokes and a very sharp knife; hold the handle in one hand and rest your other hand on top of the blade. Mince rapidly, pushing the herbs back to the center of your board as they spread out.

SLIVERING BASIL AND MINT

Wash and dry the leaves. Pile them on top of each other, and using scissors or a very sharp knife, cut crosswise into thin slivers.

turkish romaine and yogurt salad

This is much like the cucumber and yogurt salad made in Greece and Turkey, called tzatziki or cacik. Instead of cucumber, finely shredded romaine is used. The salad is quickly thrown together and makes a very refreshing appetizer. **MAKES 4 TO 5 SERVINGS**

2 cups Yogurt Cheese (page 8)
2 to 3 garlic cloves, or more to taste,
    pounded to a puree with salt
Salt and freshly ground black pepper to taste
½ pound hearts of romaine, cut into chiffonade
    (shredded; see page 37)
1 tablespoon dill or mint, chopped
1 tablespoon extra virgin olive oil (optional)

Beat together the yogurt, garlic, and salt and pepper. Stir in the lettuce and mound in a bowl. Sprinkle on the dill and drizzle on the olive oil. Serve at once.

Advance preparation: The yogurt and garlic mixture can be prepared and the lettuce cut up hours ahead; keep both in the refrigerator. The salad should be assembled just before serving.

Pureeing Garlic

The easiest way to puree garlic is to pound it in a mortar and pestle. Adding salt helps to break down the garlic. In the bowl of a mortar and pestle, combine ¼ teaspoon salt with the number of garlic cloves called for in the recipe. Pound the mixture to a paste. Pounded garlic is quite pungent.

Another way to puree garlic, without getting quite as pungent a mixture, is to set the clove of garlic on a cutting board, with ¼ teaspoon of salt next to it. Take a small sharp knife, or even a butter knife, and scrape the edge of the blade down the side of the garlic clove, picking up a little salt with the knife and mixing the scraped garlic with it as you work. Continue scraping the clove until only a bit of the clove is left, then mash what is left with the remaining salt.

Chiffonade

Chiffonade are thin, crosswise slivers of lettuce. To make them, pile up 3 or 4 leaves of clean, dry lettuce, roll the lettuce lengthwise, then cut across the roll with a sharp kitchen knife. The slivers should be about ¼ inch thick unless otherwise specified.

shredded romaine salad

Radishes and romaine lettuce go nicely together because of their compatible crunch and contrasting colors. The romaine is cut into thin strips here, rather than left whole. The dressing is much simpler than a vinaigrette, just lemon juice or vinegar, olive oil, and a small amount of yogurt. **MAKES 4 SERVINGS**

1 large romaine lettuce, washed and dried
1 bunch scallions, finely chopped
6 to 8 red radishes, sliced or quartered
Quartered hard-boiled eggs (optional)
Olives (optional)

DRESSING
2 to 3 tablespoons fresh lemon juice, or red wine vinegar or cider vinegar
¼ cup extra virgin olive oil
Salt to taste
2 to 4 tablespoons plain nonfat yogurt

1. After washing and drying the lettuce, and if not serving the salad right away, wrap in a clean dish towel, seal in a plastic bag, and refrigerate in the vegetable bin of your refrigerator for at least 1 hour.

2. Meanwhile, mix together the ingredients for the dressing and place in the bottom of your salad bowl.

3. Stack the lettuce leaves and cut into thin chiffonade (see page 37). Place in the salad bowl on top of the dressing. Add the scallions and radishes. Refrigerate until just before serving. Toss with the dressing and serve, garnished, if you wish, with quartered hard-cooked eggs and/or olives.

Advance preparation: The prepared vegetables and dressing will keep, separately, for several hours in the refrigerator.

tomato, feta, and arugula salad

This is one of the many summer salads I indulge in daily when tomatoes are in season. **MAKES 4 TO 6 SERVINGS**

1½ pounds sweet, ripe, firm tomatoes, cut into wedges
Salt to taste
1 large bunch arugula, tough stems removed, washed, and dried
        (about 4 cups)
1 ounce feta cheese, crumbled (about ¼ cup)
2 teaspoons balsamic vinegar
4 teaspoons sherry vinegar or red wine vinegar
¼ cup extra virgin olive oil or 1 tablespoon olive oil
        and 3 tablespoons plain nonfat yogurt or buttermilk
Freshly ground black pepper to taste

1. Toss the tomatoes with the salt. Add the arugula and feta.

2. Whisk together the vinegars and olive oil, or olive oil and yogurt or buttermilk. Thin with water, if desired.

3. Toss the dressing with the salad. Add the pepper and serve.

Advance preparation: The salad ingredients and the dressing can be prepared hours ahead of time and held in or out of the refrigerator. The salad is tossed with the dressing at the last minute.

mushroom and celery salad

Recipes often call for one or two stalks of celery, then you're left with the rest of the bunch. This refreshing, lemony salad, with the crunchy celery against the smooth mushrooms, is a great solution. **MAKES 4 SERVINGS**

½ pound mushrooms, very thinly sliced
4 celery stalks, very thinly sliced
2 tablespoons chopped fresh herbs,
*   such as dill, tarragon, or chives*
2 tablespoons fresh lemon or lime juice
¼ cup extra virgin olive oil
Parmesan
Salt and freshly ground black pepper to taste
Romaine lettuce leaves (optional)

Combine the mushrooms, celery, herbs, lemon juice, and olive oil in a salad bowl. Using a potato peeler, shave thin slivers of Parmesan over the salad. Season with salt and pepper and toss well. If you wish, serve on leaves of romaine lettuce.

Advance preparation: The salad can be assembled and even tossed with the dressing 2 to 3 hours before serving. Hold in the refrigerator.

asian napa cabbage slaw

The delicious, subtle play of sweet and sour flavors in this dressing and the colorful mix of vegetables are inspired by the many Southeast Asian salads I've enjoyed in restaurants. **MAKES 4 TO 6 SERVINGS**

SALAD

1 medium Napa cabbage, cored and shredded (about 7 cups)
1 red bell pepper, seeded and cut into very thin 2-inch-long slivers
1 large or 2 medium carrots, peeled and cut into thin strips
*   with a vegetable peeler*
¼ cup chopped fresh cilantro
½ to 1 red Thai chile pepper or serrano pepper,
*   minced (optional)*

DRESSING

⅓ cup rice wine vinegar
1 to 1¼ teaspoons sugar (omit if rice wine vinegar is seasoned)
Salt to taste
¼ cup peanut or canola oil

1. Toss together the salad ingredients.

2. Mix together the dressing ingredients. Make sure the sugar is dissolved, and toss with the salad.

3. Let the salad sit for 15 to 30 minutes (or longer), toss again, and serve.

Advance preparation: The salad will keep for a day or two in the refrigerator.

coleslaw

I've always had a weakness for deli coleslaw. I love the tang, and the creaminess contrasting with the crunch of the cabbage, but most of them are too mayonnaise-y. So I've used yogurt in place of most of the mayonnaise. It's important to give the coleslaw time to sit, so that the juices of the cabbage emerge to give the salad its familiar bite. **MAKES 4 SERVINGS**

DRESSING
1 cup plain nonfat yogurt or Yogurt Cheese (page 8)
1 tablespoon plus 1 teaspoon Dijon mustard or prepared horseradish,
    or more to taste
Salt and freshly ground black pepper to taste
½ teaspoon sugar, or more to taste
2 tablespoons cider vinegar
2 tablespoons milk

SALAD
4 heaped cups very finely shredded green cabbage
    (about ½ medium head)
2 medium carrots, finely grated
Finely chopped scallion (optional)
Slivered green bell pepper (optional)

1. Mix together the ingredients for the dressing. If the dressing is too thick for your taste, add another tablespoon milk to thin it out. Taste and adjust the salt and mustard or horseradish. If you like sweet coleslaw, add more sugar.

2. Toss the dressing with the cabbage, carrots, and optional ingredients.

3. Refrigerate for 30 to 60 minutes, or longer. Toss again and serve.

Advance preparation: This keeps for several days in the refrigerator.

bulgarian cucumber and yogurt salad

Versions of this salad are popular throughout Greece, Turkey, and the Balkans. The walnuts here are a feature of the Bulgarian rendition. Enjoy this for lunch, with whole wheat country bread or focaccia, or as a first course for dinner. **MAKES 4 TO 6 SERVINGS**

1 European cucumber, halved lengthwise,
*   and cut into very small dice*
Salt to taste
2 cups Yogurt Cheese (page 8)
1 to 2 garlic cloves, pounded to a puree with ¼ teaspoon salt
¼ cup shelled walnuts, crushed in a mortar and pestle
*   or very finely minced*
2 teaspoons red wine or sherry vinegar
1 to 2 tablespoons chopped dill or mint
Lots of freshly ground black pepper to taste
Paprika

1. Place the diced cucumber in a bowl or colander and salt liberally. Let sit for 30 to 60 minutes. Drain off any water that accumulates.

2. Toss the cucumber with the yogurt, garlic puree, walnuts, vinegar, dill, and pepper. Mound in a salad bowl or on individual plates. Sprinkle on the paprika and serve.

Advance preparation: You can prepare and salt the cucumber several hours ahead of assembling the salad. Keep in the refrigerator.

summer vegetable salad

I spent the summer of 1985 on the island of Korčula, off the coast of what was then Yugoslavia and now is Croatia. I have many fond food memories of that summer, but among the most vivid is the taste of the tomatoes we ate every day. They were large and firm but very juicy; and at that point in my life, they were the best tomatoes I'd ever tasted. They were always combined in a salad with cucumbers, onions, and peppers. If you have access to fresh summer tomatoes, you may end up making this salad every day, as I do during the summer months. **MAKES 4 TO 6 SERVINGS**

1 red onion, cut in half lengthwise,
*   then sliced crosswise into half circles*
5 medium or large ripe tomatoes, peeled if thick-skinned,
*   cut into wedges, the wedges cut in half*
½ European cucumber or 1 regular cucumber,
*   peeled and diced*
1 large green or yellow bell pepper, raw or roasted
*   (see page 3) and cut into 1-inch strips*
2 tablespoons red wine vinegar
3 to 4 tablespoons extra virgin olive oil
Salt and freshly ground black pepper to taste
3 ounces feta cheese, crumbled (about ¾ cup)
2 to 3 tablespoons chopped fresh parsley or mint or
*   1 teaspoon dried oregano*
2 to 3 small hot chiles, such as serranos,
*   roasted (see page 3) and cut into strips or*
*   finely chopped (optional)*
Black olives (optional)

1. Soak the onion in a bowl of cold water for at least 5 minutes. Drain.

2. Toss together the tomatoes, cucumber, bell pepper, onion, vinegar, and olive oil. Add salt and pepper to taste, remembering that feta is salty.

3. Crumble the cheese over the top. Sprinkle with the parsley. Garnish with the chiles and black olives, if you wish, and serve.

Advance preparation: The tomatoes, cucumber, bell pepper, and onion can be assembled hours before serving. Add salt and pepper. Toss with the vinegar, olive oil, and herbs and garnish with chiles and black olives shortly before serving.

Soaking and Rinsing Raw Onions

If you are not cooking an onion, once it has been chopped or sliced, you should rinse it with cold water. This removes many of the cells containing volatile juices that stay with you long after you've eaten your meal. Either place the cut-up onions in a bowl of cold water with a tablespoon of vinegar, if you wish, then drain, or place in a strainer and rinse thoroughly, or both. The longer you soak the onion, the milder it will be.

grilled pepper and tomato salad

This smoky combination can be served as a starter or as a side dish with other grilled foods. It also makes a savory topping for polenta or bruschetta. **MAKES 6 SERVINGS**

> *2 pounds (4 large or 6 medium)*
> *red or yellow bell peppers, or both*
> *1 pound ripe tomatoes*
> *Salt to taste*
> *1 teaspoon cumin seeds*
> *2 garlic cloves, or more to taste,*
> *pounded to a puree with a little salt*
> *2 tablespoons extra virgin olive oil*
> *2 tablespoons red wine vinegar or sherry vinegar*

1. Prepare a medium fire in a gas or charcoal grill or preheat the broiler.

2. Grill or broil the peppers, turning every 3 minutes or so, until uniformly charred. Remove from the heat and place in a bowl. Cover tightly and let sit for 30 minutes or longer. Peel, seed, and finely chop.

3. Grill or broil the tomatoes for a couple of minutes on each side, until blackened. Remove from the heat and transfer to a bowl. When cool enough to handle, peel and chop.

4. Combine the peppers, tomatoes, and salt in a bowl. Set aside.

5. Heat a small skillet over medium-high heat and add the cumin seeds. Shake the pan and toast the seeds; they should begin to smell fragrant and darken slightly. Once you see the color change, remove from the pan immediately and grind in a mortar and pestle or in a spice mill. Add to the peppers and tomatoes. Stir in the garlic, olive oil, and vinegar. Taste and adjust the seasonings.

6. Allow the salad to sit for at least 30 minutes or longer for the flavors to ripen.

Advance preparation: The salad keeps for several days in the refrigerator. The garlic will become more pungent over time.

new potato and asparagus salad

The dressing here makes more than you need for the salad, but any left over makes a nice dip for artichokes or vegetables, or you can drizzle it onto tomatoes or tomorrow night's salad. **MAKES 4 TO 6 SERVINGS**

SALAD
1¼ pounds red-skinned new potatoes, small ones if possible
Salt and freshly ground black pepper
1 celery stalk, thinly sliced
1 tablespoon chopped chives
1 pound asparagus, trimmed and cut into 1-inch pieces

DRESSING
3 tablespoons red wine, white wine, or sherry vinegar
2 tablespoons fresh lemon juice
1 teaspoon Dijon mustard
1 teaspoon cumin seeds, crushed
¼ cup extra virgin olive oil
6 tablespoons plain nonfat yogurt
1 tablespoon Hellmann's or Best Foods mayonnaise
Salt and freshly ground black pepper to taste

1. Cut the potatoes into quarters or large dice. Steam for 10 to 20 minutes, until just tender.

2. Meanwhile, mix together the ingredients for the salad dressing.

3. When the potatoes are cooked, remove from the heat, drain, and toss right away with the salt and pepper, celery, chives, and ⅓ cup of the dressing.

4. Steam the asparagus for 4 to 5 minutes, until just tender. Drain and rinse with cold water.

5. Toss the asparagus with the potatoes. Add additional dressing to taste and serve.

Advance preparation: Make this recipe to the point where you toss the potato salad with ⅓ cup dressing, and steam the asparagus several hours ahead of serving. Place the asparagus on top of the potatoes and hold in the refrigerator. Toss with additional dressing just before serving.

curried rice salad

Several brands of mixed rices are available in supermarkets today, and a mix of wild, brown, and white rices is suitable for this pretty salad. It's substantial enough to serve as a main-dish salad, but could also accompany a light vegetable soup, tart, or soufflé. **MAKES 4 TO 6 SERVINGS**

1 cup packaged mixed rices, cooked according to directions
    on the package; or 3 cups cooked rice, preferably
    a combination of white, brown, and wild
½ pound green beans, trimmed and broken in
    half or into thirds
1 tart apple, peeled, cored, and diced
1 tablespoon lemon or lime juice
1 bunch scallions, white and green parts,
    thinly sliced (optional)
½ European or 1 small cucumber,
    peeled, seeded if necessary
    (usually not necessary with European cucumbers),
    and diced
4 tablespoons slivered toasted almonds
2 cups arugula, baby spinach,
    or spring greens, or ½ head leaf lettuce,
    washed and dried

DRESSING
2 tablespoons fresh lime juice
1 tablespoon sherry vinegar
1 teaspoon curry powder
2 tablespoons Hellmann's or
    Best Foods mayonnaise
1 teaspoon Dijon mustard
½ cup plain nonfat yogurt
Pinch of cayenne pepper
Salt to taste

1. Cook the rice according to the directions on page 159 or follow the package directions. Allow to cool slightly.

2. Steam the green beans for 5 minutes, until just tender. Drain and rinse with cold water.

3. Toss the apple with the lemon or lime juice.

4. Combine the rice, apple, scallions, cucumber, green beans, and 2 tablespoons of the almonds.

5. Mix together the dressing ingredients and toss with the rice mixture. Taste and adjust the seasonings.

6. Line a platter or wide bowl with the greens and top with the salad. Sprinkle the remaining 2 tablespoons of the almonds over the top and serve.

Advance preparation: The salad, undressed, will hold for a day in the refrigerator. Dressed, it will hold for a couple of hours. The dressing can also hold for a day. Keep in the refrigerator.

wheat berry salad

Because wheat berries are so chewy, salads are a great vehicle for them. If you've never tried the sturdy grain before, start with this. Their texture and tawny color contrasts nicely with the crunchy, bright, chopped vegetables. The tangy salad is substantial enough to eat as a main dish. If you make it in the winter, omit the tomatoes. **MAKES 4 TO 6 SERVINGS**

1 cup wheat berries,
  preferably soaked overnight (see box)
½ teaspoon salt
1 large red bell pepper, diced
½ European or 1 medium cucumber,
  peeled, seeded if necessary, and diced
2 medium tomatoes, diced
  (optional; in season only)
½ cup chopped fresh herbs, such as parsley,
  chives, dill, or tarragon
Leaves of romaine lettuce or leaf lettuce (optional)

DRESSING
¼ cup fresh lemon or lime juice
1 garlic clove, minced
Salt and freshly ground black pepper to taste
¼ cup extra virgin olive oil
¼ cup plain nonfat yogurt

1. Drain the soaked wheat berries and combine with 3 cups water in a saucepan. Bring to a boil, reduce the heat, cover, and simmer for 1 hour. Add the salt and continue to simmer until tender, another 30 to 60 minutes. Drain off any water left in the pot.

2. Toss the wheat berries with the bell pepper, cucumber, tomatoes, and herbs.

3. Mix together the ingredients for the dressing.

4. Toss the dressing with the salad. Just before serving, line a platter or wide bowl with the lettuce, if you wish, and top with the wheat berry mixture.

Advance preparation: The salad ingredients can be assembled and tossed together hours ahead of serving. Refrigerate and toss with the dressing just before serving. The dressing will hold for an hour, in or out of the refrigerator.

Soaking Wheat Berries

Wheat berries will be much more tender if you soak them overnight and cook them for a long time in 3 times their volume of water. If you don't soak them they will still cook through, but the cooking time will be about 30 minutes longer, and they will never be as tender as when soaked.

hearts of romaine with preserved lemon and olives

This is inspired by a salad I ate at a favorite Los Angeles restaurant, Lucques. It's a simple combination, defined by clear, salty lemony flavors and contrasting crisp, clean romaine. It goes nicely with hearty Mediterranean stews, such as Couscous with Chickpeas, Greens, and Fennel. Preserved lemon can be purchased in stores that sell North African ingredients. **MAKES 4 SERVINGS**

2 to 3 romaine hearts (depending on the size),
  leaves washed, dried, and broken in half
2 teaspoons chopped preserved lemon
  or Gremolata (page 19)
8 imported black olives, pitted and cut lengthwise
  into quarters or sixths
1 to 2 tablespoons chopped fresh dill or parsley,
  or a combination
2 tablespoons fresh lemon juice
1 very small garlic clove, pureed or pressed
¼ cup extra virgin olive oil
Salt and freshly ground black pepper to taste

1. Mix together the lettuce, preserved lemon, olives, and herbs.

2. Whisk together the lemon juice, garlic, olive oil, and salt and pepper. Toss with the salad just before serving.

Advance preparation: The salad ingredients can be prepared and refrigerated hours before tossing with the dressing and serving. The dressing will hold for a few hours at room temperature.

chickpea salad

This lemony Provençal-inspired salad could be the focus of a meal, or it could complement a pasta with tomato sauce or vegetable soup, such as the Carrot and Leek Soup or the Chilled Beet Soup. A well-stocked pantry and refrigerator should provide you with most of the ingredients, so you could pull this together on a night when you haven't given much thought to dinner.

MAKES 4 SERVINGS

1 red onion, thinly sliced
Three 15-ounce cans chickpeas,
*   drained and rinsed*
1 large red bell pepper, diced
½ cup chopped fresh parsley
2 teaspoons finely chopped lemon zest
2 garlic cloves, minced

DRESSING
1 tablespoon red wine vinegar or sherry vinegar
3 tablespoons fresh lemon juice
Salt and freshly ground black pepper to taste
2 tablespoons plain nonfat yogurt
¼ cup extra virgin olive oil

1. Soak the sliced onion in a bowl of cold water while you prepare the remaining ingredients.

2. Drain the onion and toss with the chickpeas, bell pepper, parsley, lemon zest, and garlic.

3. Whisk together the vinegar, lemon juice, salt and pepper, yogurt, and olive oil.

4. Toss the dressing with the chickpeas and serve at once, or allow to sit for a little while. Refrigerate the salad if it will sit for longer than 30 minutes.

Advance preparation: You can make this several hours ahead and keep it in the refrigerator.

black-eyed peas with cumin vinaigrette

This cumin-scented bean salad is good warm or chilled. It makes an excellent buffet dish. Serve it with quesadillas or a frittata as a first course or a side dish. **MAKES 4 TO 6 MAIN-COURSE OR 8 FIRST-COURSE SERVINGS**

1 pound black-eyed peas,
    washed and picked over
1 medium onion, chopped
4 garlic cloves, minced
1 bay leaf
Salt to taste
1 medium red bell pepper, diced
1 small green bell pepper, diced
2 tablespoons chopped fresh chives
½ cup chopped fresh cilantro
3 to 4 cups baby arugula

VINAIGRETTE
¼ cup red wine vinegar or
    sherry vinegar
1 garlic clove, minced
1 teaspoon Dijon mustard
1 teaspoon ground cumin
Salt and freshly ground black pepper to taste
½ cup broth from the beans
¼ cup extra virgin olive oil

1. Combine the beans with 8 cups water in a soup pot, casserole, or Dutch oven and bring to a boil. Reduce the heat slightly and spoon off any foam. When all the foam has been spooned off, add the onion, garlic, and bay leaf. Reduce the heat, cover, and simmer for 30 minutes. Add salt (about 2 teaspoons) and continue to simmer for another 15 minutes, or until the beans are thoroughly tender but still intact. Taste the broth. Is there enough salt? Adjust the seasonings. Drain the beans over a bowl and return them to the pot.

2. Mix together the vinaigrette ingredients. Stir into the beans.

3. If you are serving the beans warm, add the bell peppers, chives, and cilantro. If you are serving the beans chilled, allow the beans to cool slightly, then refrigerate. Shortly before serving, stir in the peppers, chives, and cilantro. Taste and adjust the seasonings. Line a big salad bowl, platter, or individual plates with the arugula. Give the beans a stir, pile them onto the arugula, and serve.

Advance preparation: The dressed beans keep for 5 days in the refrigerator, but if you aren't serving the salad right away, wait and add the cilantro just before serving.

orange, onion, and olive salad

Serve this refreshing North African salad as part of a couscous dinner or with a hearty stew, such as the Mediterranean Chickpea and Vegetable Stew. The romaine hearts are the lighter, smaller inside leaves of the romaine lettuce. You can find them packaged in most supermarkets. **MAKES 4 SERVINGS**

½ to 1 small sweet red onion, sliced
4 navel or Valencia oranges
½ teaspoon cumin seeds, crushed in a mortar and pestle
12 imported black olives, pitted and halved
Salt to taste
1 to 2 romaine hearts (depending on the size),
   washed and broken into small pieces
3 tablespoons extra virgin olive oil
1 to 2 tablespoons fresh lemon juice (optional)

1. Soak the sliced onion in a bowl of cold water while you prepare the other ingredients.

2. Peel the oranges, cutting away the white pith with the peel. Hold the orange above a bowl to catch the juice as you do this. Either cut the ends off and cut the peel away in wide strips from top to bottom, or cut it away in a spiral. It's important to catch the juices for the dressing. Once peeled, cut the sections away from the membranes, holding the orange over the bowl. Toss the orange sections with the cumin, olives, and salt.

3. Place the lettuce in a salad bowl. Top with the oranges and all of the juice that has accumulated in the bowl. Drain the onion, rinse briefly, shake dry, and add to the salad. Add the olive oil and toss. Taste and adjust the salt. If you'd like the salad to be a little more tart, add the lemon juice and toss again.

Advance preparation: The oranges and onion can be prepared several hours ahead of time. Toss the salad just before serving.

Soups

Soups can be hearty and protein-rich, light and brothy, or somewhere in between. Whether robust or delicate, they always satisfy. Ingredients can be minimal: Garlic Soup, for example, has little more than garlic, water, salt, herbs, and a couple of eggs; Two-Potato and Leek Soup consists of potatoes and leeks, water or stock, and seasonings. Served with a salad and crusty bread, these simple soups make nourishing, filling dinners that are blissfully easy to prepare. Pantry items, such as lentils, onions, potatoes, and garlic can be the basis for a soup, as can the vegetables you bought last weekend at the farmers' market but haven't gotten around to cooking.

Even soups with long lists of ingredients, like Thick Minestrone, require little supervision once they're simmering. Robust bean and vegetable soups like this benefit from being made in advance; make a big pot on a Sunday and eat it through the week, or freeze the leftovers.

I often serve soup as a dinner-party first course. For example, I might serve a summer meal that begins with Corn Soup and follow that with a pasta or risotto, a vegetable tart or gratin and a salad. A big hearty soup like Thick Minestrone, however, is likely to be the focus of the meal, preceded by a green salad like Mixed Greens with Beets, Goat Cheese, and Walnuts or Shredded Romaine Salad.

I learned much about the value of soups when I lived in France. My French friends never agonized over supper, yet they always prepared a delicious meal, and often it was a soup, made from simple vegetables, such as pumpkin, potatoes, leeks, or carrots plus aromatics, water, and salt. The Mediterranean is also a rich source of hearty main-dish soups, and many of them are vegetarian. Tunisians begin their day with a chickpea soup/stew called leblebi that is served with a number of garnishes, such as chopped onion, tomato, harissa, and olive oil. Italian mine-strone and Provençal soupe au pistou are thick vegetable and bean soups that are bulked up with pasta or rice and seasoned with a basil paste. Tuscany is known for its bean soups, and throughout Provence vegetable soups, called "bouillabaisses" because they're seasoned with a pinch of saffron, are enriched at the end with poached eggs, Gruyère cheese, and garlic crou-tons.

Many soups begin by cooking aromatics—onion, carrot, celery, garlic—in oil or butter, then adding liquid and the remaining ingredients. This is one way to ensure a rich-tasting broth. But you will find recipes in this chapter where that step is omitted, and ingredients are simply combined with water or stock and cooked until fragrant, with delicious results. There are no hard and fast rules—I've seen too many great cooks in different places making wonderful dishes using varying techniques to think that only one way works.

Most vegetarian soups are quickly made. Those containing beans, such as black beans, chickpeas, white beans, and pintos—beans that must be soaked and then require 2 hours of cooking—are the exception. But lentil soups, black-eyed pea soups, and split pea soups need only 45 minutes. Soups with hard vegetables, such as potatoes, carrots, turnips, and winter squash, require only 30 to 45 minutes.

Soup Basics

- Use a heavy soup pot, such as an enamel-lined cast-iron pot, and keep the heat low. This allows a very slow simmer, and the heavy pots will keep aromatics from sticking when cooking in the small amounts of butter or olive oil that the recipes call for.

- Aromatic vegetables are vegetables that add fragrance, sweetness, and flavor to a soup. They include onions, leeks, carrots, celery, and garlic. Mushrooms add depth and a savory flavor; broth made from dried mushrooms has a meaty flavor. Sometimes aromatic vegetables are the main ingredient.

- A bouquet garni is a bundle of herbs and aromatics that is added to the simmering broth and discarded at the end of cooking. It almost always contains a bay leaf, a few sprigs of thyme and parsley, and mine sometimes includes a rind of Parmesan or the leafy part of a celery rib. These ingredients are tied together with kitchen string, or tied into a piece of cheesecloth.

- Soups don't need cream to be creamy. Add potatoes or rice to vegetable soups, then puree the mixture to get a thick, creamy potage. Potatoes add body and flavor without overpowering the other vegetables. They also add nutrients. Russet potatoes make great thickeners because they're starchy and fall apart as the soup simmers. Rice has the same effect. When soups contain beans, the beans act as thickeners because of their starch. Even if the soup isn't supposed to be a puree, you can blend up a cupful for a more substantial broth.

- Use Parmesan rinds to get a cheesy taste without adding more cheese. Simmer the hard rinds of Parmesan, those bits you usually throw away. Add one or two rinds directly to the broth, or wrap in cheesecloth along with the bouquet garni, or tie up with the bouquet garni, then remove at the end of cooking. They're great in bean and vegetable soups.

- Pureed soups should retain some texture, so rather than using a blender or food processor to blend soups, use a food mill or immersion blender. I use a hand-held immersion blender most often; this is the easiest implement. You don't have to take the soup out of the pot, you don't make a mess, and the hot soup won't bounce out of the blender jar and burn you. I do use a blender, however, for blended cold soups, such as gazpacho, or to puree a small portion of a soup in order to thicken it. Don't use a food processor for potato-thickened soups, because the potatoes become gummy against the large, fast-moving blades of the food processor. *If you do use a blender or food processor, make sure to puree in batches. If you fill it more than halfway full, the hot soup will splash out and burn you.*

- Don't simmer the life and color out of bright green vegetables; 10 to 15 minutes is usually sufficient. If you're making a large batch, or making the soup for the freezer, steam or blanch the green vegetables separately and add them at the end of cooking to heat them through in the soup.

- Unless otherwise instructed, add fresh herbs just before serving.
- Add eggs and dairy products at the end of cooking, and do not boil or they will curdle.
- Fresh herbs and garlic croutons can give a soup a bright, memorable finish. Sometimes one or two eggs are stirred into a hot soup just before serving. A small amount of high-quality Parmesan or Gruyère is appropriate for many soups. Drained plain nonfat yogurt, a squeeze of lime juice, or a drizzle of olive oil also can have a transforming effect.

Stocks

Much has been written about stocks and how they contribute dimension and depth of flavor to soups. This is true, but I have eaten many delicious soups made with water and vegetables or beans alone, so although I agree that stocks enhance the flavor, they're not absolutely necessary for most soups. Certain soups, like Corn Soup (page 84), benefit from a particular broth (in this case corncob stock). Others benefit from rich mushroom stocks or from stock made from the trimmings of the vegetables that will go into the soup. Still, it's always good to have a few fragrant vegetarian stocks in your repertoire. They can be incredibly simple, perhaps made only with the leek greens you couldn't bear to throw away. The only vegetables to avoid when making stocks are cruciferous ones, such as cabbage, cauliflower, Brussels sprouts, and broccoli, which have a strong sulfurous flavor.

easy vegetable stock

There are cooks who brown their vegetables or roast them to bring out their sugars, but a simple simmer results in a sweet-tasting, aromatic broth. You can throw everything into the pot and get the stock simmering while you prepare ingredients for a soup or risotto, adding trimmings as you work. **MAKES 7 CUPS**

1 onion, quartered
1 carrot, peeled and thickly sliced
1 celery stalk, sliced
4 to 8 garlic cloves, crushed and peeled
1 leek, cleaned and sliced
Salt to taste (about 2 teaspoons)
Vegetable trimmings, such as sliced chard stalks,
*   sliced parsley stems, cleaned and sliced leek greens,*
*   mushroom stems, and scallion trimmings*

1. Combine all of the ingredients with 8 cups water and bring to a boil. Reduce the heat, cover partially, and simmer gently for 30 minutes or longer.

2. Strain through a fine strainer. Use right away, or refrigerate or freeze.

Advance preparation: This is best used within a day of being made, or it can be frozen for 3 to 4 months.

leek-green stock

I used to regret throwing away a large portion of the leeks that I used in other dishes. Now I combine the green ends with other trimmings and a few aromatics and make stock, which I use for soups, sauces, and risottos. **MAKES 6 TO 8 CUPS**

Green ends of 4 to 8 leeks
1 onion, coarsely chopped
10 garlic cloves, crushed and peeled
1 carrot, scrubbed and thickly sliced
1 potato, scrubbed and diced (optional)
Sliced chard stalks (optional)
Parsley stems (optional)
Salt to taste (1½ to 2 teaspoons)

1. Discard the really hard outer layers of the leek greens. Run the rest under cold water to dislodge sand and mud. When thoroughly cleaned, slice and place in a soup pot or Dutch oven. Add the onion, garlic, carrot, potato, chard, parsley and 6 to 8 cups water, making sure that everything is well covered with water. Bring to a boil. Add salt, about 1 teaspoon per quart of water, reduce the heat to low, cover, and simmer for 30 to 60 minutes.

2. Strain the stock, discarding the solids. Use right away, or refrigerate or freeze.

Advance preparation: This is best used soon after it's made, but it will keep for a couple of days in the refrigerator and can be frozen for 3 to 4 months.

garlic broth

I recommend using this as a vegetarian substitute for chicken stock. It has a rich, fragrant taste, sweet rather than pungent with long-simmered garlic. **MAKES 7 CUPS**

1 bay leaf
Few sprigs thyme
Few sprigs parsley
2 heads garlic, cloves separated and peeled
2 teaspoons salt, or to taste
6 peppercorns
1 tablespoon extra virgin olive oil

1. Combine all the ingredients in the pot and add 8 cups water. Bring to a boil. Reduce the heat to very low, cover, and simmer for 1 to 2 hours.

2. Strain and discard the garlic and herbs. Taste. Is there enough salt? Add more if needed. Use right away, or refrigerate or freeze.

Advance preparation: This will keep for 4 days in the refrigerator and freezes well for 3 to 4 months.

wild mushroom broth

An intensely flavored broth made by steeping dried wild mushrooms like porcini (cèpes) in boiling water. The flavor is meaty, and it's good for hearty vegetable soups traditionally made with meat stock or such dishes as Vegetarian Borscht (page 76). If you don't add them to the soup, you can use the reconstituted mushrooms in salads, omelets, pasta sauces, and risottos.
MAKES 6 CUPS

2 ounces dried porcini (2 cups)
1 tablespoon soy sauce, preferably mushroom soy
Salt and freshly ground black pepper to taste

1. Place the mushrooms in a bowl and pour in 4 cups boiling water. Let them sit for 30 minutes. Drain the soaking water through a cheesecloth-lined strainer into a bowl. Squeeze the mushrooms over the strainer to extract all the liquid. Add more water to the soaking liquid to measure 6 cups. Add the soy sauce, if desired, and season to taste with salt and pepper.

2. Rinse the mushrooms in several changes of water. Squeeze dry and keep for another purpose.

3. Use the broth immediately or store in the refrigerator or freezer.

Advance preparation: This keeps for 2 days in the refrigerator, and it can be frozen for 3 to 4 months.

Deglazing

The term *deglaze* is usually associated with cooking meat. It means to detach tasty bits of food that may be stuck to a pan after browning by pouring liquid into the hot pan after removing the food. By stirring and scraping with a wooden spoon, the residues, which are full of flavor, will be incorporated into the liquid, which is then incorporated into the dish.

roasted vegetable stock

A rich, dark stock that can stand in for beef stock. **MAKES ABOUT 6 CUPS**

1 large onion, coarsely chopped
4 carrots, trimmed and sliced
6 large garlic cloves, peeled
1 large leek, white and light green parts,
*   cleaned and sliced*
1 parsnip, peeled and sliced
½ pound mushrooms, stems trimmed, wiped clean
1 tablespoon extra virgin olive oil
1 cup dry white wine or water
Bouquet garni made with several parsley sprigs,
*   a bay leaf, and a few sprigs of thyme*
6 whole peppercorns
Salt to taste (about 2 teaspoons)
Soy sauce to taste (1 to 2 teaspoons)

1. Preheat the oven to 400°F.

2. Combine the onion, carrots, garlic, leek, parsnip, mushrooms, and olive oil in a roasting pan and toss to coat. Place in the oven and roast for about 40 minutes, until the vegetables are browned, tossing every 10 minutes or so.

3. Transfer the vegetables to a soup pot. Pour the wine into the pan and stir the bottom of the pan to deglaze. Pour this into the soup pot. Add 8 cups water, the bouquet garni, peppercorns, salt, and soy sauce and bring to a boil. Reduce the heat, cover partially, and simmer for 45 to 60 minutes.

4. Strain the stock, discarding the solids. Taste and adjust salt. Use immediately or store in the refrigerator or freezer.

Advance preparation: This will keep for a day or two in the refrigerator, and it can be frozen for 3 to 4 months.

soy sauce bouillon

An ultra-quick broth to make when you want something with more flavor than water for a soup, but you don't have time to make a stock. Use only top-quality bouillon cubes, such as Morga.
MAKES 4 TO 6 CUPS

2 to 3 vegetable bouillon cubes
2 to 3 tablespoons soy sauce

Bring 4 to 6 cups water to a boil and dissolve the bouillon cubes in it. Add the soy sauce and use as a stock.

Advance preparation: This will hold at room temperature for several hours.

thick minestrone

I promise that none of the other soups in this book has such a long list of ingredients. Mine-strone means "big soup," in Italian, and that's exactly what this is. If you have a delicious, hearty vegetable soup in your repertoire, you will always have dinner for a crowd. Almost any soup can be eaten as a main dish, but some are heartier than others. The dried beans and pasta add substance and texture to the delicate spring vegetables, resulting in a filling soup that would even satisfy the hunger of an adolescent male. I often serve this type of soup, humble as it may be, for dinner parties. Everybody loves it, and it leaves nobody wondering when the meat course will arrive.

Although the number of ingredients may seem daunting, keep in mind that some of them are not added to the soup until after it's been simmering for 45 minutes or so. So you can pre-pare those vegetables while the soup is cooking. **MAKES 6 GENEROUS SERVINGS**

½ ounce dried porcini (about a heaped ½ cup)
1 to 2 tablespoons extra virgin olive oil
2 medium onions, chopped
2 leeks, white and light green parts only, cleaned and sliced
Salt to taste
2 medium carrots, peeled and chopped
2 celery stalks, chopped
½ small head green cabbage, shredded
    (about 4 cups)
6 large garlic cloves, minced or pressed
2 medium potatoes, scrubbed and diced
2 medium turnips, peeled and diced
One 14-ounce can tomatoes with juice,
    seeded and chopped
1 teaspoon chopped fresh oregano or
    ½ teaspoon dried
1 rind Parmesan
Few sprigs thyme
Few sprigs parsley
1 bay leaf
1 pound fresh fava beans, shelled
    (optional)

1 cup fresh peas (about 1 pound unshelled) or
    thawed frozen peas
½ pound green beans, cut into 1-inch lengths (about 2 cups)
One 15-ounce can cannellini or borlotti beans,
    drained and rinsed
¼ pound Swiss chard, stemmed, washed well,
    and chopped (about 2 cups)
½ cup soup pasta, such as elbow macaroni,
    small shells, or broken spaghetti
Freshly ground black pepper to taste
¼ to ½ cup fresh basil leaves or parsley, chopped
⅓ cup freshly grated Parmesan

1. Put the dried mushrooms in a bowl or a glass measuring cup and pour in 3 cups boiling water. Let sit for 30 minutes, while you prepare the vegetables for the soup. Line a strainer with cheesecloth or several thicknesses of paper towels, and place over a bowl. Drain the mushrooms and squeeze out any excess liquid over the strainer. Rinse the mushrooms in several changes of water and chop. Measure the soaking liquid and add enough water to make 8 cups.

2. Heat 1 tablespoon olive oil over medium-low heat in a large heavy soup pot or Dutch oven. Add the onions and cook, stirring, until they begin to soften. Add the leeks and a pinch of salt. Cook, stirring, for about 5 minutes, until the vegetables are tender and translucent but not browned. Add the carrots and celery and continue to cook, stirring often, for 5 to 10 minutes, until the vegetables are tender and fragrant. Stir in the cabbage and half the garlic, add a little more salt, and cook for about 5 minutes, until the cabbage has wilted. Add the chopped dried mushrooms and their soaking liquid, 5 cups water, the potatoes, turnips, canned tomatoes with liquid, and oregano. Bring to a boil. Tie the Parmesan rind, thyme, parsley, and bay leaf together with kitchen string, or tie in cheesecloth, and add to the pot. Add salt to taste (2 teaspoons or more), reduce the heat to low, cover, and simmer for 45 minutes.

3. While the soup is simmering, blanch the green vegetables. Bring a pot of water to a boil, drop in the shelled favas and boil for 1 minute. Remove from the water using a slotted spoon or skimmer and transfer to a bowl of cold water. Drain and pop the skins off the favas. Set aside. Bring the water in the pot back to a boil, add 1 teaspoon salt, the fresh peas, and green beans. Boil for 5 to 8 minutes, until just tender but still bright green. Remove from the water using a slotted spoon, refresh with cold water, drain, and set aside. Retain the cooking water in case you want to thin out the soup later.

4. After the soup has simmered for 45 minutes, stir in the remaining garlic and canned beans. Add the chard and the pasta to the soup and simmer for another 10 minutes, or until the pasta is cooked al dente. Stir the cooked favas, peas, and green beans into the soup. Grind in some pepper and taste. Does the soup taste vivid? Does it need more salt (probably) or garlic? It should be savory and rich-tasting. Adjust the seasonings as necessary. If it seems too thick, thin out with a little cooking water from the green vegetables.

5. Remove the Parmesan rind bundle, stir in the basil, and remove the soup from the heat. Serve in wide soup bowls, with about 1 tablespoon of Parmesan sprinkled over the top of each serving.

Advance preparation: The soup will keep for 3 or 4 days in the refrigerator, and it benefits from being cooked a day ahead of time. However, the pasta will absorb more liquid, so the soup will require thinning out. A better method is to make the soup a day ahead, but add the pasta on the day you are serving it. Make the recipe through step 3. Reheat to a boil, add the pasta, reduce the heat, and simmer 10 minutes, until the pasta is cooked at dente. Proceed with step 4.

Garlic Croutons

Croutons can be large or small and can be made with whole grain or white bread, but should be made from a country bread or baguette of high quality. I use croutons most often as soup garnishes, as a vehicle for tasty spreads and as a salad ingredient.

To make garlic croutons, cut stale or fresh bread into thin slices. Cut a large, unpeeled garlic clove in half (it's easier to hold on to it if you cut it in half crosswise). Toast the bread in a toaster oven or a medium oven (325° to 350°F). When lightly browned, remove the toast from the heat and rub one or both sides with the cut side of the clove of garlic. If you wish, brush with extra virgin olive oil. I leave croutons whole for soups and spreads, and cut or break them up for salads.

Advance preparation: The bread can be toasted hours ahead of using, but rub with garlic shortly before using for the best flavor.

lentil minestrone

From France to Italy to Lebanon to India to Mexico, lentils are appreciated for their distinctive earthy flavor. Any lentil soup can be a main dish. This one, with pasta or rice added at the end and Parmesan sprinkled over each serving, is another Italian minestrone, or "big soup." The pasta and rice absorb much of the liquid, so the soup is thick (you can add more water if you want a brothier soup). Use just enough cayenne to add a little bite. **MAKES 4 TO 6 GENEROUS SERVINGS**

1 tablespoon extra virgin olive oil
1 small onion, chopped
1 small carrot, minced (about ½ cup)
½ cup minced celery
4 large garlic cloves, minced or pressed
One 14-ounce can tomatoes with juice,
  seeded and chopped
1½ cups lentils, picked over and rinsed
1 Parmesan rind (optional)
Few sprigs parsley
Few sprigs thyme
1 bay leaf
Few pinches of cayenne pepper, or to taste
Salt to taste
½ cup small pasta, such as elbow macaroni,
  small shells, or ditalini, or Arborio rice
Freshly ground black pepper to taste
¼ to ½ cup chopped fresh parsley
¼ cup freshly grated Parmesan

1. Heat the oil over medium-low heat in a heavy soup pot or Dutch oven. Add the onion, carrot, and celery. Cook, stirring, until the vegetables are tender, about 5 minutes. Stir in half the garlic. Cook, stirring, just until the garlic smells fragrant and is beginning to color, about 1 minute. Stir in the tomatoes. Turn the heat to medium and bring the tomatoes to a simmer.

Cook, stirring often, for about 10 minutes, until the tomatoes have cooked down somewhat and smell fragrant. Stir in the lentils and 8 cups water and bring to a boil.

2. Meanwhile, tie the Parmesan rind, parsley, thyme, and the bay leaf together with kitchen twine, or tie in a piece of cheesecloth. Add to the soup. Add the cayenne, reduce the heat, cover, and simmer for 30 minutes.

3. Add salt, about 2 teaspoons to begin with (you will probably add more) and the remaining garlic. Simmer for another 15 to 30 minutes, until the lentils are tender and the broth is fragrant.

4. Add pepper, and stir in the pasta or rice. Continue to simmer for another 10 to 15 minutes, until the pasta or rice is cooked through.

5. Taste. Is there enough salt? Garlic? Adjust the seasonings, and remove the Parmesan rind bundle. Stir in the chopped parsley. Serve, topping each bowl with a generous sprinkle of Parmesan cheese.

Advance preparation: The soup is even better if it's made a day ahead of time; but don't add the pasta or rice or parsley until you reheat. Then proceed with step 4. It will keep for 5 days in the refrigerator and for 3 to 4 months in the freezer.

white bean soup with red pepper and vegetables

This is the prettiest bean soup I've ever seen—carrots, red peppers, white beans, pale onion and parsnip, and the bright green of the parsley and mint garnishes. The flavors are just as extraordinary; paprika and garlic, parsley and mint, and a pinch of hot red pepper flakes to set everything off. The recipe is adapted from a Balkan soup in Maria Kaneva-Johnson's book, *The Melting Pot: Balkan Food and Cookery*. Serve it with crusty bread and a green salad, such as the Shredded Romaine Salad (page 38), Arugula, Pear, and Walnut Salad (page 39), or Bulgarian Cucumber and Yogurt Salad (page 45). You could also follow it with a vegetable gratin or tart, such as the Asparagus and Scallion Tart (page 116). **MAKES 4 SERVINGS**

½ pound (1 heaped cup) white beans,
      rinsed and picked over
1 large onion, finely chopped
3 large garlic cloves, minced
1 large red bell pepper, cut into ½-inch squares
2 carrots, sliced
1 medium parsnip (about ¼ pound),
      peeled, cored, and diced
1 teaspoon paprika
¼ teaspoon red pepper flakes, or
      more to taste
5 flat-leaf parsley sprigs
5 mint sprigs
Salt and freshly ground black pepper to taste
1 to 2 tablespoons extra virgin olive oil (optional)
Chopped fresh parsley
Chopped fresh mint

1. Soak the beans in water to cover for 6 hours or overnight. Drain.

2. Combine the beans and 5 cups water and bring to a boil. Skim off any foam, then add the onion and 1 garlic clove. Reduce the heat, cover, and simmer for 1 hour, until the beans are just about tender but not falling apart.

3. Add the remaining 2 garlic cloves, bell pepper, carrots, parsnip, paprika, and red pepper flakes. Tie the parsley and mint sprigs together with kitchen twine, or tie in a piece of cheese-cloth. Add to the pot along with salt and pepper. Simmer for another 30 minutes, or until the beans are thoroughly tender and the broth is aromatic. Taste. Is there enough salt? Garlic? Adjust the seasonings and simmer for another 5 minutes.

4. Remove the soup from the heat and discard the bouquet garni. Drizzle in the olive oil, sprinkle with the chopped parsley and mint, and serve.

Advance preparation: The soup keeps for 3 to 4 days in the refrigerator, and it can be frozen for 3 to 4 months. Add the olive oil and fresh herbs shortly before serving.

vegetarian borscht

This is a gorgeous, red-hued, warming winter soup with great depth of flavor. The dried mushroom stock has a rich, savory, almost meaty, quality, and the beet stock, with its slightly acidic overtones, adds another layer of flavor, as well as brilliant color. My recipe is based on several Russian and Ukrainian vegetarian borschts, which have evolved over centuries of fasting in accordance with the requirements of the Russian Orthodox Church. Make sure you buy beets with a generous bunch of greens attached. You could serve this with a green salad, or with Bulgarian Cucumber and Yogurt Salad (page 45). Or follow it with a more substantial salad, such as Chickpea Salad (page 55) or Wheat Berry Salad (page 52). **MAKES 4 GENEROUS SERVINGS OR 6 FIRST-COURSE SERVINGS**

¾ ounce dried porcini (about ¾ cup)
1 bunch beets (about 4 medium) with greens;
the beets peeled and quartered, the greens stemmed,
washed, and coarsely chopped
2 garlic cloves, thinly sliced
Salt to taste
1 to 2 teaspoons sugar
1 tablespoon mild vinegar, such as rice wine vinegar or
Champagne vinegar
1 tablespoon canola oil
2 medium onions, chopped
2 small or 1 medium turnip, peeled and chopped
2 medium or 1 large carrot, sliced
2 ounces fresh mushrooms (about 4 medium or 3 large),
trimmed and chopped
2 bay leaves
10 parsley stems
6 black peppercorns
3 allspice berries
¼ cup chopped fresh parsley
1 cup Yogurt Cheese (page 8) or sour cream

1. Place the dried mushrooms in a bowl and pour in 4 cups boiling water. Let sit for 30 minutes, then strain through a cheesecloth-lined strainer. Squeeze the mushrooms over the strainer to extract any remaining flavorful liquid. Rinse the mushrooms thoroughly in several changes of water, then chop.

2. While the mushrooms are soaking, combine the beets, garlic, and 4 cups water in a saucepan. Bring to a boil. Add 1 teaspoon salt and the sugar, reduce the heat, and simmer, uncovered, for 30 minutes. Stir in the vinegar. Remove the beets from the water using a slotted spoon and rinse with cold water; allow to cool until you can handle them. Cut the beets into julienne slices, about ¼ inch wide by 1 inch long. Set the cooking water aside.

3. Heat the oil in a large, heavy soup pot or Dutch oven over medium heat. Add the onion. Cook, stirring, until just tender, 3 to 5 minutes. Add the turnips, carrots, julienned beets, the chopped dried and fresh mushrooms, the mushroom stock, and 1 cup water. Tie the bay leaves, parsley stems, allspice berries, and peppercorns together in a piece of cheesecloth. Add to the pot, along with about 1 teaspoon salt, or more to taste. Bring to a boil, reduce the heat, cover, and simmer for 40 minutes.

4. Add the chopped beet greens and simmer for another 10 minutes.

5. Stir in the cooking water from the beets. Taste. Is there enough salt? Adjust the seasonings. Remove the cheesecloth bag. Heat the soup through, sprinkle on the parsley, and serve, garnishing each bowl with a generous dollop of Yogurt Cheese.

Advance preparation: The soup keeps in the refrigerator for a few days, and it can be frozen for a few months. Add the parsley just before serving.

mushroom and barley soup

Barley and mushrooms are staples throughout Central and Eastern Europe, where many versions of this soup are widely eaten. The two complement each other beautifully. In European versions of the soup, sour cream is added at the end of cooking. This is a nice enrichment, and in my version I give you the option of using low-fat sour cream or yogurt cheese. I'm not crazy about what it does to the appearance of the soup, however; so rather than stir it into the pot, I top each serving with a dollop and diners can stir it in themselves. You could accompany this with a simple green salad, with Arugula, Pear, and Walnut Salad (page 39), or Coleslaw (page 44). **MAKES 4 TO 6 SERVINGS**

½ pound mushrooms
7 cups Wild Mushroom Broth (page 66),
    Easy Vegetable Stock (page 63), or
    Soy Sauce Bouillon (page 68)
1 tablespoon extra virgin olive oil,
    canola oil, or butter
1 medium onion, chopped
1 medium carrot, minced
Salt to taste
2 large garlic cloves, minced or pressed
1 teaspoon fresh thyme leaves or
    ½ teaspoon dried
¾ cup pearl barley
¼ cup dry white wine or dry sherry
½ pound waxy potatoes, peeled and diced
1 tablespoon soy sauce,
    such as Kikkoman or tamari
1 tablespoon fresh lemon juice (optional)
1 tablespoon chopped fresh dill
Freshly ground black pepper to taste
1 cup Yogurt Cheese (page 8) or
    low-fat sour cream

1. Trim the mushrooms and slice the caps, reserving the stems. Simmer the stems in the stock for 30 minutes while you prepare all of the ingredients.

2. Heat the oil or butter over medium-low heat in a large, heavy soup pot or Dutch oven. Add the onion and carrot. Cook, stirring, for 5 to 10 minutes, until the vegetables are tender. Add the mushrooms and a generous pinch of salt. Cook, stirring, until the mushrooms begin to release liquid, a few minutes. Add the garlic and thyme. Continue to cook, stirring, until the mushrooms are tender and the mixture fragrant. Stir in the barley and wine. Cook, stirring, until the liquid in the pot evaporates. Add the stock, potatoes, and salt to taste. Bring to a boil, reduce the heat, cover, and simmer for 1 hour, until the barley is tender and the soup is aromatic.

3. Stir in the soy sauce, lemon juice, and dill. Add pepper, taste, and adjust the salt.

4. Remove the soup from the heat and serve, topping each bowl with a generous dollop of yogurt.

Advance preparation: The soup keeps for 3 or 4 days in the refrigerator. The barley will continue to swell, so you might need to add a bit of water or stock to thin it.

winter vegetable soup

This is a comforting, pretty winter soup. Use an immersion blender or a food mill to puree the mixture, so that it retains some texture. If you have time to make a stock, use the leek greens and make the Leek-Green Stock on page 64. Follow this soup with the Mixed Greens with Beets, Goat Cheese, and Walnuts (page 33). **MAKES 6 GENEROUS SERVINGS**

6 medium or 3 large leeks, white parts only, cleaned and sliced
1 large or 2 small onions, chopped
1 to 2 garlic cloves, minced
½ pound winter squash, such as butternut, peeled, seeded, and diced
2 medium carrots, chopped
1 celery stalk, chopped
2 small turnips, peeled and diced
¾ to 1 pound russet potatoes (1 large), peeled and diced
7 cups Easy Vegetable Stock (page 63) or water
Bay leaf
1 to 2 thyme sprigs
1 to 2 parsley sprigs
Salt to taste
1 cup low-fat milk (optional)
Freshly ground black pepper to taste
> *Optional Garnishes: Yogurt Cheese (page 8)*
> *Chopped fresh parsley*
> *Grated Gruyère*

1. Combine the leeks, onion, garlic, winter squash, carrots, celery, turnips, potatoes, and stock. Tie the bay leaf, thyme sprigs, and parsley sprigs together with kitchen twine, or tie in a piece of cheesecloth. Add to the pot. Add the stock. Bring to a boil. Add salt, reduce the heat, cover, and simmer for 1 hour.

2. Remove the bouquet garni and puree the soup through the medium blade of a food mill, or with an immersion blender.

3. Return the soup to the heat and thin with milk as desired. Add abundant pepper. Taste and adjust the salt. You will need quite a bit to bring up the flavors. Serve, garnishing each bowl with a dollop of yogurt, a sprinkling of parsley, or a sprinkling of Gruyère.

two-potato and leek soup

I use two types of potatoes for this incredibly easy version of a classic French soup. Russets fall apart and thicken the broth, replacing the more traditional cream. Waxy potatoes hold their shape and give the soup texture. **MAKES 4 SERVINGS**

¾ pound leeks, white and light green parts only,
　　cut in half, cleaned, and thinly sliced
¾ pound russet potatoes (1 medium),
　　peeled, cut in half lengthwise, and thinly sliced
1 pound waxy potatoes, such as new potatoes or fingerlings,
　　scrubbed (or peeled if desired) and thinly sliced
5 cups Easy Vegetable Stock (page 63), Leek-Green Stock (page 64),
　　or water
Salt and freshly ground black pepper to taste
½ cup low-fat milk (optional)
2 tablespoons chopped fresh tarragon or chervil

1. Combine the leeks, potatoes, and stock and bring to a boil. Add salt (1½ teaspoons to start), reduce the heat, cover, and simmer for 40 minutes, until the waxy potatoes are tender and the russets are falling apart.

2. Using the back of your spoon or a potato masher, mash some of the potatoes to thicken the soup. Taste and add salt and pepper as desired. Stir in the milk and heat through.

3. Serve, garnishing each bowl with fresh tarragon or chervil.

Advance preparation: The soup can be made several hours ahead and reheated.

• COLD TWO-POTATO AND LEEK SOUP • Put the soup through the medium blade of a food mill, or puree with an immersion blender. Add an additional ½ cup milk if desired. Serve chilled, garnished, if you wish, with a dollop of plain nonfat yogurt.

kale and potato soup

This is inspired by the classic Portuguese caldo verde, the national soup that combines potatoes, greens, and Portuguese chouriço sausage. Obviously, that last ingredient isn't a part of this soup, which derives its marvelous flavor from the fresh greens and comforting potatoes. Serve with crusty bread or Garlic Croutons (page 71). A hearty soup, this can make a meal, with a Tomato, Feta, and Arugula Salad (page 41) or a green salad. You could also follow it with a vegetable tart or gratin. **MAKES 6 SERVINGS**

2 tablespoons extra virgin olive oil
1 medium onion, chopped
4 large garlic cloves, minced
1¾ to 2 pounds russet potatoes, peeled and thinly sliced
8 cups Easy Vegetable Stock (page 63) or water
Salt to taste (about 2½ teaspoons, or more)
1 pound kale, stems trimmed, washed well
Freshly ground black pepper to taste

1. Heat 1 tablespoon of the oil over medium-low heat in a large, heavy soup pot or Dutch oven. Add the onion. Cook, stirring, until tender, 3 to 5 minutes. Add the garlic. Cook, stirring, until fragrant, about 30 seconds. Stir in the potatoes and stock. Bring to a boil, add salt, reduce the heat, cover, and simmer for 30 to 40 minutes, until the potatoes are falling apart.

2. Meanwhile, prepare the greens. Stack the leaves, about six or eight to a stack, roll them up tightly, and slice crosswise into very thin ribbons.

3. Mash the potatoes in the pot with a potato masher or an immersion blender. Stir the greens into the soup and simmer for 10 to 15 minutes, until the greens turn bright green and tender.

4. Taste, adjust the salt, and add pepper. Stir in the remaining 1 tablespoon olive oil and serve.

Advance preparation: The soup keeps for a couple of days in the refrigerator.

corncob broth

This sweet broth is a summer broth for sweet-tasting vegetable soups, particularly anything with corn in it, like the recipe on page 84. **MAKES ABOUT 6 CUPS**

1 onion, quartered
3 leeks, white part only, cleaned and sliced
2 carrots, sliced
2 to 4 corncobs, broken into pieces
1 to 2 teaspoons salt

1. Combine the onion, leeks, carrots, corncobs, salt, and 7 cups water. Bring to a boil. Reduce the heat, cover, and simmer for 1 hour

2. Remove from the heat and strain. Taste and adjust salt.

Advance preparation: This is best used the day it's made.

corn soup

When corn is in season, I buy it every time I see it in the market. This behavior is a carryover from my childhood, when there was a very short growing season and we ate it every night. Now the corn season seems longer, and the corn is always sweet, due to the development of sweeter strains, but it's still a summer vegetable, and that's the only time to make this incredibly sweet soup. You will be using the corncobs here for the broth, so hold on to them. Make sure to put the finished soup through the fine blade of a food mill or through a strainer, to get rid of the corn kernel husks. **MAKES 4 SERVINGS**

1 tablespoon canola oil or corn oil
1 medium sweet white or yellow onion,
    chopped
Kernels from 6 ears corn
1 small potato, peeled and chopped
7 cups Corncob Broth (page 83)
Salt to taste
Slivered sage leaves or chopped fresh tarragon

1. Heat the oil in the soup pot over medium heat and add the onion. Cook, stirring, until tender, about 5 minutes. Add the corn kernels and stir together for a couple of minutes. Then add the potato and broth. Bring to a boil, add salt to taste, reduce the heat to low, cover partially, and simmer for 20 minutes.

2. Remove from the heat and puree in batches in a blender or with an immersion blender. Put through a strainer or the fine blade of a food mill and return to the pot.

3. Heat through, taste, and adjust the salt. Serve garnished with the slivered sage or chopped tarragon.

Advance preparation: This is best served no more than a few hours after it's made.

carrot and leek soup

This sweet, comforting soup is based on a French classic. I love its texture—it should be coarsely pureed, preferably with an immersion blender or through a food mill. Use the leek greens for the stock; even if you don't have time to make stock, you can simmer them in the water while you prepare the other vegetables. **MAKES 4 SERVINGS**

1 pound leeks
6 cups water
1 tablespoon butter
2¼ pounds carrots, finely chopped (you may use a food processor, using the pulse action)
¼ teaspoon sugar (optional); omit if carrots are very sweet
1 medium russet potato (about ½ pound), peeled and diced small
Salt to taste
½ cup low-fat milk
Freshly ground black pepper to taste
2 tablespoons chopped fresh chives, thyme, or dill

1. Clean the leeks. Chop the white and light green parts and set aside. Simmer the leek greens in the water while you prepare the other ingredients for the soup, 20 to 30 minutes. Strain and discard the greens.

2. Heat the butter over medium-low heat in a large, heavy soup pot or Dutch oven. Add the leeks. Cook, stirring often, until they are tender and fragrant, 5 to 10 minutes. Add the carrots and stir together for 1 to 2 minutes. Add the sugar, stock, and the potato. Bring to a boil. Add salt and reduce the heat. Cover partially and simmer for 30 minutes.

3. Puree the soup coarsely using an immersion blender (my choice) or a food mill fitted with the medium blade. Return to the pot and add the milk. Taste. Is there enough salt? Add a little pepper.

4. Heat through just to a simmer. Serve, topping each bowl with a sprinkling of chives.

Advance preparation: This is best served the day it's made, but it will keep for a day or two in the refrigerator.

garlic soup

I apologize to those of you who have my other books for repeating myself here, but I cannot leave garlic soup out of this cookbook. It is essential to the vegetarian cook, because it's so easy to make, so pleasing, and makes such a nutritious meal. If you can make this soup, even when you think you have nothing in the house, you can make dinner (I am assuming you will have garlic). This is the same version of Garlic Soup that I published in *Light Basics Cookbook*. **MAKES 4 SERVINGS**

4 to 6 large garlic cloves, minced
1½ to 2 teaspoons salt
1 bay leaf
¼ to ½ teaspoon dried thyme, a few sprigs of fresh thyme,
*   or 2 or 3 fresh sage leaves*
4 thick slices country-style bread or French bread
1 garlic clove, cut in half
2 large eggs, beaten
2 teaspoons extra virgin olive oil (optional)
Freshly ground black pepper to taste
2 tablespoons chopped fresh parsley
2 to 3 tablespoons freshly grated Parmesan or Gruyère

1. Bring 6 cups water to a boil in a large saucepan or soup pot. Add the minced or pressed garlic, 1½ teaspoons salt, the bay leaf, and thyme. Cover and simmer for 15 minutes. Taste. Does it taste good? Is there enough salt? Garlic? Adjust the seasonings.

2. Toast the bread. As soon as it's done, rub both sides with the cut clove of garlic and set aside.

3. Beat together the eggs and olive oil. Spoon a ladleful of the hot soup into the eggs and stir together. Then remove the soup from the heat and stir in the egg mixture. The eggs should cloud the soup but they shouldn't scramble. Stir in the pepper and parsley.

4. Place a garlic crouton in each bowl. Ladle in the soup, sprinkle cheese over the top, and serve.

Advance preparation: This is a last-minute soup.

- GARLIC SOUP WITH BROCCOLI, PEAS, GREEN BEANS, OR SUGAR SNAP PEAS •
  Add ½ pound broccoli florets, green beans, or sugar snap peas, or 1 cup fresh or thawed
  frozen peas, to the soup at the end of step 1. Simmer for 5 to 10 minutes, until the vegetables
  are tender. Meanwhile, make the croutons. Proceed with step 3.

- GARLIC SOUP WITH POTATOES • Scrub and slice ½ pound waxy potatoes, such as Yukon
  Gold, fingerlings, or white creamers, about ¼ inch thick. Add to the soup at the beginning of
  step 1. By the end of the 15 minutes, they should be tender. If they are not, continue to simmer until they are tender and proceed with the recipe. If desired, add green vegetables at the
  end of step 1.

- GARLIC SOUP WITH PASTA • Add soup pasta, such as small shells or elbow macaroni, or
  large pasta, such as fusilli, to the soup at the end of step 1. Cook the pasta al dente, then check
  again for salt, and proceed with the recipe. If desired, add green vegetables at the end of step 1.

cream of pea soup with mint

Looking for space in my freezer one day, I was dismayed to find two bags of frozen peas that I had opened, used part of the contents, and forgot about for who knows how long. That's it, I said. These are going into a soup (for I had bought yet another package of frozen peas, not realizing that I already had some). I use a potato to thicken this sweet, pale green soup, not the traditional butter and flour combination. **MAKES 4 SERVINGS**

4 cups frozen peas
1 tablespoon butter
1 onion, chopped
1 medium waxy potato, such as Yukon Gold or White Rose,
     peeled and diced
6 cups Easy Vegetable Stock (page 63) or water
Salt and freshly ground black pepper to taste
1 cup low-fat milk (optional)
Nonfat or low-fat sour cream or Yogurt Cheese (page 8)
Fresh mint leaves, slivered

1. Put the peas in a bowl or a large glass measure and cover with hot water to remove any frost. Drain.

2. Heat the butter in a large, heavy soup pot or Dutch oven over medium heat. Add the onion. Cook, stirring, until the onion softens, about 3 minutes. Add the peas, potato, and stock. Bring to a boil. Reduce the heat, cover, and simmer for 20 minutes, or until the potato is tender.

3. Remove the soup from the heat. Puree in a blender, with an immersion blender, or through the fine blade of a food mill. Strain to rid the soup of the pea skins for a really smooth soup. Return to the pot, season with salt and pepper, and heat through.

4. Serve hot or cold, garnished with a dollop of sour cream and a sprinkling of mint.

Advance preparation: The soup will keep for 2 days in the refrigerator, but the color will fade.

chilled beet soup

One of my all-time favorite cold soups, this tart beet soup is beautiful, thirst quenching, and easy. Serve it with black bread or pumpernickel or any crusty country bread. **MAKES 6 SERVINGS**

2 pounds beets, peeled and thinly sliced
1 to 1½ teaspoons salt, or to taste
Juice of 2 to 3 lemons
1 tablespoon sugar
2 garlic cloves, peeled and cut in half lengthwise
½ European cucumber or 1 small cucumber,
    peeled and finely diced
1 cup Yogurt Cheese (page 8) or
    low-fat sour cream
Chopped fresh dill (optional)

1. Combine the beets, 7 cups water, and a pinch of salt in a soup pot or Dutch oven. Bring to a boil. Reduce the heat, cover, and simmer for 30 minutes.

2. Add the juice of 2 lemons, the salt, and sugar. Continue to simmer, uncovered, for 25 to 30 minutes, until the beets are tender and the broth aromatic.

3. Remove the soup from the heat and add the garlic. Allow to cool, then cover, and chill.

4. Taste. Is there enough salt? Enough lemon juice? Adjust the seasoning. Remove the garlic cloves before serving. Garnish each serving with a spoonful of cucumber, a generous dollop of yogurt, and a sprinkling of fresh dill.

Advance preparation: The soup will keep for 3 to 4 days in the refrigerator.

cold blender tomato soup

This is a soup for summer, when tomatoes are at their height. It's somewhat like a gazpacho, but it isn't thickened with bread. **MAKES 4 SERVINGS**

½ medium sweet red or white onion,
coarsely chopped
2½ pounds ripe tomatoes,
peeled and quartered
1 large carrot, coarsely chopped
2 large garlic cloves
2 to 4 tablespoons red wine vinegar
Salt and freshly ground black pepper to taste
1 tablespoon extra virgin olive oil (optional)
½ European cucumber or 1 medium regular cucumber,
peeled and seeded if necessary, cut in very small dice
2 tablespoons slivered fresh basil leaves

1. Put the chopped onion in a bowl and cover with water. Let soak while you prepare the other vegetables. Drain.

2. Combine the tomatoes, onion, carrot, garlic, and 2 tablespoons vinegar in a blender and puree until smooth. Transfer to a bowl. Add ⅔ cup water and blend well. Season to taste with salt and pepper. Chill for several hours. Taste and add more vinegar or salt if desired.

3. Serve, garnishing each bowl with a drizzle of olive oil, a spoonful of cucumber, and a generous sprinkling of basil.

Advance preparation: This must be made several hours ahead, and it will keep for a day or two in the refrigerator. The onion and garlic flavors will become more pronounced.

EGGS *and* Cheese

The egg is my rebuttal to the argument that vegetarian cooking is too time-consuming. What could be more satisfying and quick to prepare than an omelet? And what could be more elegant than a cheese soufflé or a giant round, ten-egg, bright yellow frittata sparkling with bright peas, red peppers, chopped herbs, and onions, cut into diamonds, and served as hors d'oeuvre or cut into more substantial wedges for entrées?

Many of the dishes in this chapter depend on eggs and/or cheese for their structure or flavor, but vegetables are actually the focus of the dish. Vegetables may inspire a gratin or a tart, but eggs are required to hold them together. Dishes such as the Greens and Tomato Gratin (page 122), the Swiss Chard Frittata (page 101), and the Leek Tart (page 114) are perfect vehicles for many different types of vegetables. You will find more gratins in the vegetable chapter, but I chose to put here those that make suitable main dishes; they are like tarts without the crust.

You'll also find in this chapter a recipe for buckwheat crêpes with several fillings. Buckwheat crêpes have a memorable, earthy flavor and make a great wrap for cheese and vegetable combinations.

The cheeses I use most often in my cooking are imported Gruyère and Parmesan. For most dishes you need little more than 2 or 3 ounces to produce a dish with great depth of flavor. Goat cheese is another one whose distinctive flavor goes a long way.

Buying and Storing Eggs

People can become infected with salmonella from uncooked or soft-cooked eggs. In actual fact, the risk is very slim: two in ten thousand eggs were contaminated in a recent survey. And these were battery eggs, eggs that are intensively produced on huge, crowded chicken farms. I think that the best prevention against infected eggs is to buy free-range eggs, which are produced by smaller egg farmers. But the best reason to buy free-range eggs is that they taste at least ten times better than battery eggs. The yolk is a much deeper yellow color, the whites and the shells are firmer, they make fluffier everything, they have real flavor. I can't emphasize enough what a difference there is between the two.

Make sure to keep the eggs at the top of your shopping bag when you go grocery shopping. When you get home, don't take them out of the carton. Throw away those egg holders in your refrigerator door. Eggs absorb flavors through their thin shells, and the door is not the coldest part. Put them in a cool part of the refrigerator, in their carton.

Omelets, Frittatas, and Stratas

Omelets, frittatas, and stratas can be breakfast, lunch, or dinner. An omelet or strata with no added filling is just fine, and even better when it becomes a vehicle for vegetables and cheeses (not to mention truffles). These dishes also allow you to reformat leftovers, even humble stale bread, transforming them into entirely new meals.

How to Separate Eggs

Each cook does it a different way. If you don't mind getting egg on your hands, then you can just break an egg into a bowl and gently scoop out the yolk, or you can break the egg and let the yolk rest in your hand as you let the white slip between your fingers into a bowl.

The "pro" way is to crack the egg deftly at the equator against the surface of the bowl and separate it into two equal halves. The yolk will be in one half. Holding the egg over the bowl, pass the yolk carefully from one half to the other, while letting the white run into the bowl. Discard the yolk or transfer it to another bowl. When separating more than one egg, transfer the whites to a bowl as you do each egg, so that if you louse up and break the yolk on, say, the third egg, you won't lose all the whites (this matters only if you have to beat egg whites until stiff for a recipe).

Whichever way you choose to separate eggs, they will separate more easily if they are cold. So if a recipe calls for separated eggs at room temperature, separate them while cold, then let them come to room temperature.

Scrambled Eggs

One of our favorite suppers, simple scrambled eggs are luscious and comforting. Cook them over low heat in a nonstick pan for the creamiest results. You don't need lots of butter—a teaspoon or two for 2 eggs will suffice. Melt the butter in a small or medium nonstick pan over low heat. Meanwhile beat 2 or more eggs in a bowl. Beat in salt and freshly ground pepper to taste, and a teaspoon or two of milk (low-fat or regular) for every 2 eggs. Add the eggs to the pan and stir slowly over low heat until they set, 5 to 10 minutes (depending on the quantity of eggs). Remove from the heat while still slightly creamy, and transfer to a plate. If you like larger, harder curds, use medium heat.

quick individual omelets, flat or folded

Omelets are a snap to make, and they can be filled or embellished with a range of foods, from simple chopped herbs or grated cheese, to chopped fresh tomatoes or tomato sauce, to leftover cooked mushrooms or greens, to simple chopped steamed green vegetables, such as asparagus or broccoli. These go so quickly that they can be made in quick succession if you're feeding more than just yourself. You can keep the omelets warm in a very low oven (250°F) while you make more of them or serve at once. They can be flat, like an Italian frittata, or folded. **MAKES 1 SERVING**

2 large eggs or 1 large egg and 2 egg whites
Salt and freshly ground black pepper
1 teaspoon low-fat milk
Filling of your choice (see page 95)
2 teaspoons extra virgin olive oil or butter

1. Beat the eggs in a small bowl, using a whisk or a fork. The whites and yolks should be nicely amalgamated. Add a good pinch of salt, the pepper, milk, and the filling of your choice.

2. Heat the olive oil in an 8-inch nonstick skillet over medium-high heat. Hold your hand above the pan; it should feel hot. Drizzle in a bit of egg; if it sizzles and cooks at once, the pan is ready.

3. Pour in the egg mixture and tilt and swirl the pan to coat the bottom evenly. Gently lift the edges of the layer that has set and tilt the pan to let more egg run underneath. Shake the pan constantly but gently and continue to lift and tilt it to allow uncooked egg to run underneath the cooked egg.

FLAT OMELETS
When the top of the omelet is just about set, slide it out onto a plate and serve. The egg will continue to cook, so the omelet won't be runny.

FOLDED OMELETS
If you are folding the omelet, you can, if you want, put the filling in the middle of the omelet, once the omelet is set, and fold the omelet over it, rather than stirring it into the eggs. To fold an omelet, either fold each side in toward the middle, folding one flap over the other, or fold the

omelet in half. This is easy in a nonstick pan. Gently flip the omelet over with a spatula, or push the pan away from you and, with a jerk of the wrist, quickly pull it toward you to flip the omelet over in the pan. Cook for a few more seconds if you wish. Slide out onto a plate and serve.

Advance preparation: Although I prefer folded omelets hot, flat omelets are good at room temperature. They make wonderful picnic food, cut into wedges. They will hold for 3 to 4 hours at room temperature and for 3 days in the refrigerator.

- FINES HERBES OMELET • For each omelet, add 2 tablespoons chopped fresh herbs, such as parsley, chives, dill, basil, thyme, tarragon.

- SWISS CHARD OR SPINACH OMELET • For each omelet, add ½ cup chopped cooked Swiss chard or spinach and 1 minced garlic clove.

- STEAMED BROCCOLI OR ASPARAGUS OMELET • For each omelet, steam ⅓ to ½ cup coarsely chopped asparagus or broccoli for 5 minutes. Add to omelet along with 1 to 2 teaspoons chopped chives or parsley if desired.

- TOMATO OMELET • For each omelet, add 3 to 4 tablespoons tomato pasta sauce (home-made or commercial) or chopped fresh tomato and 1 teaspoon slivered fresh basil.

- MUSHROOM OMELET • For each omelet, heat 1 teaspoon oil or butter in a small nonstick skillet over medium heat and add 1 minced garlic clove. As soon as it begins to sizzle, add ½ cup sliced mushrooms and a bit of salt. Cook, stirring, until the mushrooms release liquid. Continue to cook until the liquid has evaporated and the mushrooms are tender, 5 to 10 minutes. Add salt, black pepper, and 1 to 2 tablespoons chopped fresh herbs, such as parsley, chives, or thyme. Remove from the heat. Allow to cool for a few minutes before adding to omelet.

Filling Omelets with Leftovers

Leftover stews and vegetables can be turned into a whole new meal when you use them to fill an omelet. For individual omelets, use about 3 to 4 tablespoons per omelet. Spread down the center of the omelet or stir into the beaten eggs for a flat omelet. For large ten-egg frittatas, use about 1½ cups filling, or more, to taste.

egg white omelet with beet greens or swiss chard

Egg whites can be used in place of whole eggs if you need to consume a very low-cholesterol diet. In order to make an omelet with body, you need a lot of filling, and the greens and garlic here work very well. This omelet is rolled or folded. **MAKES 2 SERVINGS**

Salt
½ pound beet greens or Swiss chard (from 1 small bunch),
stemmed and washed well
5 large egg whites
Freshly ground black pepper
1 large garlic clove, minced
2 teaspoons extra virgin olive oil

1. Bring a medium pot of water to a boil, and add a couple of teaspoons of salt and the greens. Cook for about 2 minutes, until tender, and transfer to a bowl of cold water. Drain, squeeze out any liquid, and chop.

2. Beat the eggs in a bowl until foamy. Add ¼ teaspoon salt, some pepper, the greens, and the garlic.

3. Heat the olive oil in a medium nonstick skillet over medium-high heat. Hold your hand above it; it should feel hot. Drop a bit of egg into the pan; if it sizzles and cooks at once, the pan is ready. It must be hot, because you want the eggs to form a cooked surface on the bottom of the pan immediately. You will be lifting this gently with a spatula and tilting the pan, so that the uncooked egg whites run underneath, and the omelet cooks layer by layer.

4. Pour in the egg mixture. Swirl the pan to distribute the eggs and filling evenly over the surface. Shake the pan gently, tilting it slightly with one hand while lifting up the edges of the omelet with the spatula in your other hand, to let the eggs run underneath during the first few minutes of cooking. When the omelet is just about set, but still a bit runny on top, gently fold it over. You can fold it in half or fold it like a letter, folding one third over toward the middle, then the other side over toward the middle. Allow it to cook for a minute or so longer. Then carefully roll or slide the omelet onto a plate. Cut in half crosswise and serve.

large frittata

All omelets are versatile, because so many foods make good fillings. Frittatas, those colorful flat omelets that the Spanish confusingly call *tortillas*, are particularly useful for entertaining, because you can make them ahead of time and serve them cold. They look beautiful on a buffet and can be cut into small diamond-shaped pieces and passed as finger food, or they can be eaten as a first course or main dish. They're also easy to transport and make great picnic or lunch fare. I make them virtually every time I entertain for a crowd, because a 12-inch frittata cut into small diamond-shaped pieces goes a very long way, and it always impresses guests. "What's that, quiche?" they ask. I answer that it's not a quiche, it's a frittata. **MAKES 6 MAIN-COURSE SERVINGS, 10 TO 12 FIRST-COURSE SERVINGS OR HORS D'OEUVRES**

Filling of your choice (see page 95)
10 large eggs
Salt to taste (about ½ teaspoon)
Generous amount of freshly ground black pepper
3 tablespoons low-fat milk
1 tablespoon extra virgin olive oil

1. Make the filling according to the recipe.

2. Beat the eggs in a large bowl. Stir in the salt, pepper, milk, and the filling.

3. Heat the olive oil in a heavy nonstick 12-inch skillet over medium-high heat. Hold your hand above it; it should feel hot. Drop a bit of egg into the pan; if it sizzles and cooks at once, the pan is ready. The reason it must be hot is that you want the eggs to form a cooked surface on the bottom of the pan immediately. You will be lifting this gently with a spatula and tilting the pan, so that the uncooked eggs run underneath, and the frittata cooks layer by layer. Pour in the egg mixture. Swirl the pan to distribute the eggs and filling evenly over the surface. Shake the pan gently, tilting it slightly with one hand while lifting up the edges of the frittata with the spatula in your other hand, to let the eggs run underneath during the first few minutes of cooking. Turn the heat down to low, cover (use a pizza pan if you don't have a lid that will fit your skillet), and cook for 10 minutes, shaking the pan gently every once in a while. From time to time, remove the lid and loosen the bottom of the frittata with a wooden spatula and jerk the pan so that the bottom doesn't burn. It will, however, turn a deep golden brown. This is fine. The eggs should be just about set; cook for a few minutes longer if they're not. Meanwhile, preheat the broiler.

4. Finish the frittata under the broiler for 2 to 3 minutes, watching very carefully to make sure the top doesn't burn (it should brown slightly, and it will puff under the broiler).

5. Remove from the heat and shake the pan to make sure the frittata isn't sticking (it will slide around a bit in the nonstick pan). Allow to cool for at least 5 minutes and up to 15 minutes. Loosen the edges with a wooden or plastic spatula.

6. Serve hot, at room temperature, or cold. As a main dish, cut into wedges like a pie and serve from the pan, or carefully slide from the pan onto a large round platter. For hors d'oeuvres, cut diamond shapes: Cut the frittata into strips, 1½ to 2 inches wide. Turn the platter and cut strips on the diagonal, to make diamonds.

Advance preparation: Frittatas will keep for 3 to 5 days in the refrigerator. Allow to cool to room temperature, cover with plastic, then with foil. It's best not to cut them ahead of serving time.

- LOW-FAT FRITTATA • Instead of 10 whole eggs, use 6 whole eggs and 10 egg whites. Proceed with recipe above.

frittata with onions, red peppers, and peas

This is the frittata I make most frequently for parties. Its jewel-like filling does not depend on a season, and it's gorgeous and versatile. Master it and you will always have an impressive dish for a brunch, buffet, or potluck. **MAKES 6 MAIN-COURSE SERVINGS, 10 TO 12 FIRST-COURSE SERVINGS OR HORS D'OEUVRES**

1 tablespoon extra virgin olive oil
1 medium onion, chopped
1 large red bell pepper, seeded and diced
Salt to taste
1 to 2 garlic cloves, minced
1½ cups fresh or thawed frozen peas

10 large eggs, preferably at room temperature
Salt and freshly ground black pepper
3 tablespoons low-fat milk
2 to 3 tablespoons chopped fresh parsley or basil, or a combination
1 tablespoon extra virgin olive oil

1. Heat 1 tablespoon oil in a heavy nonstick 12-inch skillet over medium heat. Add the onion and cook, stirring, until it begins to soften, about 3 minutes. Add the bell pepper and a little salt. Stir together and cook, stirring often, for another 5 to 8 minutes, until the onion and pepper are tender. Stir in the garlic, cook for another minute, and remove from the heat. Transfer to a bowl, and rinse and dry your pan.

2. If you are using fresh peas, steam for 5 to 8 minutes, until tender, and refresh under cold water. Drain and add to the vegetables. Frozen peas can be thawed by covering with hot water. Drain and add to the vegetables.

3. Beat the eggs in a large bowl. Whisk in ½ teaspoon salt, a generous amount of pepper, and the milk. Stir in the vegetables and the herbs.

4. Make the frittata following the directions in the basic recipe on page 97, using the remaining 1 tablespoon oil.

parsley and onion frittata

Make this when you have a great big bunch of parsley sitting in the refrigerator. Maybe you used 2 tablespoons for another recipe and you're wondering what to do with the rest of it. This is a terrific, easily assembled frittata. **MAKES 6 TO 8 MAIN-COURSE SERVINGS OR 12 FIRST-COURSE SERVINGS OR HORS D'OEUVRES**

1 large onion, finely chopped
1 tablespoon red or white wine vinegar
Leaves from 1 large bunch parsley or 2 smaller bunches,
*   washed and chopped by hand or in a food processor (about 2 cups)*
1 tablespoon extra virgin olive oil
2 large garlic cloves, minced

10 large eggs
3 tablespoons low-fat milk
½ teaspoon salt
Freshly ground black pepper to taste
1 tablespoon extra virgin olive oil

1. Place the finely chopped onion in a bowl and cover with cold water. Add the vinegar and let sit for 20 to 30 minutes.

2. Beat the eggs in a bowl and stir in the milk, salt, pepper, and the parsley. Let sit for 15 to 30 minutes.

3. Drain the onion. Heat 1 tablespoon oil in a heavy nonstick 12-inch skillet over medium-low heat. Add the onion and cook, stirring, until the onion is tender, about 5 minutes. Stir in the garlic, cook for another minute, or until the garlic is fragrant. Remove from the heat. Stir to cool for a minute, then scrape into the eggs.

4. Make the frittata following the directions in the basic recipe on page 97, using the remaining 1 tablespoon olive oil.

Advance preparation: The frittata can be made up to 1 day ahead. Allow to cool, cover with plastic, then foil, and refrigerate.

swiss chard frittata

This chard-packed frittata is based on a classic Provençal omelet called *truccha*. It's one of my favorites, partly because it's so easy. I once worked in a Provençal restaurant in Cannes, where a garlicky *truccha* was on the daily menu. There was one kitchen assistant whose entire job appeared to be stripping chard leaves from the stems and blanching them. The *trucchas* were so popular, I suppose they needed one person just to do this task. But it's not a very daunting one if all you are making is one large omelet. **MAKES 6 MAIN-COURSE SERVINGS OR 10 TO 12 FIRST-COURSE SERVINGS OR HORS D'OEUVRES**

> 2 generous bunches Swiss chard (2 pounds or more,
> depending on the thickness of the stalks)
> Salt to taste
>
> 10 large eggs
> 2 to 4 large garlic cloves, minced or pressed
> Freshly ground black pepper
> 3 tablespoons low-fat milk
> 1 tablespoon extra virgin olive oil

1. Bring a large pot of water to a boil while you strip the chard leaves from their stems. Discard the stems or set them aside for another purpose and wash the leaves thoroughly. When the water comes to a boil, add about 1 tablespoon of salt and the chard leaves. Blanch for 2 minutes and transfer to a bowl of cold water. Drain, squeeze out any water, and chop. You should have about 3 cups chopped chard.

2. Beat the eggs in a large bowl. Add ½ to ¾ teaspoon salt, the garlic, pepper, and milk. Beat together well. Stir in the chopped chard and mix together.

3. Make the frittata following the directions in the basic recipe on page 97, using the remaining 1 tablespoon olive oil.

Advance preparation: The frittata can be made a day ahead. Allow to cool, cover with plastic wrap, then foil, and refrigerate.

onion and tomato frittata

One summer weekend I found myself having a big spontaneous lunch party. With the food I had on hand, I made this beautiful tomato-studded omelet as the main dish. Make sure to drain the tomatoes before adding them to the eggs, or the mixture will be too watery and the omelet won't hold together. **MAKES 6 MAIN-COURSE SERVINGS OR 12 FIRST-COURSE SERVINGS OR HORS D'OEUVRES**

1 pound ripe tomatoes, peeled, seeded, and finely diced
Salt
1 large or 2 medium sweet onions, finely chopped
1 tablespoon red or white wine vinegar
1 tablespoon extra virgin olive oil
2 large garlic cloves, minced

10 large eggs
3 tablespoons low-fat milk
Salt and freshly ground black pepper to taste
¼ cup chopped fresh basil or parsley, or a combination
1 tablespoon extra virgin olive oil

1. Place the tomatoes in a strainer set over a bowl, salt lightly, and let drain for 1 hour. This is to prevent the omelet from being watery. Place the finely chopped onion in a bowl and cover with cold water. Add the vinegar and let sit for 20 to 30 minutes.

2. Heat 1 tablespoon oil in a heavy nonstick 12-inch skillet over medium-low heat. Drain the onions, shake off any water, and add to the pan. Cook, stirring, until thoroughly tender, about 10 minutes. Stir in the garlic and cook for another minute, or until the garlic is fragrant. Remove from the heat.

3. Beat the eggs in a bowl and stir in the milk, salt, pepper, and the onions, tomatoes, and herbs.

4. Make the frittata following the directions in the basic recipe on page 97, using the remaining tablespoon olive oil.

Advance preparation: This can be made a day ahead and refrigerated, but it may become watery. Allow to cool, cover with plastic, then foil, and refrigerate.

strata

This couldn't be easier to throw together. It makes a perfect meal solution for those nights when all you seem to have on hand is bread that's getting stale. The dish, known as a strata, is a layered casserole made with bread, eggs, milk, and cheese. More cheese and a richer milk, and maybe cream, might be used in a traditional version, but I love this one; I eat the leftovers cold for lunch. **MAKES 4 GENEROUS SERVINGS**

½ pound bread, slightly stale if possible,
sliced about ½ inch thick
1 large garlic clove, cut in half
2 to 3 cups low-fat milk
¾ to 1 pound tomatoes (3 to 4 medium), sliced
Salt and freshly ground black pepper to taste
1 teaspoon fresh thyme leaves or ½ teaspoon dried
2 ounces Gruyère, grated (½ cup)
4 large eggs

1. Preheat the oven to 350°F. Oil or butter a 2-quart baking or gratin dish.

2. If the bread is soft, toast it lightly and rub both slices with the cut clove of garlic. If it's stale, just rub with garlic. If the bread is so stale that it's difficult to slice, soak the loaf in 1 cup milk just until it is soft enough to slice—about 1 minute—then slice. Layer half of the slices in the baking dish. Top with half the tomato slices. Sprinkle the tomato slices with salt, pepper, and thyme. Top with half the cheese. Repeat the layers.

3. Beat together the eggs and 2 cups milk. Add a scant ½ teaspoon salt and a few twists of the pepper mill. Pour over the bread.

4. Bake for 40 to 50 minutes, until firm and browned. Remove from the oven and serve hot or warm.

Advance preparation: The bread and tomato layers can be assembled hours before beating together the eggs and milk and completing the casserole.

strata with swiss chard

This is much like the previous recipe, with the addition of Swiss chard. You could also make the strata with spinach. **MAKES 4 GENEROUS SERVINGS**

¾ to 1 pound (1 large bunch) Swiss chard, stemmed and cleaned
Salt to taste
One 14-ounce can diced tomatoes, drained, or 4 medium fresh tomatoes,
*   peeled, seeded, and chopped*
3 large garlic cloves, 2 minced, 1 cut in half
1 teaspoon fresh thyme leaves, or ½ teaspoon dried thyme (optional)
Freshly ground black pepper to taste
½ pound bread, slightly stale if possible, sliced about ½-inch thick
2 to 3 cups low-fat milk
2 ounces Gruyère, grated (½ cup)
4 large eggs

1. Preheat the oven to 350°F. Oil or butter a 2-quart baking or gratin dish.

2. Bring a pot of water to a boil and add 1 tablespoon of salt and the chard. Blanch for 2 to 4 minutes, until tender. Transfer to a bowl of cold water, then drain, squeeze out water, and coarsely chop. Toss with the tomatoes, minced garlic, thyme, and salt and pepper to taste.

3. If the bread is soft, toast it lightly and rub both sides with the cut clove of garlic. If the bread is stale, just rub with garlic. If the bread is so stale that it's difficult to slice, soak in 1 cup milk just until until soft enough to slice—about 1 minute—then slice. Layer half of the slices in the baking dish. Top with half the tomato-chard mixture. Sprinkle on half the cheese. Repeat the layers.

4. Beat together the eggs and 2 cups milk. Add a scant ½ teaspoon salt and a few twists of the pepper mill. Pour over the bread mixture.

5. Bake for 40 to 50 minutes, until firm and browned. Remove from the oven and serve hot or warm.

Advance preparation: The bread and chard layers can be assembled hours before beating together the eggs and milk and completing the casserole.

Vegetable Tarts

Call it a quiche and it's a cliché, a throwback to the vegetarianism of the 1970s. But a vegetable tart, enriched with cheese and bound with eggs, is one of the most comforting and delicious of main dishes. It's one of the best ways I can think of to get kids to eat vegetables or to get a confirmed meat-eater to enjoy a vegetarian meal. Everybody loves a tart. Serve it with a salad or soup and salad, and you've got dinner. Pack leftovers in a lunch box, or cut them into squares or diamonds and serve as an hors d'oeuvre.

A traditional savory tart, the type you would find in France, has a short crust or a puff pastry crust. But go south to the Mediterranean, and you will find a number of vegetable tarts, some double-crusted, some not, made with olive oil pastry and brimming with vegetables. Olive oil and water-based crusts are easier to roll out than butter-based short crusts. When baked, the tart will have a hard, crisp edge, more like a pizza than a piecrust, and it will be easier to cut with a scissors than a knife, at least the edges will be (see instructions below). The crust underneath the filling is not at all tough or hard, but tender and somewhat bready, a real treat. The recipes make two crusts, so you can use one for tonight's dinner and freeze the other for a quick meal next week.

Cutting Oil- and Water-Based Crusts

The edges of the Mediterranean and Yeasted Olive Oil piecrusts that follow can be hard, and I find that I can get neater slices if I use kitchen scissors. Make your wedges with the tip of a sharp knife, cutting from the middle to the edge. If the rim feels hard and difficult to cut neatly with the knife, clip the exposed edges of the crust with scissors. Scissors, by the way, are also useful for slicing pizza.

mediterranean piecrust

2¼ cups unbleached all-purpose flour or
1¼ cups unbleached all-purpose flour and
1 cup whole wheat flour or whole wheat pastry flour,
plus flour for rolling out dough
¾ teaspoon salt
2 teaspoons baking powder
3 tablespoons extra virgin olive oil

1. Sift the flour, salt, and baking powder into a mixing bowl.

2. TO MIX BY HAND

Make a well in the flour mixture and add the olive oil and ¾ cup water. Using a fork, gradually mix the liquid into the flours. When it is no longer possible to use the fork, lightly flour your hands and use them to finish bringing the mixture together. Then turn out the mixture onto a lightly floured board and very gently knead until the dough is smooth.

TO MIX USING A MIXER OR FOOD PROCESSOR

Transfer the flour mixture to the bowl of your food processor, fitted with the steel blade, or mixer, fitted with the paddle. If you are using the food processor, turn on and add the olive oil, then ¾ cup water. When the dough comes together in a ball, turn off the machine. If you are using a mixer, make a well in the flour mixture. Add the olive oil and ¾ cup water. Mix at low speed until the dough comes together. Scrape out of the food processor or mixer, and knead very gently on a lightly floured board just until the dough is smooth. Do not overwork or the dough will be tough.

3. Divide the dough into two equal pieces and shape each piece into a ball. Press each ball into a disk, about 4 inches in diameter. Dust lightly with flour if the dough is sticky. Wrap in plastic, then place in a plastic bag, and let rest for 1 hour or longer, in or out of the refrigerator.

4. Sprinkle a small amount of unbleached flour over your work surface. Put the piece of dough on it, and lightly dust the top with more flour. Roll the dough from the center to the far edge, in one direction only, turning the dough, until it is quite thin, with a diameter of at least 12 inches. Keep dusting lightly with flour if the dough sticks.

5. Brush or spray a 10-inch pie pan or tart pan with olive or canola oil. Gently fold the circle of dough in half and lift onto the pan, with the fold in the middle of the pan. Unfold the dough so that it covers the pan. Press gently into the pans (this is called "easing" the dough into the pans). If the dough is uneven and doesn't cover the edge of the pan in places, cut a little of the over-lapping bits from the edges that do extend over the pan and pinch them together with the edges that fall short. Pinch an attractive lip around the rim of the pan.

6. Repeat with the second piece of dough. Use immediately, or cover with plastic and refriger-ate, or cover with plastic, then with foil, and freeze.

Advance preparation: You can freeze the dough without rolling it out. But it will make your life easier when you want another tart if it's frozen in the pan, ready to go. The dough or crust will keep for several months in the freezer. If freezing without rolling out, allow 2 to 3 hours for the dough to thaw at room temperature. You can take your crust directly from the freezer, pre-bake and fill it, and bake as directed.

yeasted olive oil pastry

This crust is a little more delicate than the Mediterranean Piecrust (page 106) and, just like that dough, extremely easy to work with. The important thing to remember here is to roll the dough very thin so that it won't be too bready. **MAKES TWO 10-INCH PIECRUSTS**

1½ teaspoons active dry yeast
¼ teaspoon sugar
1 large egg, at room temperature
3 tablespoons extra-virgin olive oil
2 to 2½ cups unbleached all-purpose flour
¾ teaspoon salt

1. Dissolve the yeast in ½ cup lukewarm water, add the sugar, and let it sit for 5 to 10 minutes, until creamy.

2. Beat in the egg and the olive oil. Combine 2 cups of the flour and the salt, and stir in. (This can be done in an electric mixer; combine the ingredients using the paddle, then switch to the kneading hook; or it can be done in a food processor fitted with the steel blade.) Work the dough until it comes together in a coherent mass, adding flour as necessary if it is very moist and sticky.

3. Turn out onto a lightly floured surface. Knead for a few minutes, adding flour as necessary, until the dough is smooth. Shape the dough into a ball. Do not overwork. Place in a lightly oiled bowl, rounded side down first, then rounded side up. Cover the bowl tightly with plastic wrap, and let rise in a warm spot for 1 hour, or until doubled in volume.

4. When the pastry has risen and softened, punch it down gently and shape into a ball. Cut into two equal pieces and shape each piece into a ball. Cover each ball loosely with plastic wrap and let them rest for 10 minutes. Butter or oil two 9- or 10-inch tart pans or pie pans.

5. On a lightly floured surface, roll each ball of dough very thinly, about ⅛ inch thick, about 1 inch bigger than the circumference of your pans. Line the pans with the dough. An easy way to do this is to fold the dough in half and lift onto the pan, with the fold in the middle of the pan. Unfold the dough so it covers the pan. Ease gently into the pans. You should have a bit of overhang around the edges of the pans. Roll the dough in and pinch an attractive lip around the edge of each pan. If you are not baking right away, cover with plastic wrap, and place in the freezer to prevent the dough from rising and becoming too bready.

6. Bake as directed.

Advance preparation: The crust will keep for several months in the freezer, wrapped in plastic, then foil. Remove from the freezer very shortly before baking.

yeasted butter pastry

This is a softer, more delicate dough than the olive oil pastries on pages 106 to 108, but it's also higher in saturated fat. I use it for tarts and galettes. **MAKES ENOUGH FOR TWO 10-INCH TARTS**

1½ teaspoons active dry yeast
¼ teaspoon sugar
1 large egg, at room temperature
2 to 2½ cups unbleached all-purpose flour
¾ teaspoon salt
4 tablespoons unsalted butter, softened

1. Dissolve the yeast in ½ cup water. Add the sugar and let sit for 5 to 10 minutes, until creamy.

2. Beat in the egg. Combine 2 cups of the flour and the salt. Stir in 1 cup. Stir in the butter. (This can be done in an electric mixer; combine the ingredients using the paddle, then switch to the kneading hook; or in the food processor using the pulse action.) Add another cup of the flour mixture and process or stir, adding additional flour as necessary until the dough comes together in a coherent mass.

3. Turn the dough out onto a lightly floured surface. Knead, adding flour as necessary, just until the dough is smooth. Shape the dough into a ball. Do not overwork.

4. Place in a lightly oiled or buttered bowl, rounded side down first, then rounded side up, cover the bowl tightly with plastic wrap, and let rise in a warm spot for 1 hour, or until doubled.

5. When the pastry has risen and softened, punch it down gently and shape into a ball. Cut into two equal pieces and shape each piece into a ball. Cover the dough with plastic wrap and let it rest for 10 minutes. Butter two pie or tart pans.

6. Roll out each ball of dough on a lightly floured surface. Roll the dough very thin, about ⅛ inch thick. It should be about 1 inch bigger than the circumference of your pans. Line the pans with the dough. An easy way to do this is to fold the dough in half, then place on one half of the pan and unfold. Ease gently into the pans. You should have a bit of overhang around the edges of the pans. Roll the dough in and pinch an attractive lip around the edge of each pan.

If you are not baking right away, cover with plastic wrap and place in the freezer, to prevent the dough from rising and becoming too bready. Remove from the freezer very shortly before baking.

7. Bake as directed.

FOR GALETTES

Roll out the dough on a lightly floured surface to a thin circle (about ⅛ inch thick), 14 to 15 inches in diameter, dusting each side of the dough lightly with flour so that it doesn't stick to your rolling pin or the table. Transfer to a baking sheet. Top as instructed, leaving a 2- to 3-inch lip all the way around. Fold the edge over the filling, draping it in folds all the way around.

Advance preparation: This will keep for several months in the freezer. You can freeze the dough before rolling out. Wrap the ball of dough in plastic wrap, seal in a plastic bag, and freeze. Allow the dough to thaw for several hours in the refrigerator before rolling out. Or roll out the dough, fit into the tart pan, cover with plastic, then foil, and freeze. It can be filled and baked without defrosting. You can also keep the dough, before rolling out, in the refrigerator for a day. You will need to dust it generously with flour when you roll it out.

spinach and cheese tart

This is a classic, always popular with family and guests, and the best way I can think of to get kids to eat spinach. Serve it with Carrot and Leek Soup (page 85) and a green salad. In summer accompany this with a Summer Tomato Gratin (page 255) or corn on the cob. **MAKES 6 SERV- INGS**

½ recipe Mediterranean Piecrust (page 106),
    Yeasted Olive Oil Pastry (page 108), or
    Yeasted Butter Pastry (page 110)
3 large eggs or 2 whole eggs and 2 egg whites
1 pound fresh spinach (1 large bunch or two 10-ounce bags),
    cleaned, wilted, squeezed dry, and chopped, or
    two 10-ounce boxes frozen chopped spinach
1 tablespoon extra virgin olive oil
1 small or ½ medium onion,
    chopped (about ⅔ cup)
1 cup low-fat milk
2 tablespoons nonfat dry milk
½ teaspoon salt
Freshly ground black pepper to taste
2 ounces Gruyère, grated (½ cup)
1 ounce Parmesan, grated (¼ cup), or
    omit and use ¾ cup grated Gruyère

1. Preheat the oven to 375°F.

2. Fit the pastry into a 9-inch or 10-inch tart pan. Beat the eggs and lightly brush the surface of the crust with the eggs. Bake for 7 minutes. Cool on a rack.

3. Heat the oil in a heavy nonstick skillet over medium heat and add the onion. Cook, stirring, until tender, 3 to 5 minutes. Remove from the heat and set aside.

4. Meanwhile, wilt the spinach. Bring a large pot of water to a boil while you strip the stems and wash the spinach in two changes of water. When the water comes to a boil, add about a tablespoon of salt and the spinach leaves. Blanch for 1 minute and transfer to a bowl of cold water. Drain, squeeze out the water, and chop. Alternately, wilt the spinach in the water left on its leaves after washing. Heat a large, preferably nonstick skillet over high heat while you stem and wash the spinach. Add to the pan in batches, and stir until the water sizzles and the leaves wilt, a couple of minutes once the water boils. Remove from the pan, rinse with cold water, squeeze out the water and chop. If using frozen spinach, thaw in a microwave or in a bowl at room temperature, and squeeze out the water; it will be easier to squeeze out the water from frozen spinach if you wrap the spinach, which is already chopped, in a clean dish towel and squeeze the towel.

5. In a blender or bowl with a whisk, blend together the milk and dry milk. Add the salt, eggs, and pepper, and blend together well. Stir in the onion, spinach, and cheeses. Pour into the pre-baked crust.

6. Bake for 30 to 40 minutes, until the custard is set (it shouldn't jiggle when you touch the top lightly) and the top is browned. Cool on a rack. Serve hot, warm, or at room temperature.

Advance preparation: The tart can be made a day ahead and reheated in a 250° to 300°F oven for 20 minutes, or serve at room temperature.

leek tart

This is a vegetarian version of a French classic, *flamiche aux poireaux*. I use an olive oil crust here instead of the traditional puff pastry or short crust. Serve this as a main dish, with Mediterranean Greens (page 238), Asian Greens (page 239), or steamed broccoli, and Arugula, Pear, and Walnut Salad (page 39). Or cut into smaller wedges or squares and serve as an hors d'oeuvre. **MAKES 6 MAIN-COURSE SERVINGS OR 12 HORS D'OEUVRES**

½ recipe Mediterranean Piecrust (page 106),
Yeasted Olive Oil Pastry (page 108), or
Yeasted Butter Pastry (page 110),
made with unbleached all-purpose flour
3 large eggs or 2 whole eggs and 2 egg whites
2 pounds leeks
1 tablespoon unsalted butter
¾ teaspoon salt
Freshly ground black pepper to taste
1 cup low-fat milk
2 tablespoons nonfat dry milk
3 ounces Gruyère, grated (¾ cup)

1. Preheat the oven to 375°F.

2. Fit the pastry into a 9-inch or 10-inch tart pan. Beat the eggs and lightly brush the surface of the crust with the eggs. Bake for 7 minutes. Cool on a rack.

3. Cut away the ends of the leeks and the tough green stems. Cut in half lengthwise and place in a bowl of cold water. Run each leek under cold water, making sure any sand caught between the layers runs out. Shake dry and coarsely chop. I do this by cutting the halves in half again lengthwise, then slicing across the quartered leeks.

4. Heat the butter in a heavy nonstick skillet over medium-low heat. Add the leeks and ¼ teaspoon of the salt. Stir, then cover the pan, and cook, stirring occasionally, until very tender, 10 to 15 minutes. The leeks should not brown. If they begin to stick to the pan, add 1 tablespoon water. Add pepper to taste and remove from the heat. Spread in an even layer over the tart crust.

5. In a blender or bowl with a whisk, blend together the milk and dry milk. Add the remaining ½ teaspoon salt and eggs, and blend together well. Stir in the cheese. Pour into the crust.

6. Bake for 30 to 40 minutes, until the custard is set and the top is golden brown. Cool on a rack. Serve hot or warm.

Advance preparation: This can be made a day ahead and reheated in a 250° to 300°F oven for 20 minutes, or served at room temperature. The crust will remain crisp.

asparagus and scallion tart

A beautiful spring/summer tart, this makes a welcoming hors d'oeuvre as well as a main dish. Follow it with a risotto (pages 165 to 175) or serve it with a Summer Vegetable Salad (page 46) when tomatoes are in season. **MAKES 6 MAIN-COURSE SERVINGS OR 10 HORS D'OEUVRES**

½ recipe Mediterranean Piecrust (page 106), Yeasted Olive Oil Pastry
(page 108), or Yeasted Butter Pastry (page 110)
3 large eggs or 2 whole eggs and 2 egg whites
¾ pound asparagus, trimmed and cut into ¾-inch pieces
1 tablespoon extra virgin olive oil
2 bunches scallions, white and light green parts, trimmed and sliced
2 ounces Gruyère, grated (½ cup)
1 ounce Parmesan, grated (¼ cup)
1 cup low-fat milk
2 tablespoons nonfat dry milk
½ teaspoon salt
Freshly ground black pepper to taste
2 tablespoons chopped fresh dill or parsley (optional)

1. Preheat the oven to 375°F.

2. Fit the pastry into a 9-inch or 10-inch tart pan. Beat the eggs and lightly brush the surface of the crust with the eggs. Bake for 7 minutes. Cool on a rack.

3. Steam the asparagus for 5 minutes, until just tender. Remove from the heat, refresh under cold water, and allow to drain. Transfer to a bowl.

4. Heat the oil in a medium heavy nonstick skillet and add the scallions. Cook, stirring, until tender, about 3 minutes. Toss with the asparagus and add the cheeses.

5. In a blender or bowl with a whisk, blend together the milk and dry milk. Add the salt, eggs, and pepper, and blend together well. Stir in the herbs.

6. Spread the asparagus, scallions, and cheese in an even layer in the crust. Pour in the milk mixture. Bake for 35 to 40 minutes, until the tart is firm and the top lightly browned. Cool on a rack. Serve hot or warm.

vegetable tart using leftovers

A tart is a reliable vehicle for leftover vegetables, whether complex stews like the Roasted Vegetable Stew with Bulgur or Rice (page 242) or simpler steamed or roasted vegetables. **MAKES 6 MAIN-COURSE SERVINGS OR 12 HORS D'OEUVRES**

*½ recipe Mediterranean Piecrust (page 106), Yeasted Olive Oil Pastry
    (page 108), or Yeasted Butter Pastry (page 110)
3 large eggs or 2 whole eggs and 2 egg whites
2 to 3 cups leftover cooked vegetables
    (a stew, grilled vegetables, or plain steamed vegetables)
1 cup low-fat milk
2 tablespoons nonfat dry milk
½ teaspoon salt
Freshly ground black pepper to taste
2 ounces Gruyère, grated (½ cup)
1 ounce Parmesan, grated (¼ cup)*

1. Preheat the oven to 375°F.

2. Fit the pastry into a 9-inch or 10-inch tart pan. Beat the eggs and lightly brush the surface of the crust with the eggs. Bake for 7 minutes. Cool on a rack.

3. Spread the leftovers in an even layer over the crust.

4. In a blender or bowl with a whisk, blend together the milk and dry milk. Add the salt, eggs, and pepper, and blend together well. Stir in the cheeses. Pour into the crust.

5. Bake for 30 to 40 minutes, until the custard is set and the top is just beginning to brown.

6. Cool on a rack. Serve hot or warm.

Advance preparation: The tart can be made a day ahead and reheated in a 300°F oven for 20 minutes, or served at room temperature. The crust will remain crisp.

cheese soufflé

The soufflé is the pinnacle of egg and cheese cookery, a pillow of egg white and cheese surrounding a moist, saucy interior. Soufflés are wonderful for dinner parties, as long as you know when you're going to sit down at the table. The different parts can be prepared ahead of time, so that all you have to do at the last minute is fold the elements together and put the dish into the oven. And here's your chance to learn to make a béchamel, the classic creamy white sauce that is used in other dishes, including gratins. **MAKES 6 SERVINGS**

SOUFFLÉ

1 ounce grated Parmesan (¼ cup)
6 large eggs, separated and at room temperature
2 egg whites
¼ teaspoon cream of tartar
Pinch of salt
3 ounces grated Gruyère (¾ cup)

BÉCHAMEL

1½ cups low-fat milk
2 tablespoons unsalted butter
3 tablespoons sifted unbleached all-purpose flour
Salt and freshly ground white pepper to taste
Tiny pinch of nutmeg

1. Butter the inside of a 2-quart soufflé dish. Sprinkle in 2 tablespoons Parmesan, and tap the dish so that the cheese coats the sides.

2. Make the béchamel. Heat the milk in a small saucepan, just until simmering. Meanwhile, melt the butter in a heavy 2-quart saucepan over medium-low heat. When the butter is bubbling, stir in the flour. Stir to a smooth paste; this is called a *roux*. Cook the roux for a few minutes, stirring constantly with a wooden spoon. It should not brown, but it should bubble; you are trying to rid the flour of its raw flavor. Now whisk in the hot milk. Whisk vigorously to make sure there are no lumps. Turn the heat to medium and continue to whisk, making sure all of the roux is incorporated from the edges of the pot into the milk, until the mixture comes to a simmer and thickens. Turn the heat to low and simmer, stirring often to bring the sauce up from the sides and bottom of the saucepan, for 5 minutes. The sauce should be quite thick (thicker than a normal béchamel, because you will be adding the egg yolks). Season to taste with salt (½ to 1 teaspoon), a small amount of white pepper, and nutmeg. Remove from the heat and stir for another minute.

3. Preheat the oven to 375°F.

4. Beat the egg yolks into the béchamel, one at a time. Set aside.

5. Beat the egg whites in the bowl of an electric mixer until they begin to foam. Add the cream of tartar and a pinch of salt, and beat until they are satiny and form peaks that hold their shape when lifted with the spatula or beater. Do not overbeat; the peaks should be satiny and not dry.

6. Combine the remaining 2 tablespoons Parmesan and the Gruyère in a bowl. Stir one-fourth of the beaten egg whites into the béchamel, using a rubber spatula. This lightens the sauce and makes it easier to fold into the egg whites. Now pour the sauce into the middle of the beaten egg whites. Fold the egg whites into the sauce with your spatula by gently scooping the sauce from the middle of the bowl, under the egg whites to the side of the bowl, up over the egg whites, and back to the middle of the bowl. With each fold, sprinkle in a handful of the cheese mixture and give the bowl a quarter turn. Fold until the mixture is homogeneous and all the cheese has been added, working rapidly but with a light hand.

7. Carefully spoon the soufflé mixture into the prepared dish. Place in the middle of the oven and bake for 25 to 35 minutes, until puffed and browned. Remove from the oven and serve at once, spooning the runny middle part over the fluffy outer section with each portion.

Advance preparation: The béchamel can be made and any vegetable additions (below) prepared a day ahead. To store the béchamel, allow it to cool slightly, then lay a piece of plastic wrap on the surface, and cover with the pot lid. Refrigerate. When you remove it from the refrigerator, it will be quite solid. Allow to come to room temperature and whisk vigorously over very low heat. Remove from the heat, stir for a minute, then whisk in the egg yolks. You can do this hours before you bake. Then just beat the egg whites and fold in. But make sure that everything is at room temperature.

• BROCCOLI SOUFFLÉ • Prepare 2 cups finely chopped steamed broccoli (you can do this in a food processor after the broccoli has been steamed, or use a sharp knife and large cutting board). Stir into the béchamel with the egg yolks.

potato and chard gratin with goat cheese

When I buy greens at the farmers' market each week, I rarely know what I'm going to do with them, but they're always inspiring. Greens and potatoes merge beautifully here in a comforting gratin bound with milk, egg, and goat cheese. Chard, either red or green, is the green to use here. **MAKES 4 MAIN-COURSE SERVINGS OR 6 SIDE-DISH SERVINGS**

3 large garlic cloves, peeled
1 pound Swiss or red chard, stemmed and washed
Salt to taste
1½ pounds waxy potatoes, such as Yukon Gold or
 red or white new potatoes,
 scrubbed and sliced about ¼ inch thick
2 large eggs, beaten
2½ cups low-fat milk
4 ounces fresh mild goat cheese,
 such as Montrachet (about 1 cup)
Freshly ground black pepper to taste
Pinch of nutmeg, freshly grated if possible

1. Preheat the oven to 400°F. Cut a garlic clove in half and rub the inside of a 2½- or 3-quart gratin dish or baking dish with the cut side. Brush with about 1 teaspoon olive oil.

2. Bring a large pot of water to a boil while you stem and wash the chard. When the water comes to a rolling boil, add 1 tablespoon salt and the chard. Cook for 1 minute, drain, and rinse with cold water. Squeeze out any water and chop coarsely; you should have about 1½ cups chopped chard.

3. Toss together the chard and potatoes with a little salt and pepper in a large bowl.

4. Turn on a food processor fitted with the steel blade and drop in the garlic, including the cut clove you used for seasoning the baking dish. When the garlic adheres to the sides of the bowl, stop the machine and scrape down the sides. Add the eggs, milk, cheese, and about ½ teaspoon salt or more to taste. Process until smooth. Combine with the potatoes and chard. Add pepper and a pinch of nutmeg.

5. Turn into the gratin dish. Bake for 1 to 1½ hours, until all the milk is absorbed and the gratin is brown and crusty on the top. During the first 40 minutes, stir every 10 minutes or so to bring the potatoes up from the bottom and break up. Serve hot or warm.

Advance preparation: You can assemble this hours before you bake it, and prep the chard the day before. The finished dish can sit for a couple of hours and be gently reheated in a 250° to 300°F oven for 20 minutes.

greens and tomato gratin

Here's a summery Mediterranean gratin that can be made with your choice of greens, alone or in combination. Once the greens are washed and blanched, the gratin is easily thrown together and can be eaten hot or at room temperature, so it's a great do-ahead dish. **MAKES 4 MAIN-COURSE OR 6 SIDE-DISH SERVINGS**

*2 pounds greens, such as beet greens, Swiss chard, kale, or
    spinach, stemmed and washed well*
Salt
2 tablespoons extra virgin olive oil
1 large garlic clove, minced
3 large eggs or 2 whole eggs and 2 egg whites, beaten
¾ cup low-fat milk
2 tablespoons nonfat dry milk
Freshly ground black pepper to taste
*1 teaspoon chopped fresh rosemary or
    ½ teaspoon crumbled dried*
2 ounces Gruyère, grated (½ cup)
2 medium tomatoes, thinly sliced
¼ cup dry or fresh bread crumbs

1. Preheat the oven to 375°F. Oil a 2-quart baking dish or gratin dish.

2. Bring a large pot of water to a boil and add 1 tablespoon salt and the greens. Blanch the greens for 2 minutes and transfer to a bowl of cold water. Drain and squeeze dry. Chop coarsely. You should have about 1½ cups chopped greens.

3. Heat 1 tablespoon of the oil in a large, heavy nonstick skillet over medium heat. Add the garlic. Cook, stirring, for about 30 seconds, until the garlic just begins to color. Add the greens. Stir together for 1 minute, until the greens are coated with oil and infused with garlic, and remove from the heat.

4. Beat together the eggs, milk, nonfat dry milk, ½ teaspoon salt, pepper to taste, and rosemary. Stir in the cheese and greens. Scrape into the prepared baking dish. Layer the sliced tomatoes over the top. Lightly salt and pepper the tomatoes and sprinkle on the bread crumbs. Drizzle on the remaining 1 tablespoon oil.

5. Bake for 40 to 45 minutes, until the top is browned and the gratin is sizzling and firm to the touch. Serve hot, warm, or at room temperature.

Advance preparation: The greens can be prepared a day or two ahead and held in the refrigerator. The gratin can be assembled and baked hours before serving; reheat if desired in a 250° to 300°F oven for 20 minutes.

yellow squash and rice gratin

Provence is the source of many of my gratin recipes. Vegetables are such a vital part of the cuisine in this Mediterranean region of France, and they all find their way into gratins. Many of the Provençal gratins are bound with a mixture of rice and eggs. This is an economical way to make a substantial dish out of vegetables. I love the chewy texture that the rice contributes. **MAKES 4 SERVINGS**

½ cup long-grain or Arborio rice
2 tablespoons extra virgin olive oil
Salt to taste
1 medium onion, minced
1 pound yellow summer squash, diced
2 garlic cloves, minced
Freshly ground black pepper to taste
2 large eggs
2 ounces Gruyère or Parmesan, or a mixture, grated (½ cup)
½ cup chopped fresh parsley
1 teaspoon fresh thyme leaves or ½ teaspoon dried
2 tablespoons fresh or dry bread crumbs

1. Bring 1 cup water to a boil in a 1-quart lidded saucepan. Add the rice and ¼ teaspoon salt. When the water comes back to a boil, stir once and once only, turn the heat down to low, and cover the pot tightly. Simmer 15 minutes, until the water has evaporated. Turn off the heat, uncover the pot, and cover the top of the pot with a clean dish towel. Return the lid to the pot and let sit for 10 minutes undisturbed.

2. Preheat the oven to 375°F. Brush a 2-quart baking dish or gratin dish with olive oil.

3. Heat 1 tablespoon of the oil in a large, heavy nonstick skillet over medium heat. Add the onion. Cook, stirring, until tender, about 5 minutes. Add the squash, garlic, salt, and pepper, and cook, stirring often, for 8 to 10 minutes, until the squash is tender but not mushy. Remove from the heat and allow to cool slightly.

4. Beat the eggs in a bowl. Stir in the squash and onion, the cheese, parsley, rice, and thyme. Stir together, taste, and add more salt and pepper, if desired. Transfer to the baking dish. Sprinkle the bread crumbs over the top and drizzle on the remaining 1 tablespoon oil.

5. Bake for 45 minutes, until firm and browned on the top. Cool on a rack. Serve warm or at room temperature.

Advance preparation: This can be made a day ahead of time and held in the refrigerator, tightly wrapped. Reheat in a 250° to 300°F oven for 20 minutes or serve at room temperature.

beet and beet green gratin with goat cheese

One of my favorite appetizers at Spago restaurant in Los Angeles combines sliced beets and goat cheese. That marriage, and my love for Provençal-style gratins that are bound with rice and a little egg, inspired me to make this beautiful, red gratin (it looks like a dessert!). It's a great way to make use of the greens at the end of the beets. Shop for beets with generous bunches attached. If you make this in a loaf pan, try unmolding it and serving it in slices as a first course or main dish. **MAKES 4 MAIN-COURSE SERVINGS OR 6 TO 8 FIRST-COURSE SERVINGS**

2 medium beets
2 large eggs
½ cup Arborio or short-grain rice
Salt to taste
2 tablespoons extra virgin olive oil
1 medium onion, minced
2 garlic cloves, minced
¾ to 1 pound beet greens (from the bunch),
*   stemmed, washed thoroughly, and coarsely chopped*
Freshly ground black pepper to taste
2 ounces fresh, mild goat cheese, such as Montrachet,
*   crumbled (about ½ cup)*
1 teaspoon fresh thyme leaves or
*   ½ teaspoon dried*
2 tablespoons fresh or dry bread crumbs

1. Preheat the oven to 425°F.

2. Cut away the beet greens by slicing across the top end of each beet about ½ inch above where the stems and root meet. Scrub the beets under warm water with a vegetable brush. Place in a baking dish and add about ¼ inch water. Cover and bake for 30 to 60 minutes, depending on the size of the beets. Medium-size beets take about 45 minutes, small ones 30 minutes, and very large ones take an hour. Test for doneness by sticking a knife into a beet. It should slide in easily. Remove from the heat and allow to cool. When the beets are cool, it will be easy to slip their skins off. Skin and cut into small dice.

3. Turn the oven down to 375°F. Brush a 2-quart gratin dish or an 8½ × 4½-inch nonstick loaf pan with olive oil.

4. While the beets are roasting, cook the rice. Bring 1 cup water to a boil in a 1-quart lidded saucepan. Add the rice and ¼ teaspoon salt. When the water comes back to a boil, stir once and once only, turn the heat down to low, and cover the pot tightly. Simmer 15 minutes, until the water has evaporated. Turn off the heat, uncover the pot and cover the top of the pot with a clean dish towel. Return the lid to the pot and let sit for 10 minutes undisturbed.

5. Heat 1 tablespoon of the oil in a large, heavy nonstick skillet over medium-low heat and add the onion. Cook, stirring, until tender, about 5 minutes. Add the garlic and cook, stirring, for another 30 to 60 seconds, until the garlic is fragrant. Rinse the greens if they are no longer wet from washing. Stir in the wet greens and cook, stirring, until they wilt, 4 to 5 minutes (they should retain a bright green color). Add salt and pepper and remove from the heat.

6. Beat the eggs in a bowl. Stir in the greens and onions, the cheese, rice, thyme, and diced beets. Stir together, taste, and add more salt and pepper if desired (I usually do). Transfer to the baking dish. Sprinkle the bread crumbs over the top and drizzle on the remaining 1 tablespoon oil.

7. Bake for 45 to 60 minutes (it will take longer in a loaf pan than in a gratin dish), until firm, sizzling (the bubbles will be a dazzling red), and browned on the top. Cool on a rack. Serve warm or at room temperature.

Advance preparation: This keeps well for a couple of days, tightly wrapped, in the refrigerator. Serve at room temperature or reheat in a 250° to 300°F oven for 20 minutes.

zucchini, red pepper, and corn gratin

Serve this beautiful, bright, summer gratin with the Tomato, Feta, and Arugula Salad (page 41) or Bulgarian Cucumber and Yogurt Salad (page 45) for a perfect, light summer meal. It would also go with a more substantial salad, such as Wheat Berry Salad (page 52) or Chickpea Salad (page 55). **MAKES 4 MAIN-COURSE OR 6 SIDE-DISH SERVINGS**

1 tablespoon extra virgin olive oil
1 medium or large red bell pepper, diced
3 medium zucchini (1¼ to 1½ pounds), diced
1 to 2 large garlic cloves, minced or pressed
Salt and freshly ground black pepper to taste
Kernels from 1 ear corn
1 teaspoon fresh thyme leaves or ½ teaspoon dried
3 large eggs or 2 whole eggs and 2 egg whites
¾ cup low-fat milk
1 to 2 ounces Gruyère, grated (¼ to ½ cup)

1. Preheat the oven to 375°F. Oil a 2-quart baking dish or gratin dish.

2. Heat the oil in a large, heavy nonstick skillet over medium heat. Add the bell pepper and cook, stirring, until it begins to soften, about 3 minutes. Add the zucchini, garlic, and about ¼ teaspoon salt and continue to cook, stirring often, until the zucchini is translucent, but still bright green, 5 to 10 minutes. Stir in the corn, ground pepper, and thyme and cook, stirring, for another few minutes, until the corn is barely tender. Remove from the heat and transfer to the baking dish.

3. Beat together the eggs and milk. Add about ½ teaspoon salt, pepper to taste, and the cheese; stir together. Pour over the zucchini mixture.

4. Bake for 30 to 40 minutes, until firm and lightly browned. Serve hot or at room temperature.

Advance preparation: This can be made several hours ahead of serving. Serve at room temperature or reheat in a 250° to 300°F oven for 20 minutes.

quesadillas

Quesadillas are quick and satisfying, the kind of dish you could get to the table for supper on a night when one child is rushing to baseball practice, the other to a play rehearsal, and you have to get back to work. I use corn tortillas rather than flour. I like their earthy flavor and the charred taste when they brown. It's also nice to know that they are virtually fat free. **MAKES 1 SERVING**

1 corn tortilla
2 heaped tablespoons grated Monterey Jack or
    white cheddar
Salsa (homemade or commercial)

Heat the tortilla in a dry nonstick skillet over medium-high heat. Turn it over and sprinkle the grated cheese over the surface. When the cheese begins to melt, fold the tortilla over with the help of a spatula. Heat for about half a minute, then flip it over and continue to heat until the tortilla is lightly browned in places. Remove from the heat and serve with salsa.

Advance preparation: Quesadillas should be made to order.

- QUESADILLAS WITH BEANS • For each quesadilla, sprinkle on the cheese as directed, and top the cheese with 2 tablespoons cooked or refried black or pinto beans. Fold over and proceed with the recipe above.

- QUESADILLAS WITH GREENS • For each quesadilla, sprinkle on the cheese as directed and top the cheese with 2 tablespoons cooked chopped greens, such as spinach or chard, and a spoonful of salsa. Fold over and proceed with the recipe above.

buckwheat crêpes

I've put these wonderful crêpes in this chapter because they are made with dairy products, eggs, and buckwheat flour, and cheese is a traditional filling or ingredient in the filling. Fillings needn't be complicated—eggs, cheese, spinach, mushrooms—these complement the unmistakable buckwheat flavor. **MAKES ABOUT 15 CRÊPES**

1 cup low-fat milk
3 large eggs
½ teaspoon salt
⅔ cup buckwheat flour
½ cup unbleached all-purpose flour
2 tablespoons melted unsalted butter, plus additional for cooking

1. Combine the milk, ⅓ cup water, eggs, and salt in a blender or food processor. With the motor running, add the flours, then the melted butter, and blend for 1 minute. Transfer to a bowl, cover, and refrigerate for 1 to 2 hours before making the crêpes.

2. Heat a 6- to 7-inch seasoned crêpe pan or nonstick skillet over medium heat and brush lightly with butter. When the pan just begins to smoke, remove from the heat, and pour or ladle in about 3 tablespoons batter per crêpe, enough to thinly coat the bottom of the pan. Tilt or swirl the pan to distribute the batter in an even layer. Return the pan to the heat and cook the crêpe for about 1 minute, until it is easy to loosen the edges with a thin spatula or butter knife. The bottom of the crêpe should be nicely browned and should not stick to the pan. Flip the crêpe over and cook for 30 seconds on the other side, until it is speckled. Turn out onto a plate.

3. Cook all of the crêpes like this, whisking the batter from time to time, until all of the batter is used up. Use right away or stack between pieces of waxed paper. Seal in a plastic bag and refrigerate, or wrap in foil, then seal in a bag, and freeze.

Advance preparation: Crêpes keep for a few days in the refrigerator and for 3 or 4 months in the freezer. They thaw quickly in a dry nonstick skillet or wrapped in foil in a 300°F oven for about 15 minutes. Don't use the microwave because it dries them out too much. They will also thaw in less than an hour at room temperature.

buckwheat crêpes with gruyère cheese

When I tested this recipe I experienced the most wonderful Proustian reverie. The flavors of the Gruyère and the buckwheat brought me right back to the Paris street corner where I used to eat these crêpes for lunch. **MAKES 4 TO 6 SERVINGS**

12 Buckwheat Crêpes (page 130)
3 to 6 ounces Gruyère cheese, grated (¾ to 1½ cups)

Heat the crêpes, one by one, in a dry nonstick skillet over medium-high heat. Sprinkle 1 to 2 tablespoons of the grated cheese onto the crêpe while it's in the pan. When the cheese melts, fold the crêpe into quarters, flip over a couple of times, and transfer to a plate. Serve at once or keep warm in a low oven (low setting) while you heat and fill all of the crêpes.

Advance preparation: These should be made just before serving.

Filling Crêpes

Crêpes can be folded in half like an omelet, rolled like an enchilada, or folded into quarters. The nature of the filling and whether or not you're going to reheat the crêpes will help you determine how to fill the crêpe. If it is a substantial filling with some bulk, like a mushroom filling, then folding in half or rolling the crêpe is the best way to fill it. If it is spreadable, or a simple filling like grated cheese, then the crêpe can be folded (quartered) and served right away. To quarter a crêpe, spread or sprinkle the filling over the crêpe, then fold it in half, then in half again. To roll it, spread the filling on the crêpe and roll up like an enchilada. To fold in half, put the filling in the middle or on one side and fold the crêpe over it.

mushroom and cheese crêpes

MAKES ENOUGH FOR 12 CRÊPES, 4 SERVINGS

1 tablespoon extra virgin olive oil
1 pound cultivated or wild mushrooms
    (such as shiitakes or oyster mushrooms),
    or a combination, trimmed and thickly sliced
Salt to taste
2 large garlic cloves, minced
2 tablespoons chopped fresh parsley
Freshly ground black pepper to taste
12 Buckwheat Crêpes (page 130)
2 ounces Gruyère, grated (½ cup)

1. Heat the oil in a large, heavy nonstick skillet over medium heat. Add the mushrooms and a generous pinch of salt. Cook, stirring, until the mushrooms begin to release water. Add the garlic and continue to cook, stirring, until the liquid has cooked off, and the mushrooms are tender and lightly glazed, 5 to 10 minutes. Stir in the parsley and pepper and remove from the heat. Taste and adjust seasonings. Keep warm.

2. Heat each crêpe in a dry nonstick skillet over medium-high heat. Sprinkle 1 to 2 tablespoons of the grated cheese onto the crêpe while it's still in the pan. Top with a spoonful of mushrooms. When the cheese has melted, fold the crêpe over or roll it up. Serve hot.

Advance preparation: The mushroom filling will keep for a day in the refrigerator. Reheat gently in a skillet and stir in a spoonful of water or wine if it has dried out.

Remove the stems from 1 pound spinach and wash the leaves well. Place in a large nonstick skillet over high heat. Cook, stirring, until the water on the leaves sizzles and the leaves wilt, which will take a few minutes once the water boils. You may have to do this in batches. Remove from the pan and rinse with cold water. Squeeze out any water and chop. Rinse and dry the pan, and return to the heat. Cook the mushrooms as directed in the recipe above. Stir in the spinach and mix together well. Heat the crêpes and top with the cheese and the spinach and mushroom mixture as directed above. Fold the crêpes and serve.

Advance preparation: The filling will keep for a day in the refrigerator.

goat cheese and herb crêpes

ENOUGH FOR 12 CRÊPES, 4 SERVINGS

1 cup nonfat cottage cheese
2 tablespoons plain nonfat yogurt
2 ounces goat cheese, crumbled (about ½ cup)
½ cup chopped fresh herbs, such as parsley,
*   basil, tarragon, chives, chervil, or dill*
Salt and freshly ground black pepper to taste
1 to 2 garlic cloves, minced (optional)
12 Buckwheat Crêpes (page 130)

1. Blend the cottage cheese in a food processor fitted with the steel blade until fairly smooth. Add the yogurt and goat cheese and continue to blend until completely smooth. Stir in the herbs, salt, pepper, and garlic.

2. Heat each crêpe in a dry nonstick skillet over medium-high heat. Spread a heaped tablespoon of the filling on each warm crêpe, fold the crêpe into quarters, and serve.

Advance preparation: These crêpes are best assembled hot and served right away.

GRAINS *and* beans

Grains are synonymous with food for most of the world's population, and each culinary tradition has its way of approaching the grain that is its staple. Copious amounts of rice accompany smaller quantities of aromatic vegetable, meat, and fish dishes throughout China and Southeast Asia, where it is also fried with other foods. In the Middle East and in India, rich, saffron-hued pilafs surprise the palate with fragrant and pungent spices. Italians bring out the best in their starchy round-grained Arborio rice in their gorgeous risottos, and transform humble cornmeal into creamy polentas that can be topped with a number of sauces. Mountains of couscous accompany complex stews throughout North Africa. Buckwheat, cooked whole as kasha, which means "grain" in Russian, or ground into flour for pancakes called blini, gives sustenance throughout the long Eastern European winters. In

Africa, grains such as millet are pounded and made into porridges that are topped with "sauces," which are actually stews.

For the vegetarian, grains and legumes are important sources of protein, calories, and sustenance. They can be a great source of pleasure for vegetarians and meat-eaters alike. Each grain has its own unique nutty, chewy characteristics and lends itself to particular types of dishes; in today's restaurant kitchens, American chefs are discovering what these attributes are. Barley and wild rice risottos, quinoa pilafs, and wheat berry salads are just some of the dishes you are bound to see on today's menus. Often served as side dishes when meat or fish is the focus of the meal, grains can just as easily take center stage.

Although these pages do not include recipes for all of the different grains, there may be some here that are unfamiliar to you. When I first became interested in vegetarian cooking, these were the foods I had to learn about. I went to the health-food store and bought some of everything I'd never cooked before—millet, bulgur, buckwheat groats, wheat berries—and began cooking. I discovered a world of food and learned about many different cuisines in my search to find recipes. In this chapter I've given you basic cooking instructions for each grain, followed by recipes for more elaborate dishes.

Although some grains, such as wheat berries, have long cooking times, many are actually secret convenience foods, and for this reason, if for no other, they should be pantry staples. Bulgur and couscous require only reconstituting and a short steam. White rice and quinoa take only 15 to 20 minutes to cook and, with the exception of risotto, most grains require unsupervised cooking. Polenta, which used to require a lot of time and energy before I learned the convenient oven method of cooking it, is now one of the easiest of foods to prepare.

Beans are incredibly versatile and flavorful, and their protein and fiber content is excellent. Certain beans, such as black beans and pintos, yield a rich, soupy broth when cooked, and make a great meal served on their own, as they are in the Tasty Pot of Beans (page 180). Legumes can be the foundation of a dish, or added to it, contributing flavor and protein to pilafs and salads, soups, pastas, and stews. They're also made into delicious, filling purees like hummus. Bean soups, salads, spreads, pasta with beans, and bean and vegetable ragouts make important and delicious contributions to the vegetarian diet. They're key ingredients in recipes throughout most of this book, not just in this chapter.

Like certain grains, beans can be a convenience food, particularly canned beans, which should be a pantry staple. I know I can transform salads, soups, pastas, or pilafs into satisfying main dishes just by adding a can of these high-protein, tasty nuggets.

Note: Many of the recipes in this chapter call for either water or stock, with references to some of the vegetable stocks in "Soups." Chicken stock would also be appropriate if it is included in your diet.

barley

Barley is a roundish, beige grain that looks somewhat like short-grain rice but has a chewier, heartier texture. "Pearl" barley has had the tough outer hull removed, and this is the type I recommend using. My favorite use for barley is the classic one, in a soup with lots of mushrooms (page 78). But it can also stand in for rice in a risotto or pilaf, or as a side dish or accompaniment to a vegetable stew. **MAKES ABOUT 3½ CUPS, 4 TO 6 SERVINGS**

3 cups water or stock
(Wild Mushroom Broth on page 66 is a good choice)
1 cup pearl barley
¼ to ½ teaspoon salt

1. Bring the water to a boil in a 2- or 3-quart saucepan. Add the barley and salt. When the water returns to a boil, reduce the heat, cover, and simmer for 30 to 45 minutes, until tender.

2. Pour off any liquid remaining in the pan and let sit for 10 minutes, covered, before serving.

Advance preparation: This keeps well in the refrigerator for 3 or 4 days. Reheat in the oven or in a microwave. To reheat in the oven, place the barley in a lightly oiled baking dish, cover tightly with foil, and reheat in a 350°F oven for 20 minutes. To reheat in a microwave, place the barley in a microwave-safe bowl, cover tightly with plastic wrap, then pierce the plastic with a knife. Microwave for 1 minute. Let sit for 1 minute, carefully remove plastic, and fluff with a fork. Repeat one more time, if needed.

barley and asparagus risotto

When cooked like a risotto, barley gives up its starch like Arborio rice, resulting in a creamy dish. But the grains remain quite chewy, so a barley risotto is heartier than one made with rice. The asparagus contributes color as well as flavor here. **MAKES 4 GENEROUS SERVINGS**

1½ pounds asparagus, trimmed (save trimmings)
*   and cut into 1-inch lengths*
6 to 7 cups vegetable, garlic stock, or mushroom,
*   preferably homemade (pages 63, 65, 66)*
2 tablespoons extra virgin olive oil
½ medium or 1 small onion,
*   minced (⅓ to ½ cup)*
1 cup pearl barley
2 garlic cloves, minced
½ cup dry white wine
Salt and freshly ground black pepper to taste
1 ounce Parmesan, grated (¼ cup)
¼ cup chopped fresh parsley
*   or a combination of parsley and other herbs,*
*   such as chives and tarragon*

1. Add the asparagus trimmings to the stock and bring to a simmer while you prepare the remaining ingredients. Keep the stock at a simmer on low heat in a saucepan. You can remove the stems from the stock or continue to simmer them, but don't let them get into the risotto.

2. Heat the oil in a large nonstick skillet over medium heat. Add the onion. Cook, stirring, until the onion begins to soften, about 3 minutes. Add the barley and garlic. Cook, stirring, until the grains of barley are separate, about 3 minutes.

3. Stir in the wine and continue to cook, stirring constantly. The wine should bubble, but not too quickly. You want some of the flavor to cook into the barley before it evaporates. When the wine has just about evaporated, stir in 2 cups of the simmering stock and cook, without stirring, until the liquid has just about evaporated. Now begin adding the stock, a ladle or two at a time, enough to just cover the barley. The stock should bubble slowly. Cook, stirring often, until the first portion is just about absorbed. Add the asparagus and another ladle or two of the stock and continue to cook in this fashion, not too fast and not too slowly, adding more stock when the barley is almost dry, for 20 to 25 minutes. Taste a bit of the barley. Is it cooked through? It should be chewy but not hard in the middle. If it is still hard in the middle, you need to add another ladle of stock and continue cooking until the barley is tender. Now is the time to ascertain if there is enough salt. Add if necessary.

4. Add another ladle of stock to the barley. Stir in the Parmesan and herbs, and remove from the heat. The mixture should be creamy, but the grains should be chewy. Add freshly ground pepper, taste one last time, and adjust the salt. Stir once and serve right away.

Note: If you are using canned broth instead of homemade stock, you can dilute the broth, using 1 part broth to 1 part water.

Advance preparation: Although the best way to make risotto is to cook it all the way through and serve immediately, this might not be the most convenient method if you don't have an open kitchen where you can visit with family and friends while you're making it. I've taken to cooking risotto halfway through, then returning it to the heat and finishing it just before serving, with good results. You can begin up to several hours before serving: Proceed with the recipe and cook halfway through step 3, that is, for about 15 minutes. The barley should still be hard when you remove it from the heat. Spread it in an even layer in the pan and keep it away from the heat until you resume cooking. About 20 minutes before serving, resume cooking as instructed.

bulgur

Bulgur is wheat that has been precooked, dried, and cracked. Since it's been precooked and dried, it needs only a soak in boiling water. I love its nutty flavor and often serve it in place of rice. **MAKES ABOUT 3 CUPS, 4 SERVINGS**

1 cup fine or medium bulgur
¼ to ½ teaspoon salt
1 teaspoon butter or olive oil (optional)

1. Place the bulgur in a bowl and add salt to taste. Stir with a spoon or mix with your hands to distribute the salt evenly. Pour in 2½ cups boiling water. Let sit for 15 to 20 minutes, until the bulgur is soft.

2. Drain off any excess water through a strainer and press the bulgur in the strainer to extract more water.

3. Reheat in a pan over low heat or in a microwave for about 30 seconds, adding the butter or oil, if desired.

Advance preparation: Bulgur keeps well in the refrigerator for 3 or 4 days. Reheat in the oven or in a microwave. To reheat in the oven, place the bulgur in a lightly oiled baking dish, cover tightly with foil, and reheat in a 350°F oven for 20 minutes. To reheat in a microwave, place the bulgur in a microwave-safe bowl, cover tightly with plastic wrap, then pierce the plastic with a knife. Microwave for 1 minute. Let sit for 1 minute, carefully remove plastic, and fluff with a fork. Repeat one more time, if needed.

bulgur pilaf with cumin and chickpeas

This easy pilaf is a perfect marriage of Middle Eastern ingredients. **MAKES 4 TO 6 SERVINGS**

1 cup medium bulgur
½ teaspoon salt, or more to taste
1 tablespoon extra virgin olive oil
1 teaspoon cumin seeds,
    crushed in a mortar and pestle
1 small onion, chopped
1½ cups cooked chickpeas
    (one 15-ounce can or ¾ cup dried, cooked
    according to the directions on page 144)
2 to 3 tablespoons fresh lemon juice (optional)
Plain nonfat yogurt

1. Place the bulgur in a bowl and add the salt. Stir with a spoon or mix with your hands to distribute the salt evenly. Pour in 2½ cups boiling water. Let sit for 15 to 20 minutes, until the bulgur is soft. Drain off any excess water through a strainer and press the bulgur in the strainer to extract more water.

2. Heat the oil in a large, heavy nonstick skillet over medium heat. Add the cumin seeds. Cook, stirring, just until they begin to color and smell fragrant, about 1 minute. Stir in the onion. Cook, stirring, until tender, about 5 minutes. Stir in the bulgur and chickpeas. Heat through, stirring. Then add the lemon juice, if desired.

3. Remove from the heat, taste, and adjust the salt. Serve hot or warm, topped with yogurt.

Advance preparation: Reconstituted bulgur keeps for a few days in the refrigerator, so you can have the bulgur on hand and make this at the last minute, or make it with leftover bulgur.

COUSCOUS

We think of couscous as a grain, but the grainlike particles are actually tiny pellets of semolina pasta. However, couscous isn't cooked like pasta, nor should it be cooked following the directions on most boxes of instant couscous, which will result in soggy couscous. Like bulgur, couscous has already been cooked once and dried, so all it needs is soaking to reconstitute it. However, the grains will be much lighter and fluffier and, according to some authorities, more digestible, if they are steamed once reconstituted. This is easily done by placing the couscous in a colander above the simmering stew with which you are serving it, or in the oven or micro-wave. The quantities of couscous that are called for in a given recipe are usually large compared to other grain recipes. **MAKES ABOUT 5 CUPS, 4 SERVINGS**

2 cups couscous
½ to ¾ teaspoon salt
2½ cups hot stock, such as Easy Vegetable Stock
 (page 63), or warm water

1. Measure out the couscous into a bowl and add the salt to taste. Mix the salt through the couscous with your hands so that it's well distributed. Pour the stock or water over the couscous. The couscous should be completely submerged, with about a half inch of liquid to spare. Let it sit for 20 minutes, until the water is absorbed. Stir every 5 minutes with a wooden spoon or rub the couscous between your moistened thumbs and fingers, so that it doesn't clump. The couscous will be reconstituted but slightly al dente; fluff it with a fork or with your hands. Taste the couscous and add salt, if necessary.

2. Place the couscous in a colander, sieve, or the top part of a *couscoussière* and set it over the stew you are serving it with, or over boiling water, making sure that the bottom of the colander does not touch the liquid (remove some of the liquid if it does). Wrap a towel between the edge of the colander and the pot if there is a space, so that steam doesn't escape. Steam, uncovered, for 20 minutes. Then transfer to a large bowl or platter.

ALTERNATE STEAMING METHODS

The couscous can also steam in the oven or the microwave. To steam in the oven, place the couscous in a lightly oiled baking dish, cover tightly with foil, and place in a 350° oven for 20 minutes. To steam in a microwave, transfer to a microwave-safe bowl, cover tightly with plastic wrap, and pierce the plastic with a knife. Microwave for 1 minute. Let sit for 1 minute, carefully remove the plastic, and fluff with a fork. Repeat one more time if desired.

Advance preparation: You can steam the couscous twice. Proceed as above—this can be done hours before you are ready to eat—and repeat one more time just before eating.

couscous with chickpeas, greens, and fennel

This is the kind of hearty main dish that is fabulous for a dinner party, because everything can be done ahead of time. The couscous gets its final steam when you reheat the chickpea and greens stew. The complexity of spicy flavors in the stew is typical of many North African dishes. This one comes from Tunisia. A hearty main dish, the chickpea and couscous combination is a perfect example of a complete protein, as the amino acids in the grains complement those in the beans. The dish, incidentally, is a great one for vegans. It is filling and satisfying and needs little more than a crisp green salad or Orange, Onion, and Olive Salad (page 58) and a fruity dessert.

When you prepare all of the greens here, you may wonder at the quantity; but once they cook down in the stew, contributing some of their own water and their nutrients to the mix, you'll see that the amount is just right. **MAKES 6 SERVINGS**

1 pound chickpeas (2 heaped cups), soaked in 3 times their volume of water
for 6 hours or overnight
2 tablespoons extra virgin olive oil
1 medium onion, chopped
2 leeks, white and light green parts only, cleaned and sliced
4 large garlic cloves, minced
1 teaspoon coriander seeds, ground
1 teaspoon caraway seeds, ground
2 tablespoons Harissa, or more to taste, plus additional for serving
(page 20; or substitute ¼ to ½ teaspoon ground cayenne pepper
if harissa is unavailable)
2 tablespoons tomato paste
Salt to taste
2 fennel bulbs, with tops, rinsed and chopped
2 pounds greens, such as Swiss chard, spinach, or turnip greens, stemmed,
washed thoroughly, and coarsely chopped
1 large bunch fresh parsley, stemmed, washed, and chopped
3 cups couscous

1. Drain the chickpeas and transfer to a large pot. Add 8 cups water. Bring to a boil, reduce the heat, and simmer for 1 hour. Meanwhile prepare the remaining ingredients.

2. Heat the oil over medium heat in a heavy casserole or Dutch oven, or if you have one, in the bottom of a *couscoussière*. Add the onion and leeks and cook, stirring, until tender, about 5 minutes. Add the garlic, ground coriander, and ground caraway and stir together for about 30 seconds, until the garlic is fragrant. Add the harissa and the tomato paste and stir together for another minute or two. Add the chickpeas with their cooking liquid, plus another 1 cup water, stir together and bring back to a simmer. Add salt to taste; you will need a generous amount—about 1 tablespoon. Cover and simmer 30 to 60 minutes, until the chickpeas are thoroughly tender and the broth fragrant.

3. Stir in the fennel and fennel tops. Gradually stir in the greens, allowing each handful to cook down a bit before adding the next. Simmer for 10 to 15 minutes, until the fennel and greens are tender. Stir in the parsley. Remove from the heat. Taste and adjust the seasonings, adding salt, garlic, or harissa as desired. Strain off 1 cup of the liquid and reserve.

4. Reconstitute and steam the couscous. Place the couscous in a bowl with 1 teaspoon salt. Combine 2½ cups hot water with the reserved cup of strained cooking liquid. Pour it over the couscous. The couscous should be completely submerged, with about a half inch of liquid to spare. Let it sit for 20 minutes, until the water is absorbed. Stir every 5 minutes with a wooden spoon or rub the couscous between your moistened thumbs and fingers, so that the couscous doesn't lump. The couscous will now be fairly soft; fluff it with a fork or with your hands. Taste the couscous and add salt, if necessary.

5. Have the stew at a simmer, or you can steam the couscous over a small amount of water in a large pot, if you don't want to keep cooking the greens. Place the couscous in a colander, sieve, or the top part of a *couscoussière* and set it over the stew or boiling water, making sure that the bottom of the colander does not touch the liquid (remove some of the liquid if it does). Wrap a towel around the edge of the colander and the pot if there is a space, so that steam doesn't escape. Steam for 15 to 20 minutes. (Alternately, steam in the oven or microwave, following instructions on page 143.)

6. Transfer the couscous to a wide serving bowl, such as a pasta bowl, or directly to wide soup plates. Spoon on the stew, and serve, passing additional harissa at the table.

Note: You can steam the couscous twice: Proceed as above—this can be done hours before you are ready to eat—and repeat one more time just before eating.

Advance preparation: The stew will keep for 3 or 4 days in the refrigerator. You may need to add a small amount of water when you reheat it.

kasha (buckwheat groats)

Dara Goldstein, Russian scholar and cookbook author, says that the reason Russian buckwheat groats are so good in comparison to what we often get in this country is that they are much coarser, so they don't turn to mush. You can find coarse-cut buckwheat groats in whole foods stores, however. This cooking method is based on her recipe in *The Vegetarian Hearth*. **MAKES ABOUT 3 CUPS, 4 SERVINGS**

> 2 cups Easy Vegetable Stock (page 63), Wild Mushroom Broth (page 66), or
>   water
> 1 cup coarse-cut buckwheat groats
> ½ teaspoon salt
> 1 tablespoon unsalted butter, cut into small pieces (optional)

BAKED METHOD

1. Preheat the oven to 350°F. If you are not using an ovenproof casserole for both the top of the stove and for baking, butter or oil a 2-quart baking dish, preferably earthenware, with a cover.

2. Bring the water or stock to a boil in a saucepan.

3. Stir the buckwheat groats in a large heavy skillet or lidded ovenproof and flameproof casserole over medium-high heat until all of the grains are toasty and beginning to brown, about 5 minutes. Transfer to the casserole and add the salt. Pour in the boiling water or stock and dot with the butter. Cover and bake for 20 minutes, or until the liquid has been absorbed.

TOP OF THE STOVE METHOD

Bring the water or stock to a boil in a 3-quart saucepan. Toast the buckwheat groats in a skillet as directed, then stir into the water along with the salt. Reduce the heat to low, cover, and simmer until the liquid is absorbed, 7 to 20 minutes depending on the brand.

Advance preparation: Cooked kasha will keep for about 3 days in the refrigerator and can be frozen for 3 to 4 months. To reheat, place the kasha in a lightly oiled baking dish, cover tightly with foil, and reheat in a 350°F oven for 20 minutes. To reheat in a microwave, place the kasha in a microwave-safe bowl, cover tightly with plastic wrap, then pierce the plastic with a knife. Microwave for 1 minute. Let sit for 1 minute, carefully remove plastic, and fluff with a fork. Repeat one more time, if needed.

kasha with parsnips

I like the contrast of flavors in this Central European dish: the sweet parsnips in a bed of earthy, nutty buckwheat. It's a fine winter dish. In this recipe, another common method is used for cooking the buckwheat. The groats are coated with egg before being stirred in the pan. This is supposed to help keep the grains separate and fluffy. You can use this method or the method in the previous recipe for the dish; they both work. **MAKES 4 TO 6 SERVINGS**

2½ cups Easy Vegetable Stock (page 63), Wild Mushroom Broth (page 66),
  or water
1 cup coarse-cut buckwheat groats
1 large egg, beaten
1 tablespoon butter or canola oil
1 small onion, chopped
½ pound parsnips, peeled, cored, and diced
½ teaspoon salt unless stock is quite salty
Freshly ground black pepper to taste
2 tablespoons finely chopped chives
½ cup Yogurt Cheese (page 8)

1. Bring the stock to a simmer in a saucepan.

2. In a bowl, stir together the buckwheat groats and the egg.

3. Heat the butter in a large, heavy nonstick skillet or 3-quart saucepan over medium heat. Add the onion. Cook, stirring, until tender, 3 to 5 minutes. Add the groats and the parsnips. Cook, stirring, until the kasha has absorbed the egg, and the grains are separate and smell toasty, 3 to 5 minutes. Pour in the stock and add salt. When the liquid comes to a boil, reduce the heat, cover, and simmer for 20 to 30 minutes, until the buckwheat groats are tender and the liquid is absorbed.

4. Remove from the heat and allow to sit, covered, for 10 minutes. Transfer to a serving bowl, toss with pepper and the chives, and serve, passing the yogurt at the table.

Advance preparation: This dish will keep for a couple of days in the refrigerator. Reheat in a 325°F oven for 15 to 20 minutes. Cooked kasha also freezes well for a few months.

millet

These small, yellow, round grains may be familiar only to those of you who buy birdseed, but they are also widely eaten by humans. Millet is a hearty grain with a nutty flavor. **MAKES ABOUT 3 CUPS, 4 TO 6 SERVINGS**

2½ cups stock or water
1 cup millet
¼ to ½ teaspoon salt (optional)

1. Bring the stock or water to a simmer in a saucepan. Place the millet in another heavy saucepan and heat over medium-high heat, stirring, until it begins to smell toasty, about 3 minutes. Pour in the simmering stock or water, add salt, if you are using water, and reduce the heat so that the liquid is simmering. Cover and simmer for 35 to 45 minutes, until the grains are tender and the liquid is absorbed. Let sit for 10 minutes, covered.

2. Transfer the millet to a bowl and fluff with forks to separate the grains.

Advance preparation: This keeps well in the refrigerator for 3 to 4 days. Reheat in the oven or in a microwave. To reheat in the oven, place the millet in a lightly oiled baking dish, cover tightly with foil, and reheat in a 350°F oven for 20 minutes. To reheat in a microwave, place the millet in a microwave-safe bowl, cover tightly with plastic wrap, then pierce the plastic with a knife. Microwave for 1 minute. Let sit for 1 minute, carefully remove plastic, and fluff with a fork. Repeat one more time, if needed.

millet soufflé

This comforting, fragrant, sage-flecked dish is a great way to use up leftover cooked millet, but it's also reason enough to make a pot. **MAKES 4 SERVINGS**

1 tablespoon extra virgin olive oil
1 medium onion, chopped
2 garlic cloves, minced
3 egg yolks
½ cup low-fat milk
½ to ¾ teaspoon salt, depending on how salty the cooked millet is
Freshly ground black pepper to taste
2 ounces Gruyère, grated (½ cup)
1 tablespoon chopped fresh sage (6 to 8 good-size leaves)
About 3 cups cooked millet, fluffed with forks (1 cup uncooked)
4 egg whites

1. Preheat the oven to 375°F. Butter a 1½- or 2-quart soufflé or gratin dish.

2. Heat the oil in a nonstick skillet over medium heat. Add the onion. Cook, stirring, until tender, about 5 minutes. Stir in the garlic. Cook, stirring, until the garlic begins to color and smells fragrant, another 30 to 60 seconds. Remove from the heat.

3. Beat the egg yolks in a medium bowl. Add the milk, salt, and pepper and beat together well. Stir in the cheese, sage, millet, and cooked onion and garlic.

4. Beat the egg whites with an electric beater or whisk until they form stiff but not dry peaks. Stir one fourth of the beaten egg whites into the millet mixture. Gently fold in the rest, one third at a time. Turn into the buttered dish.

5. Bake for 40 minutes, until puffed and browned.

6. Serve hot.

Advance preparation: Cooked millet will keep for a few days in the refrigerator. The cooked onion and garlic will hold at room temperature for a couple of hours.

polenta

Polenta is coarse cornmeal that is cooked in simmering water until it forms a stiff puddinglike mixture. Any number of sauces and toppings can be served with it, and once cooled it can be sliced and grilled or toasted. The oven-cooking method below makes any polenta dish a cinch. This recipe makes a lot of polenta, but it's worth cooking twice what you need so that you can slice and grill or toast leftovers for quick meals. Serve with the topping of your choice or as a side dish with a vegetable gratin. **MAKES 8 SERVINGS**

2 cups polenta
2½ teaspoons salt
1 to 2 tablespoons butter

1. Preheat the oven to 350°F.

2. Combine the polenta, salt, butter, and 8 cups water in a 3- to 4-quart baking dish. Stir together.

3. Bake for 1 hour and 20 minutes. Remove from the oven, stir, and return to the oven for 10 more minutes.

4. Remove from the oven and let sit for 5 minutes, and serve.

Note: This recipe can be halved (see those that follow). But when making only 1 cup of polenta, bake for 1 hour only, not 1 hour and 20 minutes. Then stir the polenta and return to the oven for 10 minutes as in the above recipe.

Advance preparation: If you are serving the polenta hot with a topping, it's best to serve it when it comes out of the oven, though it can sit for more than the required 5 minutes. It will keep, once cooked, for several days in the refrigerator and is delicious cut into pieces and grilled, toasted, or broiled.

polenta with tomato sauce, sage, and beans

The topping here is enough for 4 generous servings, which is why only a half recipe of the polenta is required. **MAKES 4 SERVINGS**

½ recipe Polenta (page 150)
1 recipe tomato sauce (page 194)
One 15-ounce can cannellini beans,
*   drained and rinsed (or 1½ cups cooked beans)*
6 to 12 fresh sage leaves (to taste), cut in slivers
1 ounce Parmesan, grated (¼ cup)

1. Prepare the polenta according to the recipe directions. While the polenta is baking, make the tomato sauce. Stir the beans and sage into the sauce. Taste and adjust seasonings.

2. Remove the polenta from the oven. Let it sit for 5 minutes, then spoon on the tomato and bean topping. Sprinkle on the Parmesan and serve. (If you have made a full recipe of polenta, spoon the polenta onto each plate, top with the sauce, sprinkle on the Parmesan, and serve.)

Advance preparation: The tomato and bean combination will keep for a few days in the refrigerator. Reheat gently in a saucepan or frying pan.

- POLENTA WITH TOMATO SAUCE, MINT, AND FETA • Substitute 2 tablespoons chopped fresh mint and ⅓ cup crumbled feta for the sage and Parmesan. Stir half the mint into the tomato sauce and sprinkle the remaining mint and the feta over the top after you have sauced the polenta.

polenta with oyster mushrooms and chipotles

A mix of cultures comes together in this dish; but even though polenta is Italian, corn itself couldn't be more Mexican. The topping here is a hot and smoky mixture of oyster mushrooms, available now at most supermarkets, tomatoes, and canned chipotle chiles, which are sold in supermarkets that sell Mexican ingredients. If you can't find oyster mushrooms, make the dish with regular mushrooms. When you seed the chiles, wear rubber gloves to protect your hands (and anything you rub with them) from the heat. Mexican queso fresco, found in the cheese section of supermarkets, is the perfect cheese for this; but if you can't find it, you can use Monterey Jack. You will probably have extra polenta, which you can serve grilled or broiled later in the week. **MAKES 6 SERVINGS**

1 recipe Polenta (page 150)
1 tablespoon extra virgin olive oil
1 medium or large onion, chopped
1½ pounds oyster mushrooms, cleaned, stems trimmed,
*   and quartered or thickly sliced*
Salt to taste
¼ cup dry, fruity red wine,
*   such as a Beaujolais or Côtes du Rhône*
2 to 3 chipotle chiles en adobo,
*   drained, seeded, and chopped*
1 teaspoon dried oregano
2 to 4 large garlic cloves, minced
1½ pounds (6 medium or 3 large) tomatoes, peeled and chopped,
*   or one 28-ounce can tomatoes, drained and chopped*
½ cup crumbled queso fresco
*   (use grated Monterey Jack if unavailable)*
Slivered epazote leaves (optional)

1. Prepare the polenta according to the recipe directions. While the polenta is baking, prepare and cook the mushrooms. Heat the olive oil in a large, heavy nonstick skillet over medium heat. Add the onion. Cook, stirring, until the onion is tender, about 5 minutes. Add the mushrooms. Sprinkle with salt and cook over medium-high heat until the mushrooms begin to release liquid. Cook, stirring, until the mushrooms begin to stick to the pan, 5 to 10 minutes. Add the red wine, chipotle chiles, and oregano. Turn the heat down to medium and cook, stirring, until the wine is just about gone, about 5 minutes. Add the garlic and stir together for a minute, until the garlic begins to color. Add the tomatoes and salt to taste, and bring to a simmer. Simmer for 15 minutes, stirring often, until the tomatoes have cooked down and the mixture is fragrant. Remove from the heat, taste, and adjust the seasonings.

2. When the polenta is done, spread the mushroom mixture over the surface and sprinkle on the cheese. Return to the oven and bake until the cheese has melted and the mixture is sizzling, 10 to 15 minutes.

3. Sprinkle the epazote on just before serving. Serve hot.

Advance preparation: The mushroom mixture will keep for a couple of days in the refrigerator.

grilled vegetables and polenta with red and green sauces

Grilled vegetables are a standard vegetarian entrée on restaurant menus. Although the vegetables always taste good if they're in season, I find the usual presentation—an assortment of grilled vegetables, usually sliced, and usually undercooked (they have a tasty charred surface, but a close-to-raw texture) rather uninteresting. I like to grill vegetables until they are fairly soft, with a nicely charred surface. Polenta diamonds, grilled until just golden, make the perfect accompaniment. But without the complex sauces, this would be just another restaurant-style mixed grilled vegetable plate. One sauce is an adaptation of an orange Catalan roasted (or grilled) vegetable and almond sauce called Romesco, the other a green Republic of Georgia–inspired cilantro sauce. They transform this meal into a feast.

Grilling vegetables is not a precise art, particularly grilling over coals. Times will vary according to where your vegetables are placed in relation to the hottest coals, how hot those coals are, and how you like your food grilled. **MAKES 6 TO 8 SERVINGS**

1 recipe Polenta (page 150)
6 to 8 ears corn, husks on (optional)
2 large or 3 medium sweet red or white onions,
    thickly sliced
6 to 8 small yellow summer squash,
    cut in half lengthwise
6 to 8 small zucchini, cut in half lengthwise
3 to 4 medium tomatoes,
    cut in half across their equators
4 portobello mushrooms, stems removed
Salt and freshly ground black pepper
⅓ cup extra virgin olive oil,
    or more as needed
Cilantro Sauce (page 14)
Romesco Sauce (page 16)

1. Prepare the polenta according to the recipe directions. Cool. Cut the polenta into 3- to 4-inch diamonds or squares.

2. Soak the corn in water to cover for 1 hour. Soak the onion slices in a bowl of cold water for at least 10 minutes.

3. Prepare a medium-hot fire in a gas or charcoal grill.

4. Place the other vegetables on baking sheets, sprinkle with salt and pepper, and brush lightly on both sides with olive oil. Grill the onions until tender and charred, 8 to 10 minutes on each side. Turn them over every few minutes so they don't blacken too much.

Grill the corn until the outer leaves are blackened, about 20 minutes, turning once. Remove from the grill and let sit until you can handle it, then remove the leaves and silk.

Grill the mushrooms until softened and golden brown, about 15 minutes, turning once.

Grill the squash until charred on the surfaces and tender in the middle, 3 to 5 minutes on the cut side and 5 to 8 minutes on the rounded side.

Grill the tomatoes until the surface is colored with grill marks, and the tomatoes are softened but still hold their shape, 3 to 5 minutes on each side.

5. Brush the polenta lightly with olive oil on both sides, and grill until golden with grill marks, 3 to 4 minutes per side.

6. Arrange the vegetables and polenta on platters or plates, and pass the sauces in bowls. Serve warm.

Advance preparation: The cooked polenta will keep for 3 days in the refrigerator. You can prepare the vegetables hours before you grill them.

quinoa

This high-protein grain has its origins in Peru. It's a wonder grain that is high in iron, potassium, magnesium, and lysine as well as protein. And it also happens to be delicate, with an appealing nutty flavor. The grains cook in 15 minutes, making them a convenience food as well. Always rinse quinoa before cooking, to make sure that there are no bits of its bitter protective coating; this is removed during processing, but some may linger. **MAKES ABOUT 3 CUPS, 4 TO 6 SERVINGS**

1 cup quinoa
2 cups water or Easy Vegetable Stock (page 63)
¼ teaspoon salt, or more to taste

1. Place the quinoa in a bowl and rinse thoroughly in several changes of cold water, draining the quinoa through a fine sieve each time.

2. Bring the water or stock to a boil in a 2-quart saucepan. Add the quinoa and the salt. Reduce the heat, cover, and simmer for 12 to 15 minutes, until the liquid is absorbed and little spirals appear in the grain.

3. Remove from the heat and let sit, covered, for 5 minutes. Season to taste with additional salt.

Advance preparation: Quinoa will keep for 3 or 4 days in the refrigerator. Reheat in the oven or in a microwave. To reheat in the oven, place the quinoa in a lightly oiled baking dish, cover tightly with foil, and reheat in a 350°F oven for 20 minutes. To reheat in a microwave, place the quinoa in a microwave-safe bowl, cover tightly with plastic wrap, then pierce the plastic with a knife. Microwave for 1 minute. Let sit for 1 minute, carefully remove plastic, and fluff with a fork. Repeat one more time, if needed.

quinoa and butternut squash gratin

This gratin is a heavenly vehicle for both quinoa and butternut squash. The chewy grains are enveloped by the velvety butternut squash and cheese, resulting in a dish whose luscious textures match its sweet and nutty flavors. **MAKES 4 TO 6 SERVINGS**

1 large butternut squash (about 2 pounds),
quartered or cut into large pieces, seeds removed
1 cup quinoa
Water or Easy Vegetable Stock (page 63), as needed
½ teaspoon salt, or to taste
2 tablespoons extra virgin olive oil
1 small onion, chopped
2 garlic cloves, minced
Freshly ground black pepper to taste
2 large eggs, beaten
2 ounces Gruyère, grated (½ cup)
2 tablespoons fresh or dry bread crumbs

1. Place the squash in a steaming basket above 1 inch of boiling water, cover, and steam until tender but not mushy, about 15 minutes. Remove from the heat and transfer the squash to a strainer set over a bowl. Allow to drain for 10 minutes. If any liquid drains from the squash, combine it with water or stock to measure 2 cups. Peel the squash when cool enough to handle and cut into small dice (about ¼ inch).

2. Cook the quinoa. Wash the grains in several changes of water and drain through a fine sieve. Transfer the squash and water mixture to a 2-quart saucepan and bring to a boil. Add ½ teaspoon salt and the quinoa. Reduce the heat, cover, and simmer for 15 minutes, or until the liquid is absorbed and the grains display a spiral shape. Remove from the heat and let stand, covered, for 5 minutes.

3. Preheat the oven to 400°F. Oil a 2-quart gratin dish or baking dish.

4. Heat 1 tablespoon of the oil over medium heat in a heavy nonstick skillet. Add the onion and cook, stirring, until tender, 3 to 5 minutes. Stir in the garlic. Cook, stirring, just until the garlic begins to color and smell fragrant, 30 to 60 seconds. Gently stir in the squash and quinoa. Stir together and remove from the heat.

5. Beat the eggs in a bowl, add about ½ teaspoon salt and plenty of pepper. Add the quinoa mixture and the cheese. Toss to combine. Taste and add more salt if desired. Turn into the baking dish. Sprinkle on the bread crumbs and drizzle on the remaining 1 tablespoon oil.

6. Bake for 35 to 45 minutes, until the top is golden brown and the mixture is sizzling.

7. Serve hot, warm, or at room temperature.

Advance preparation: This can be assembled and refrigerated hours before you bake it. It will also keep, once baked, for a couple of days. Reheat in a 325°F oven for 15 to 20 minutes.

Rice

There are many, many types of rice and each has its own particular cooking method. The types of rice used in this book are:

- ARBORIO RICE • The round, starchy Italian rice used for risottos.

- WHITE RICE • I use long-grain and medium-grain white rice varieties. This widely used rice has been hulled and the germ removed, and is fairly quick-cooking.

- BASMATI RICE • The fragrant rice used in Indian and Middle Eastern cooking.

- BROWN RICE • Brown rice has been husked, but it still contains all of its bran and germ, so it has more B vitamins, fiber, and trace minerals than white rice. It takes twice as long to cook and has a chewier, heartier texture.

- WILD RICE • This is not actually a rice but a grass and it is often not wild. The popular grain, which used to be harvested from the lakes of northern Minnesota, is now cultivated as far afield as California. The dark brown grains have a marvelous nutty flavor.

rice

MAKES ABOUT 2½ CUPS, 4 SERVINGS

1 cup rice
½ to ¾ teaspoon salt (I use the lesser amount)

1. Bring 2 cups water to a boil in a 1- or 2-quart lidded saucepan. Add the rice and salt. When the water comes back to a boil, stir *once* and once only, turn the heat down to low, and cover the pot tightly. Simmer for 15 minutes.

2. Remove the lid and look and listen. There will be holes in the mass of rice, into which you can peer to see if the water has evaporated. You will hear it sizzle and crack, as well. If you're really not sure, stick a chopstick, not a spoon, down, to see if a small layer of rice is beginning to stick to the bottom of the pan. If there is still water simmering, return the lid to the pan and check again in 5 minutes. When all the water has evaporated, turn off the heat, return the lid to the pan, and let the pan sit without touching it for 10 minutes (or longer). The rice will continue to steam and grow fluffy. For really fluffy rice, put a clean dish towel over the top of the pot and put the lid over it; the towel will absorb steam and the rice will be drier.

• BROWN RICE •

Use 2¼ cups water for 1 cup brown rice. Cook as above, for 35 to 50 minutes. Check after 35 minutes, as above.

wild rice

MAKES ABOUT 3 CUPS, 4 TO 6 SERVINGS

> *3 cups stock, such as Easy Vegetable Stock (page 63),*
> *Soy Sauce Bouillon (page 68), or water*
> *1 cup wild rice*
> *½ to ¾ teaspoon salt, or to taste*

Bring the liquid to a boil in a large saucepan. Rinse the rice well and add, along with the salt, if the stock isn't salted. When the liquid comes back to a boil, reduce the heat, cover, and simmer for 40 minutes, or until the rice is tender and the kernels have burst open. Remove from the heat. Drain off any liquid that remains.

basmati rice

I probably give a new method for cooking basmati rice with each cookbook I write. They all work, but I keep finding better methods. I often use the same method I use for white rice, except I rinse the basmati rice several times first. The first method is recommended by Julie Sahni, writer of highly regarded Indian cookbooks. She doesn't call for salt, but I always use it. The second method (which, come to think of it, I also learned from Julie Sahni) is one I have used for years with good results. It is quicker than the first method, but the resulting rice is not as fluffy. **MAKES 4 SIDE-DISH SERVINGS**

1 cup basmati rice
¼ to ½ teaspoon salt

METHOD 1

1. Place the rice in a strainer and rinse thoroughly with cold water. Transfer to a bowl and cover with water. Remove any particles that float to the top of the water. Drain and transfer to a saucepan. Cover with 1¾ cups water and let sit for 30 minutes to 2 hours (no longer).

2. Bring the water in the saucepan to a boil over medium-high heat. Add the salt, cover partially, and cook at a fairly brisk boil for 8 to 10 minutes, until the water is absorbed and steam holes appear. Cover the pot and turn the heat very low. Cook for another 5 minutes. Turn off the heat and let sit, covered, for 5 minutes.

METHOD 2

1. Place the rice in a bowl and fill with water. Drain and repeat the process a few times, until the water runs fairly clear. Cover with water and soak for 30 minutes.

2. Bring a large pot of water to a boil. Add ¼ teaspoon salt and the rice. Stir until the water comes back to a boil to make sure the rice doesn't stick to the bottom of the pot. Boil for 4 to 5 minutes. Test the rice for doneness. It should be tender.

3. Drain through a strainer or colander. Shake out the water and serve at once.

Advance preparation: Spread the cooked rice in a lightly oiled baking dish and allow to cool uncovered. To reheat, cover with foil and reheat in a 350°F oven for 20 minutes.

basmati rice pilaf with indian spices and peas

This fragrant pilaf is subtly spiced with roasted cumin, coriander seeds, cardamom, and saffron. You could serve it as a main course topped with yogurt, thickened or plain, with a cooling cucumber salad (page 45) on the side. Or you could serve it alongside pan-cooked tofu, an omelet, or a gratin. **MAKES 4 TO 6 SERVINGS**

1 cup basmati rice
1 tablespoon canola oil, peanut oil, or butter
½ medium onion, minced
4 green cardamom pods
½ teaspoon coriander seeds,
*   crushed in a mortar or spice mill*
¾ teaspoon roasted cumin seeds
2 cups Easy Vegetable Stock (page 63),
*   Garlic Broth (page 65), or water*
½ to ¾ teaspoon salt (omit if the stock is salty)
Pinch of saffron
1 cup defrosted frozen peas, or 1 cup shelled fresh peas
*   (they must be very sweet)*
Freshly ground black pepper to taste
Yogurt Cheese (page 8)

1. Wash the rice in several rinses of cold water until the water runs clear. Soak in water to cover while you prepare the remaining ingredients. Drain.

2. Roast the cumin seeds. Heat a small skillet over medium-high heat and add the cumin seeds. Shake the pan and toast the seeds; they should begin to smell fragrant and darken slightly within a minute. Once you see the color change, remove the pan from the heat and immediately transfer the seeds to a bowl.

3. Heat the oil over medium heat in a heavy 3- or 4-quart saucepan. Add the onion and cook, stirring, until it begins to soften, about 3 minutes. Add the cardamom, coriander, and cumin and cook, stirring, until the onion is tender and the spices fragrant, another couple of minutes.

Stir in the rice. Cook, stirring, until the grains of rice are separate, about 3 minutes. Pour in the stock. Bring to a boil, add salt if necessary, and the saffron, reduce the heat to medium-low, and cover partially. Cook for 10 minutes, until steam holes cover the surface of the rice and most of the water has evaporated.

4. Add the peas to the surface of the rice (do not stir in). Cover the pot, turn the heat to low, and steam the rice another 5 to 10 minutes. Remove from the heat and let it sit for 5 to 10 minutes without disturbing it.

5. Transfer the rice to a serving bowl, toss and stir the peas into the rice, and serve, topped with Yogurt Cheese (page 8).

Advance preparation: This can be made a few hours ahead and reheated, though the peas will shrivel. Follow the recipe, but right after the rice has sat off the heat for 10 minutes, remove the lid, transfer the rice to a lightly oiled baking dish, and allow to cool in a single layer. Cover the dish and heat through for 20 minutes in a 350°F oven.

rice pilaf with chickpeas

Chickpeas contribute protein, texture, and their wonderful nutty flavor to this pilaf. Serve it with a Summer Tomato Gratin (page 255) and any pan-cooked vegetables, such as Mediterranean Greens (page 238) or Pan-Cooked Mushrooms with Gremolata (page 245), with a vegetable stew, or as a side dish with one of the vegetable tarts on pages 112 to 117. Follow it with a green salad or a Summer Vegetable Salad (page 46). **MAKES 4 SERVINGS**

1 tablespoon butter or extra virgin olive oil
1 medium onion, chopped
1 cup long-grain or basmati rice (rinse if using basmati)
1 cup cooked chickpeas (canned, or ½ cup dried)
2½ cups stock, such as Easy Vegetable Stock (page 63), or water
½ teaspoon salt, or to taste
Pinch of saffron (optional)
Freshly ground black pepper to taste

1. Heat the butter in a heavy saucepan over medium heat. Add the onion and cook, stirring, until tender, about 5 minutes. Stir in the rice, chickpeas, and water. Bring to a boil. Add the salt and saffron, if using. Reduce the heat to low, cover, and simmer for 15 to 20 minutes, until the liquid has just about been absorbed. Remove from the heat.

2. Place a clean, dry dish towel over the pan and cover tightly with the lid. Allow to sit, covered, for 15 to 20 minutes. Serve hot.

Advance preparation: You can make this in advance, following the recipe as written. Then transfer the rice to a lightly oiled 2-quart baking dish. Spread it in an even layer and allow it to cool completely. Cover with foil. Reheat for 20 minutes in a 350°F oven.

risotto

Risotto, one of the world's great dishes, dispels all misconceptions that anybody might have about vegetarian cooking (that it is bland, for example, or ascetic). It tastes rich without necessarily being rich (though some risottos are). The creamy dish is made with a particular type of rice, the round starchy Italian Arborio rice that yields up its sauce-thickening starch as it slowly cooks, while retaining its chewy texture. Homemade risotto is better than any risotto I have ever eaten in a restaurant, no matter how good, because it is a dish that should go from the pan to your plate immediately.

If you are confident about making risotto, you will never lack ideas for company dazzlers as well as everyday meals. Risottos are a vital part of my repertoire; virtually any vegetable in season can be used for a main-dish risotto, and this basic plain version can serve as either a side dish—say with a vegetable gratin or a soup, such as Carrot and Leek Soup (page 85) or Garlic Soup (page 86), and green salad—or as a main dish.

The stock is important in a risotto, because it seasons the rice as it cooks. Vegetarian stocks include Garlic Broth (page 65) and the Easy Vegetable Stock on page 63. For risottos containing mushrooms, use the Wild Mushroom Broth (page 66). I will admit that I have also made perfectly acceptable risottos with good-quality vegetable bouillon; if I don't have a stock on hand or the time to make one, I don't let that stand in the way of making the dish. If you are not a vegetarian, chicken stock, preferably homemade or good-quality canned, is a good choice. A dry white wine such as Pinot Grigio or Fumé Blanc is the best wine to use. Don't use Chardonnay, which is too oaky and not dry enough. **MAKES 4 GENEROUS SERVINGS**

6 to 7 cups vegetable stock or garlic broth,
      preferably homemade (pages 63 and 65),
      but in a pinch use broth made from bouillon cubes or
      canned broth (see Note)
2 tablespoons unsalted butter or extra virgin olive oil, or
      1 tablespoon each
½ medium or 1 small onion, minced (⅓ to ½ cup)
1½ cups Arborio rice
2 garlic cloves, minced (optional)
½ cup dry white wine
Salt and freshly ground black pepper to taste
1 ounce Parmesan, grated (¼ cup)

1. In a saucepan, bring the stock or broth to a simmer on the stove, with a ladle nearby or in the pot. Make sure that it is well seasoned with salt. It should remain at a simmer the entire time you are making the risotto, and you will add it a ladle or two at a time to the rice.

2. Heat the butter or oil in a wide, heavy nonstick skillet over medium heat. Add the onion, which also seasons the rice, and cook gently until it is just tender but not browned, 3 to 5 minutes.

3. Stir in the rice and garlic, if using. Traditional risottos call for more fat than mine, and the rice absorbs it before you add the other ingredients. In this case, you will stir the rice just until the grains become separate, which doesn't take very long, 2 to 3 minutes.

4. Add the wine and cook, stirring, until it is absorbed, about 3 minutes. The wine is important for flavor, as it adds a delicious acidity to the dish. The alcohol boils off. The heat should be moderate; the wine should bubble as soon as you add it to the rice, but it should not boil off so quickly that the rice doesn't have time to absorb its flavor.

5. Begin adding the simmering stock, a couple of ladles (about ½ cup) at a time. The stock should just cover the rice and should be bubbling, not too slowly but not too quickly. Stir often; you don't have to stand there and stir constantly as I used to think we did—you can be preparing the vegetables you are going to add, or something else—but you do have to stir often, to keep the grains separate and distribute their starch throughout the mixture, and also to ascertain when it's time to add the next portion of stock. The rice will be cooked through but still be chewy after 20 to 25 minutes of this cooking—adding the stock in increments and stirring. When the rice is tender all the way through but still chewy, it is done. Taste and correct the seasoning.

6. Add another ladle of stock to the rice. Stir in the Parmesan, and remove from the heat. The mixture should be creamy. Add pepper, taste one last time, and adjust the salt. Stir once and serve right away.

Note: If you are using canned broth, you can dilute the broth, using 1 part broth to 1 part water.

Advance preparation: Although the best way to make risotto is to cook it all the way through and serve immediately, this might not be the most convenient method if you don't have an open kitchen where you can visit with family and friends while you're making it. I've taken to cooking risotto halfway through, then returning it to the heat and finishing it just before serving, with good results. You can begin up to several hours before serving: Proceed with the recipe and cook halfway through step 5, that is, for about 15 minutes. The rice should still be hard when you remove it from the heat, and there should not be any liquid in the pan. Spread it in an even layer in the pan and keep it away from the heat until you resume cooking. About 15 minutes before serving, resume cooking as instructed. These advance preparation directions apply to all the risottos that follow.

- RISOTTO WITH ASPARAGUS OR PEAS • To the above recipe, add 1½ pounds asparagus, trimmed and cut into 1-inch pieces, or 2 cups fresh or thawed frozen peas to the risotto after the first 10 minutes, so that they cook with the rice for 10 to 15 minutes. Stir in 2 to 4 table-spoons chopped flat-leaf parsley along with the Parmesan and proceed as instructed.

- RISOTTO WITH GREEN BEANS • I'm not always sure that my green beans will cook to the right color or texture if I cook them with the risotto, as I do with peas and asparagus, so I blanch them in the stock, then add them to the risotto at the end. Bring the stock to a boil and add ½ pound green beans, trimmed and broken in half or into thirds if very long. Cook for 5 to 6 minutes, until just tender, and remove from the stock with a slotted spoon or deep-fry skimmer. Refresh with cold water. Proceed with the recipe and add the green beans to the risotto with the final ladle of stock.

red risotto with beet greens or red chard

When I buy beets with a big bunch of greens still attached, I'm getting two dishes in one. This is a beautiful pink-tinged risotto, the more so because I use red instead of white wine. You can use red chard as well. I often blanch greens when I get them home from the market so that they won't wilt or rot in the refrigerator if I don't get around to cooking them right away. If you do this, and want to use them for a risotto, chop the blanched greens and set aside. Add them to the risotto during the last few minutes of cooking, just to heat them through and amalgamate into the dish. The color will not be as red. **MAKES 4 GENEROUS SERVINGS**

> 6 to 7 cups stock, either vegetable or garlic,
>   preferably homemade (pages 63 and 65)
> 1 bunch beet greens or red chard (¾ to 1 pound),
>   stemmed and washed
> 1 tablespoon unsalted butter or extra virgin olive oil
> 1 small or ½ medium onion, minced (⅓ to ½ cup)
> 1½ cups Arborio rice
> 2 garlic cloves, minced
> ½ cup red wine
> Salt to taste
> 1 ounce Parmesan, grated (¼ cup)
> Freshly ground black pepper to taste

1. Have the stock simmering on low heat in a saucepan. Cut the greens crosswise into 1-inch-wide strips.

2. Heat the oil in a large nonstick skillet over medium heat. Add the onion. Cook, stirring, until the onion begins to soften, about 3 minutes. Add the rice and garlic. Cook, stirring, until the grains of rice are separate, 2 to 3 minutes.

3. Stir in the wine and cook over medium heat, stirring constantly. The wine should bubble, but not too quickly. You want some of the flavor to cook into the rice before it evaporates.

4. When the wine has just about evaporated, after about 3 minutes, stir in a ladle or two of the simmering stock, enough to just cover the rice. The stock should bubble slowly. Cook, stirring often, until it is just about absorbed. Add another ladle of the stock and continue to cook in this fashion, not too fast and not too slowly, adding more stock when the rice is almost dry, for 10 minutes.

5. Stir in the greens and continue adding more stock, a ladle at a time, and stirring, for another 10 to 15 minutes. Taste a bit of the rice. Is it cooked through? It should taste chewy but not hard in the middle, and definitely not soft like steamed rice. If it is still hard in the middle, you need to add another ladle of stock and cook for another 5 minutes or so. Now is the time to ascertain if there is enough salt. Add, if necessary.

6. Add another small ladle of stock to the rice. Stir the Parmesan into the rice and immediately remove from the heat. Add pepper, taste one last time, and adjust the salt. The rice should be creamy. Stir once and serve.

risotto with peas or green beans and corn

Make this with frozen corn and peas or green beans in winter, or you can make it at the height of summer with fresh ingredients. Either way, it's a pretty risotto. **MAKES 4 GENEROUS SERVINGS**

1 cup fresh or frozen corn kernels
1 cup fresh or frozen peas or ½ pound fresh or
    frozen green beans, trimmed and broken
    in half if fresh (2 cups)
6 to 7 cups stock, either vegetable or garlic,
    preferably homemade (pages 63 and 65)
1 tablespoon extra virgin olive oil or unsalted butter
1 small onion or ½ medium onion,
    minced (⅓ to ½ cup)
1½ cups Arborio rice
2 garlic cloves, minced
½ cup dry white wine
Salt to taste
¼ cup chopped fresh herbs, such as parsley, sage, chives,
    thyme, or tarragon
1 ounce Parmesan, grated (¼ cup)
Freshly ground black pepper to taste

1. If you are using frozen vegetables, thaw in a microwave or by putting them in a bowl and covering with boiling water. Drain when thawed. If you are using fresh green beans, bring 8 cups water to a boil in a medium saucepan and add 1 teaspoon of salt and the green beans. Cook for 5 minutes, drain, rinse with cold water, and set aside. Fresh corn and peas can be cooked directly in the risotto, but the beans are better if cooked separately.

2. Have the stock simmering over low heat in a saucepan.

3. Heat the oil or butter in a large nonstick skillet over medium heat. Add the onion. Cook, stirring, until the onion begins to soften, about 3 minutes. Add the rice and garlic. Cook, stirring, until the grains of rice are separate and beginning to crackle, about 1 minute.

4. Stir in the wine and cook over medium heat, stirring constantly. The wine should bubble, but not too quickly. You want some of the flavor to cook into the rice before it evaporates. When the wine has just about evaporated, after about 3 minutes, stir in a ladle or two of the simmering stock, enough to just cover the rice. The stock should bubble slowly. Cook, stirring often, until it is just about absorbed. Add another ladle of the stock and continue to cook in this fashion, not too fast and not too slowly, adding more stock when the rice is almost dry, for 15 minutes.

5. Stir in the corn and peas or beans and continue to cook as above, for another 10 minutes. Taste a bit of the rice. Is it cooked through? It should taste chewy, but not hard in the middle and definitely not soft like steamed rice. If it is still hard in the middle, you need to add another ladle of stock and cook for another 5 minutes or so. Now is the time to ascertain if there is enough salt. Add, if necessary.

6. Add another small ladle of stock to the rice. Stir in the herbs and Parmesan and immediately remove from the heat. Add pepper, taste one last time, and adjust the salt. The rice should be creamy. Stir for a couple of seconds, and serve.

mushroom risotto

This risotto is a great winter standby. The porcini mushrooms give its broth a rich, meaty, complex flavor, yet making it couldn't be simpler. **MAKES 4 GENEROUS SERVINGS**

1 ounce (about 1 heaped cup) dried porcinis
2 tablespoons soy sauce
1 teaspoon salt, plus more to taste
2 tablespoons unsalted butter or extra virgin olive oil
½ or 1 small onion, minced (⅓ to ½ cup)
¾ pound fresh cultivated or wild mushrooms, cleaned, trimmed,
*   and cut into thick slices*
2 large garlic cloves, minced
½ to 1 teaspoon chopped fresh rosemary or ¼ to ½ teaspoon
*   crumbled dried*
½ to 1 teaspoon fresh thyme leaves or
*   ¼ to ½ teaspoon dried*
1½ cups Arborio rice
½ cup dry white wine
1 ounce Parmesan, grated (¼ cup)
¼ cup chopped fresh parsley
Freshly ground black pepper to taste

1. Place the dried mushrooms in a bowl or glass measuring cup and pour in 3 cups boiling water. Let sit for 30 minutes. Line a strainer with cheesecloth or with a double thickness of paper towels, place it over a bowl, and drain the mushrooms. Squeeze the mushrooms over the strainer to extract all the liquid, then rinse them in several changes of water to remove sand. Chop coarsely and set aside. Combine the mushroom soaking liquid with about 4 cups additional water to make 7 cups. Add the soy sauce and salt. Taste and adjust the salt. It should be well seasoned. Transfer to a saucepan and bring to a low simmer.

2. Heat 1 tablespoon of the oil or butter in a large nonstick skillet over medium heat. Add the onion. Cook, stirring, until the onion begins to soften, about 3 minutes. Add the dried and fresh mushrooms. Cook, stirring, until the mushrooms begin to release liquid, 3 to 5 minutes. Add the garlic, rosemary, and thyme. Cook, stirring, until the mushroom liquid has just about evaporated. Add the remaining 1 tablespoon oil and the rice. Cook, stirring, until the grains of rice are separate and beginning to crackle, about 1 minute.

3. Stir in the wine and cook over medium heat, stirring constantly. The wine should bubble, but not too quickly. You want some of the flavor to cook into the rice before it evaporates. When the wine has just about evaporated, after about 3 minutes, stir in a ladle or two of the simmering stock, enough to just cover the rice. The stock should bubble slowly. Cook, stirring often, until it is just about absorbed. Add another ladle of the stock and continue to cook in this fashion, not too fast and not too slowly, adding more stock when the rice is almost dry, for 20 to 25 minutes.

4. Taste a bit of the rice. Is it cooked through? It should taste chewy but not hard in the middle, and definitely not soft like steamed rice. If it is still hard in the middle, you need to add another ladle of stock and cook for another 5 minutes or so. Now is the time to ascertain if there is enough salt. Add, if necessary.

5. Add another small ladle of stock to the rice. Stir in the Parmesan and parsley, add freshly ground pepper, taste one last time, and adjust the salt. The rice should be creamy. Serve at once.

zucchini risotto

Zucchini becomes almost creamy when cooked in a risotto. **MAKES 4 GENEROUS SERVINGS**

6 to 7 cups stock, either vegetable or garlic,
*   preferably homemade (pages 63 and 65)*
1 tablespoon extra virgin olive oil or unsalted butter
1 small onion, minced (⅓ to ½ cup)
1 pound zucchini, finely chopped
2 large garlic cloves, minced
Salt to taste
1½ cups Arborio rice
½ cup dry white wine
1 large egg, beaten (optional)
1 ounce Parmesan, grated (¼ cup)
Freshly ground black pepper to taste

1. Have the stock simmering on low heat in a saucepan.

2. Heat the oil in a large nonstick skillet over medium heat. Add the onion. Cook, stirring, until the onion begins to soften, about 3 minutes. Add the zucchini, garlic, and about ¼ teaspoon salt. Cook, stirring, until the zucchini begins to soften, about 3 minutes. Add the rice. Cook, stirring, until the grains of rice are separate and beginning to crackle, about 1 minute.

3. Stir in the wine and cook over medium heat, stirring constantly. The wine should bubble, but not too quickly. You want some of the flavor to cook into the rice before it evaporates. When the wine has just about evaporated, after about 3 minutes, stir in a ladle or two of the simmering stock, enough to just cover the rice. The stock should bubble slowly. Cook, stirring often, until it is just about absorbed. Add another ladle of the stock and continue to cook in this fashion, not too fast and not too slowly, adding more stock when the rice is almost dry, for 20 to 25 minutes.

4. Taste a bit of the rice. Is it cooked through? It should taste chewy but not hard in the middle, and definitely not soft like steamed rice. If it is still hard in the middle, you need to add another ladle of stock and cook for another 5 minutes or so. Now is the time to ascertain if there is enough salt. Add, if necessary.

5. Add another small ladle of stock to the rice. Beat together the egg and the Parmesan, stir into the rice, and immediately remove from the heat. (If you are not using the egg, just stir in the Parmesan with the last ladle of stock.) Add pepper, taste one last time, and adjust the salt. The rice should be creamy. Stir for a couple of seconds and serve.

wheat berries

Wheat berries are the whole wheat kernels that flour is milled from. The grains are hearty and chewy and benefit from soaking before cooking. I think they lend themselves best to salads (see page 52) and soups. **MAKES ABOUT 4 CUPS, 6 SERVINGS**

1 cup wheat berries
½ teaspoon salt, or to taste

1. Soak the wheat berries in water to cover by an inch for several hours or overnight if possible, and drain.

2. Combine the wheat berries and 3 cups water and bring to a boil. Reduce the heat, cover, and simmer for 1 hour. Add salt and continue to simmer for another 30 to 60 minutes, until the grains are tender. They will still be chewy. Drain off any water remaining in the pot.

Advance preparation: Wheat berries will keep for about 5 days in the refrigerator, and for 3 to 4 months in the freezer. To reheat in the oven, place in a lightly oiled baking dish, cover tightly with foil, and reheat in a 350°F oven for 20 minutes. To reheat in a microwave, place in a microwave-safe bowl, cover tightly with plastic wrap, then pierce the plastic with a knife. Microwave for 1 minute. Let sit for 1 minute, carefully remove plastic, and fluff with a fork. Repeat one more time, if needed.

wheat berries with broccoli and mushrooms

Wheat berries' meaty texture begs for a meaty-tasting broth for cooking. Dried porcini mushrooms provide just such a medium. **MAKES 4 GENEROUS SERVINGS**

1 cup wheat berries, rinsed and soaked overnight or
for several hours and drained
½ ounce (about ½ cup) dried porcini
2 tablespoons soy sauce (preferably mushroom soy)
Salt to taste
1 tablespoon extra virgin olive oil
1 medium onion, chopped
½ pound fresh cultivated or wild mushrooms,
trimmed and thickly sliced
2 large garlic cloves, minced
½ cup dry white wine or dark beer
1 pound broccoli florets
Freshly ground black pepper to taste
2 to 4 tablespoons chopped fresh parsley
1 ounce Parmesan, grated (¼ cup; optional)

1. Place the drained wheat berries in a pot, add water to cover by a couple of inches, and bring to a boil. Reduce the heat, cover, and simmer for 1 hour. Drain.

2. Meanwhile, place the dried mushrooms in a bowl or large glass measuring cup. Pour in 3 cups boiling water. Let sit for 15 to 30 minutes, until softened. Line a strainer with cheesecloth or a double layer of paper towels and place over a bowl. Drain the mushrooms and squeeze them over the strainer to extract the fragrant liquid. Rinse the mushrooms in several changes of water to remove sand, then squeeze dry, and chop. Add water, if necessary, to the mushroom soaking liquid to make 3 cups. Add the soy sauce and salt to taste; it should be well seasoned. Bring to a simmer in a saucepan.

3. Heat the oil in a heavy saucepan, Dutch oven, or skillet over medium heat. Add the onion. Cook, stirring, until just about tender, 3 to 5 minutes. Add the fresh mushrooms and a large pinch of salt and cook, stirring, until the mushrooms begin to release liquid, about 3 minutes.

Add the garlic and the wheat berries. Stir together for a couple of minutes and add the wine. Cook, stirring, until the wine has just about evaporated, about 3 minutes. Stir in the simmering stock. Bring to a boil, reduce the heat, cover, and simmer for 30 to 60 minutes, until the wheat berries are tender. If there is still a lot of liquid in the pot, pour it off.

4. While the wheat berries are cooking, steam the broccoli. Bring 1 inch of water to a boil in a saucepan with a steaming rack in place. Add the broccoli, cover, and steam for 5 minutes. Remove from the heat and refresh with cold water. Set aside.

5. Check to make sure the wheat berries are tender. They will be chewy no matter how long they cook, but they should be cooked through. Taste and correct seasoning. Add pepper and stir in the broccoli and parsley. Stir in the Parmesan, if using, and serve.

Advance preparation: This keeps well for a day in the refrigerator. It's best to add the broccoli and the parsley just before serving. To reheat in the oven, place in a lightly oiled baking dish, cover tightly with foil, and reheat in a 350°F oven for 20 minutes. To reheat in a microwave, place in a microwave-safe bowl, cover tightly with plastic wrap, then pierce the plastic with a knife. Microwave for 1 minute. Let sit for 1 minute, carefully remove plastic, and fluff with a fork. Repeat one more time, if needed.

A Tasty Pot of Beans

No one food is essential to the vegetarian diet, but dried beans have always been an important element in mine. Sustaining and versatile, a good pot of beans can stand alone—it is really like a main-dish soup—or be a building block for another dish, such as tacos or enchiladas, main-dish salads, stews, and hearty soups.

A good pot of beans usually begins with onion and garlic. These two ingredients, plus salt, can be all it takes to ensure a rich, flavorful broth. Chickpeas don't even need the onion and garlic, because they have such a nutty flavor. But chickpeas, unlike rich-tasting beans like black beans and pintos, rarely stand alone as a dish, because they don't produce the marvelous broth that black beans and pintos produce.

You can make a meal of a savory bowl of black beans or pintos. When you eat beans with corn tortillas or other grains, the protein you are getting is complete. I usually accompany this dish with corn tortillas or cornbread and a salad. Sometimes, for a more substantial meal, I stir some cooked rice into my beans or top the beans with crumbled Mexican cheese, goat cheese, or feta.

- HOW TO MAKE A POT OF BEANS TASTY • There are three essential ingredients: onion, garlic, and salt. Add the salt after the beans have softened, and let the beans simmer with the salt for another 30 to 60 minutes. I was taught that the beans won't soften properly if you add the salt too early; now there seems to be some disagreement about this, but it's a habit I stick with. The important thing is to add enough. I begin with 1 teaspoon of salt for each cup of beans, which may sound like a lot, but trust me, they need it. If there is a lot of broth, the dish will probably require more than this.

- OTHER FLAVORINGS • It depends on the bean, but when cooking black beans or pintos, I use southwestern and Mexican seasonings. Cilantro is the easiest to get, and I almost always use it. I also use a Mexican herb called epazote, which gives the beans an earthy quality and also seems to give the broth a richer texture. See specific recipes for other seasoning ideas.

- WHY TAKE THE TIME TO MAKE BEANS WHEN MOST BEANS COME IN CANS? • The answer is simple: The beans that you make at home will taste better. Canned beans are perfectly fine, and I am a big advocate of them, for using in salads, pastas, soups, purees, and other dishes. But if you want a bowl of beans with a fantastic broth, or if the broth is important in the dish you are making the beans for, then you'll have to cook them yourself. The broth in canned beans is usually sweet or too thick, which is why you should rinse canned beans when adding them to most dishes. Remember to plan in advance so you have enough time to soak the beans.

tasty pot of beans

1 pound black beans or pinto beans (2 heaped cups),
washed and picked over (to make sure there are
no stones mixed in with the beans)
1 medium onion, chopped
4 large garlic cloves, minced
1 sprig fresh epazote (optional)
2 tablespoons chopped cilantro,
plus additional for garnish
Salt to taste (about 2 teaspoons or more)

1. Place the beans in a large bowl and pour in 8 cups water. Soak for at least 6 hours or overnight.

2. Transfer the beans with their soaking liquid to a large, heavy bean pot, casserole, or Dutch oven. They should be covered by an inch of water. Add another cup if they are not and bring to a boil. Reduce the heat to medium and skim off any foam that rises. Continue to skim off the foam for another few minutes, until there isn't any more. Then add the onion and half the garlic. If using epazote, add now. Reduce the heat to low, cover, and simmer for 1 hour.

3. Add the salt, the remaining 2 garlic cloves, and cilantro. Continue to simmer for another hour, until the beans are quite soft and the broth is thick and fragrant. Taste the broth. Is there enough salt? Does it need more garlic? Add, if necessary. Taste the beans and make sure they are very soft.

4. Let the beans sit overnight in the refrigerator for the best flavor. Heat through and serve, garnishing each bowl with additional chopped cilantro.

Advance preparation: Beans will keep in the refrigerator for about 4 days. They get better overnight. They also freeze well and will keep, frozen, for 3 to 4 months.

white beans

MAKES ABOUT 3 CUPS, 4 TO 6 SERVINGS

> *1 pound white beans, such as navy beans or*
> *cannellini beans (2 heaped cups),*
> *washed and picked over (to make sure there*
> *are no stones mixed in with the beans)*
> *1 medium onion, chopped*
> *2 to 4 large garlic cloves, minced*
> *1 large bay leaf*
> *Salt to taste (about 2 teaspoons, or more)*

1. Soak the beans in 6 cups of water for at least 6 hours or overnight. Drain.

2. Combine the beans and 8 cups of water in a large, heavy bean pot, casserole, or Dutch oven. Bring to a boil and skim off any foam that rises. Add the onion, half the garlic, and the bay leaf. Make sure the beans are covered by at least 1 inch of water and add more if not. Reduce the heat to low, cover, and simmer for 1 hour.

3. Add the salt and the remaining garlic. Continue to simmer for 30 to 60 minutes, until the beans are soft but not mushy, and the broth is fragrant. Taste. Is there enough salt? Add if necessary.

Advance preparation: Beans will keep in the refrigerator for about 4 days. They get better overnight. They also freeze well, but do not drain if freezing. They will keep for 3 to 4 months in the freezer.

• BORLOTTI OR CRANBERRY BEANS • Use the same seasonings for these that you use for white beans. Follow the cooking instructions for white beans, above.

• BLACK-EYED PEAS • These cook quickly and require no soaking. Wash and pick over for stones. Combine with 8 cups water and bring to a boil. Skim off any foam that rises. Add the onion, half the garlic, and a bay leaf. Reduce the heat, cover, and simmer for 30 minutes. Add salt and the remaining garlic. Simmer for another 15 to 30 minutes, until soft but not mushy. Taste and adjust seasonings.

- LENTILS • Like black-eyed peas, these require no soaking. Follow the instructions for black-eyed peas, above.

- CHICKPEAS • These need no aromatics, just salt. Soak 1 pound beans in 6 cups water. Drain. Combine the beans and 8 cups water in a large pot and bring to a boil. Skim off any foam. Reduce the heat, cover, and simmer for 1 hour. Add about 2 teaspoons salt and continue to simmer for another 30 to 60 minutes, until thoroughly tender.

baked beans with mint and paprika

This is one of the best versions of baked beans I've ever eaten. This recipe is inspired by a recipe in Maria Kaneva-Johnson's *The Melting Pot: Balkan Food and Cookery*. Serve it with a green salad and good crusty bread or cornbread. **MAKES 4 TO 6 SERVINGS**

1 pound white beans, such as navy beans or
cannellini beans (2 heaped cups),
washed and picked over (to make sure there
are no stones mixed in with the beans)
1 bay leaf
1 dried or fresh hot red chile pepper
2 tablespoons extra virgin olive oil
2 medium onions, chopped
1 teaspoon paprika
2 to 3 large garlic cloves (to taste), minced
Salt and freshly ground black pepper to taste
1 tablespoon fresh mint leaves, chopped
2 to 3 tomatoes, cut in rounds
2 red bell peppers, seeded and
cut into strips or rounds
1 teaspoon unbleached all-purpose flour
Chopped fresh parsley or mint

1. Soak the beans in 6 cups of water for at least 6 hours or overnight.

2. Drain the beans and combine with 4 cups water, the bay leaf, and the chile pepper in a large pot or ovenproof Dutch oven. Bring to a boil, reduce the heat, and simmer for 45 to 60 minutes, until the beans are tender but intact. Discard the chile pepper. If the pot is not ovenproof, transfer the beans with their liquid, to an ovenproof casserole or Dutch oven.

3. Preheat the oven to 325°F.

4. Heat 1 tablespoon of the oil in a large nonstick skillet over medium heat. Add the onion. Stir together, cover, and cook, stirring occasionally, for 5 to 10 minutes, until soft. Uncover and continue to cook, stirring, until lightly browned, about 5 more minutes. Remove from the heat and stir in the paprika, garlic, salt (1 teaspoon or more), pepper, and mint. Stir in about ¼ cup hot water to give the mixture a saucelike consistency. Stir this into the beans and blend thoroughly. Taste and adjust the salt.

5. Arrange the tomatoes and bell peppers over the top. Sprinkle on the flour and the remaining 1 tablespoon oil.

6. Bake, uncovered, for 1 hour, or until the beans are very tender. If the water evaporates before the beans are soft, add a little more. Sprinkle the parsley or additional mint over the top and serve, hot or warm.

Advance preparation: The beans will keep for 3 to 5 days in the refrigerator. The dish can be made hours ahead and reheated just before serving.

• QUICK BAKED CANNED BEANS • The disadvantage to using canned beans is that you don't get the tasty broth. The obvious advantage is the time-saving element. In order to add a liquid dimension, I've added a can of chopped tomatoes with liquid. Substitute three 15-ounce cans white beans, drained and rinsed, for the dried beans. Omit the bay leaf. Add one 14-ounce can chopped tomatoes with liquid. Combine the canned beans, chile pepper, and tomatoes in an ovenproof casserole or Dutch oven. Proceed with the recipe, beginning with step 2.

refried beans

These have an important place in my repertoire. They are absolutely delicious and never fail to impress guests. I serve them on nachos, as part of a larger Mexican meal, and for everyday dining as the filling or topping for soft tacos or quesadillas. The beans are not really fried, as they are traditionally in lard, but cooked down in their own broth, resulting in an intense, savory dish. Use pintos or black beans for these; black beans are my favorite. **MAKES 6 SERVINGS**

Tasty Pot of Beans (page 180)
1½ to 2 tablespoons canola oil
1 tablespoon ground cumin
2 teaspoons pure ground chile powder
Salt to taste

1. Cook the beans as directed.

2. Drain off about 1 cup of liquid from the beans, retaining it in a separate bowl to use later for moistening the beans, should they dry out. Mash half the beans coarsely in a food processor or with a bean or potato masher. Don't puree them, however. You want texture. Stir the mashed beans back into the pot.

3. Heat 1½ tablespoons of oil in a large, heavy nonstick frying pan over medium heat. Add the cumin and ground chile. Cook, stirring, for about 1 minute, until the spices begin to sizzle and cook. Turn the heat to medium-high and add the beans (this can be done in batches, in which case, cook the spices in batches as well, using 1 tablespoon of oil for each batch). Fry the beans, stirring and mashing often, until they thicken and begin to get crusty on the bottom and aromatic. The broth should be bubbling briskly. Stir up the crust each time it forms, and mix into the beans. Cook for 20 to 25 minutes, stirring often and mashing the beans with the back of your spoon or a bean masher. The beans should be thick but not dry. Add liquid you saved from the beans if they seem too dry, but save some of the liquid for moistening the beans before you reheat them, if you are serving them later. They will continue to dry out once you turn off the heat. Taste the refried beans and adjust the salt, and serve.

4. Set aside in the pan if you are serving within a few hours. Otherwise, transfer the beans to a lightly oiled baking dish and cover with foil.

Advance preparation: Refried beans will keep for 3 days in the refrigerator and for several months in the freezer. Keep the liquid you retained in a jar, so that you can moisten the beans before reheating (this keeps less well, only a couple of days; use water if you need to throw out the broth). The *frijoles* can be reheated in a nonstick pan or in a lightly oiled baking dish. Cover the dish with foil and reheat for 30 minutes in a 325°F oven. However, if you are storing the beans in the refrigerator in a baking dish, cover first with plastic or waxed paper before you cover with aluminum, so that the beans don't react with the aluminum. Remember to remove the plastic before reheating.

- QUICK REFRIED BEANS • Although canned beans never taste as good as the beans you cook with lots of onion, garlic, and herbs, they are suitable for making refried beans in a hurry. For 2 cups of refried beans you will need two 15-ounce cans black beans or pinto beans (four cans yields the same amount as this recipe). Do not drain off the liquid, or even puree the beans. Heat the oil and fry the spices as directed. Pour in the beans with their liquid, and mash with a bean masher or the back of a large wooden spoon, right in the pan. Cook, stirring, exactly as instructed for the refried beans above. There is less liquid in a can of beans than you get when you cook them, so you will have to add water as the refried canned beans will dry out considerably.

soft tacos with black beans and greens

I like to serve these as open-faced tacos. Greens and beans are a classic combination the world over. **MAKES 4 SERVINGS**

1 tablespoon canola oil

2 teaspoons ground cumin

2 to 3 large garlic cloves, minced

2 pounds greens, such as chard, kale, or spinach, stemmed, washed well, and coarsely chopped

3 cups cooked black beans (Tasty Pot of Beans, page 180) or two 15-ounce cans, plus ½ to 1 cup of the bean broth or water

Salt to taste

1 ounce Mexican queso fresco or feta, crumbled (¼ cup)

12 corn tortillas

Salsa Fresca (page 12) or commercial red salsa

1. Heat the oil in a large, heavy nonstick skillet over medium heat. Add the cumin. Cook, stirring, until it sizzles, smells fragrant, and browns lightly, a minute or less. Add the garlic and cook, stirring, until it begins to color and smell fragrant, about 1 minute. Turn up the heat to medium-high and add the chard. There should be water remaining on the leaves after washing. If it seems dry, add about ¼ cup water to the pan. Cook, stirring often, for 5 minutes after the greens begin to sizzle. Add the beans (with liquid) and salt. Bring to a simmer, reduce the heat to low, and simmer for 10 minutes, stirring often. With the back of your spoon, mash the beans to thicken the mixture. Taste and adjust seasonings.

2. Heat the tortillas using one of the following methods: Heat them on a dry heavy frying pan, turning them once, until flexible; wrap all of them in foil and heat in a 350°F oven for 10 minutes; wrap them in waxed paper or a clean dish towel and heat through for 1 minute in a microwave; or wrap in a kitchen towel and steam for 1 minute above 1 inch of boiling water, then allow to sit, covered, for 10 minutes.

3. Lay two tortillas flat on each plate. Top with a generous helping of beans and greens. Sprinkle on the cheese, spoon on the salsa, and serve, with more salsa on the side.

mediterranean chickpea
and vegetable stew

This is like a ratatouille with added chickpeas and Middle Eastern seasonings. Serve it alone or over bulgur, couscous, or rice. Like most stews, it is best when made a day ahead. **MAKES 6 SERVINGS**

1 large eggplant, cut in half lengthwise

2 tablespoons extra virgin olive oil, plus more as needed

1 large onion, sliced

4 to 6 large garlic cloves, minced

2 red bell peppers, or 1 red bell pepper and
    1 green or yellow bell pepper,
    seeded and cut into 1-inch squares

Salt to taste

2 medium zucchini, cut in half lengthwise,
    then in ½-inch-wide slices

2 medium waxy potatoes (about ½ pound), scrubbed and diced

1½ pounds fresh tomatoes, peeled, seeded,
    and coarsely chopped

1 tablespoon tomato paste

1 bay leaf

2 teaspoons chopped fresh thyme leaves or 1 teaspoon dried

1½ to 2 teaspoons ground cumin

1 teaspoon coriander seeds,
    cracked in a spice mill or mortar and pestle

One 15-ounce can chickpeas,
    drained and rinsed

Freshly ground black pepper to taste

Pinch of cayenne

½ cup chopped fresh parsley

Juice of ½ lemon (optional)

1. Preheat the oven to 450°F. Brush or rub a baking sheet with olive oil.

2. Score the eggplant halves with a lengthwise cut down the middle, down to, but not through, the skin. Place on the baking sheet (or baking sheets if one isn't big enough) cut side down. Bake for 15 to 20 minutes, until the skins begin to shrivel and the edges against the pan are browning. Remove from the heat, transfer the eggplant halves to a colander, cut side down so they can drain, and allow to cool and release some of their juice. Meanwhile, turn the oven down to 350°F and prepare the rest of the vegetables. When the eggplant is cool enough to handle, cut the halves in half lengthwise along the score line. Peel away the skin if you wish, and cut into ¾-inch dice. Set aside.

3. Oil a large heavy-bottomed lidded casserole, preferably earthenware, with olive oil.

4. Heat 1 tablespoon of the olive oil in a large, heavy nonstick skillet over medium heat. Add the onion. Cook, stirring, until softened, about 5 minutes. Add 2 of the garlic cloves and cook, stirring, for another couple of minutes, until the onion has just begun to color. Remove from the heat and transfer to the casserole.

5. Heat the remaining 1 tablespoon of oil in the skillet over medium heat. Add the bell peppers. Stir for a couple of minutes. Add about ¼ teaspoon salt or ½ teaspoon coarse sea salt. Continue to cook, stirring often, until the peppers begin to soften, about 5 minutes. Add the zucchini and half the remaining garlic. Continue to cook, stirring, for another 5 minutes, until the zucchini looks translucent. Transfer to the casserole with the onions. Add the diced eggplant, the potatoes, half the tomatoes, and the tomato paste to the casserole. Stir in the bay leaf, thyme, cumin, crushed coriander seeds, and salt. Stir everything together and cover.

6. Bake for 30 minutes. Remove the casserole from the oven and give the mixture a good stir with a long-handled wooden spoon. Cover and bake for another 30 minutes.

7. Remove the casserole from the oven and stir in the remaining tomatoes and garlic, and the chickpeas. Taste and adjust the salt. Add pepper and a touch of cayenne and bake for another 30 minutes, covered.

8. Remove from the oven and allow to cool slightly or completely. Stir in the parsley and lemon juice. Serve warm, at room temperature, or chilled.

Advance preparation: This is better the day after it's made and will keep for 3 to 5 days in the refrigerator.

broccoli raab with garlic, red pepper, and beans

This is an adaptation of a southern Italian dish. Beans and greens always marry well, especially in this garlicky, slightly *piccante* dish. **MAKES 4 SERVINGS**

1 tablespoon salt, plus more to taste
1½ pounds broccoli raab, washed and tough stems discarded
2 tablespoons extra virgin olive oil
2 to 3 garlic cloves, minced
1 dried hot chile, seeded and crumbled,
    or ¼ teaspoon red pepper flakes
1½ cups White Beans with ½ cup of their liquid (page 181) or
    one 15-ounce can navy or cannellini beans, drained and rinsed

1. Bring a large pot of water to a boil while you prepare the other ingredients. When the water comes to a boil, add 1 tablespoon of salt and the broccoli raab. Boil for 5 minutes, until the stems are tender. Remove ½ cup of water from the pot and drain the broccoli raab.

2. Heat the oil in the large, heavy nonstick skillet over medium heat. Add the garlic and chile. Cook, stirring, for about 30 seconds, or until it begins to color. Stir in the broccoli raab, the beans, and ½ cup of their liquid, or the liquid you retained from the broccoli raab. Heat through, stirring, until the broccoli raab is well coated.

3. Add salt and taste. Do you need to add more? Could it use more garlic? Adjust the seasonings, remove from the heat, and serve.

Advance preparation: This can be made several hours ahead of time and reheated gently. The broccoli raab can be boiled and held in the refrigerator for a couple of days.

Pasta, pizza, and Bruschetta

In the United States, pasta is probably the most accessible vegetarian food, and pasta dishes the easiest for the beginning vegetarian cook to make. So many pasta dishes are familiar and well liked, and many of the classics are also meatless.

What I love most about pasta is its versatility and its universal appeal. A tomato sauce alone is quite enough to make a great pasta dinner, and any number of vegetables, beans, and other condiments can be added to this. But tomato sauce is just one possibility; a creamy sauce, or a Gremolata (page 19) and olive oil, with a green vegetable like broccoli or asparagus, is another way to go. Because of pasta, I know that I can impulse buy at the farmers' market. Any vegetable that looks good will be good with pasta. And these are just the simple toppings. In fact there is hardly a vegetable dish that can't be tossed with noodles to make a meal. Those with Mediterranean flavors go with Italian pastas, and Asian dishes can be served with buckwheat noodles (soba), Chinese noodles, Japanese wheat noodles (somen), or angel hair pasta. So once you've worked your way through the recipes in this chapter, go and take a look at the vegetable stews and ragouts in the vegetable side-dish chapter and the tofu stir-fries in the tofu chapter, and try some of them with pasta.

Just about any sauce or topping that tastes good with pasta also tastes good on a thick slice of toast rubbed with garlic. These open-faced sandwiches, called bruschetta, make the kind of supper I like to eat late at night, when we come home from the theater or a movie. Thick slices of bread go into the toaster oven until nicely browned, then I rub them with a cut clove of garlic and pile on leftover pasta sauce, or roasted pepper and a little cheese, or one of the dips or spreads in the dips and spreads chapter.

We rarely think of making pizza at home, but when we do it's always such a treat. I find that most of the pizzas I can buy, either at restaurants or stores, have too much cheese and oil. The ones you'll find here are much lighter, with a focus on beautiful vegetables. If you can find frozen or prepared dough, by all means use it. But the one in this chapter is easy and tasty, and it's a great way to learn to work with bread dough.

How to Cook Italian Pasta

Bring a large pot of water to a boil. Meanwhile, place a large colander in your sink unless you are using a pasta pot. Get out a big ceramic bowl to serve the pasta in (or you can toss the pasta with your sauce in the frying pan if it's large enough).

When the water comes to a boil, add 1 tablespoon of salt. Then, making sure the water is boiling hard, gradually add the pasta. The water will stop boiling momentarily when you add the noodles. Take a long-handled wooden spoon or pasta spoon and stir the pasta up from the bottom of the pot so that it doesn't stick. Some cooks say to cover the pot until the water comes back to the boil; I rarely bother, but the water will return to a boil more quickly if you do. Once the water returns to a boil and the pasta is moving around in it, you can mostly leave it alone, but every once in a while give the pasta a stir and the bottom of the pot a scrape with the wooden spoon, just in case some noodles are sticking. Meanwhile, ladle a spoonful or two of the boiling water into your serving dish, to warm it, and heat your sauce or topping over low heat.

Sometimes the cooking time is written on the pasta box or bag, but often it isn't; in any case, these cooking times aren't always accurate. Thin angel hair pasta cooks in a few minutes. Most pastas take 7 to 12 minutes. With the exception of angel hair or cappellini, I begin checking after about 7 minutes. Spoon out a piece of pasta, or grab a piece with tongs. If it's spaghetti and it doesn't even bend much, don't bother for a few more minutes. Run the piece of pasta under cold water so you don't burn your tongue. Bite into it. It shouldn't be hard in the middle. But it shouldn't be floppy or mushy either. Al dente (recipes are always instructing you to cook pasta al dente) means firm to the teeth. Not mushy. Test again in a minute or two. When you test and it's cooked all the way through, but still a bit firm in the middle—that is, it resists your teeth—you're ready to drain and serve.

Empty the water from the serving bowl, which should now be warm from the hot water you ladled into it. Turn off the heat under your pot (it's easy to forget if you put it off), and carefully bring your pot over to the sink. Slowly drain the pasta into the colander, or lift your pasta basket out of the pasta pot right at the stove. The noodles don't have to be completely dry, but give the colander one shake, then pour the noodles into your warm serving dish or into the pan with the sauce. Immediately top with the sauce and serve.

pasta with tomato sauce

The first thing I ever learned to cook was spaghetti sauce. Knowing how to make a good tomato sauce, a basic Italian marinara made with seasoned tomatoes, is fundamental. Pasta with nothing more than this sauce and a sprinkling of Parmesan always makes a great meal, and there are many variations on the theme. You can add green vegetables or chickpeas or white beans to the equation, or enrich the sauce with goat cheese, heat it up with hot red pepper flakes, and more.

I use canned tomatoes much more often than fresh tomatoes for pasta. There are just so many months in the year when good fresh tomatoes at a reasonable price are not available. When they are, I tend to make uncooked tomato sauces. This recipe makes about 1½ cups tomato sauce, which might not seem like a lot to you; but pasta should be seasoned, not drowned, in a sauce. It's enough for ¾ pound pasta, to serve four, or 1 pound pasta, to serve six. **MAKES 4 TO 6 SERVINGS**

1 tablespoon extra virgin olive oil
2 to 3 large garlic cloves, minced
One 28-ounce can tomatoes,
  drained of all but about ½ cup of the juice,
  seeded, and crushed (not pureed) in a food processor
  with the retained juice, or finely chopped
⅛ teaspoon sugar
2 tablespoons slivered fresh basil leaves,
  or ¾ teaspoon dried oregano or thyme, or a combination
Freshly ground black pepper to taste
¾ to 1 pound dried pasta
⅓ cup freshly grated Parmesan

1. Begin heating a large pot or pasta pot filled with water for the pasta.

2. Heat the oil in a large, heavy nonstick skillet over medium heat. Add the garlic and cook for 30 to 60 seconds. Don't let the garlic turn hard or brown. It should just become translucent and fragrant, and the color should become slightly golden. As soon as the garlic begins to color, add the tomatoes and their liquid, the sugar, ½ to ¾ teaspoon salt, and dried herbs, if using. Cook, stirring often, for 10 to 20 minutes, until the tomatoes are cooked down, fragrant, and just beginning to stick to the pan, but not dry. Stir in the fresh basil, if using. Add pepper, a few grinds of the mill. Taste. Does the sauce taste vivid? Is there enough salt? Garlic? Adjust seasonings and turn off the heat.

3. When the pasta water reaches a rolling boil, add 1 tablespoon salt and the pasta. Cook until the pasta is al dente, firm to the bite, and drain. Toss at once with the sauce and serve, passing the grated cheese.

Advance preparation: This sauce can be made hours ahead of time and kept on the stove. Reheat gently, adding a little water if it seems dry. It will keep in the refrigerator for a couple of days and freezes well for 6 months.

- PASTA WITH TOMATO SAUCE AND A GREEN VEGETABLE • To add a green vegetable to the meal, add one of the following to the pasta water 3 to 5 minutes after adding the pasta (4 to 5 minutes before the end of cooking): ½ pound green beans, trimmed, strings removed if necessary, and broken in half; or ½ to 1 pound broccoli, broken into florets, stems discarded, or peeled and sliced; or ½ pound sugar snap peas, strings removed; or 1 pound fresh peas, shelled; or 1 cup frozen peas (thawed or still frozen). Drain and toss with the tomato sauce as above. Proceed as above.

- PASTA WITH TOMATO SAUCE AND CHICKPEAS • Make the tomato sauce as directed. Drain one 15-ounce can chickpeas and rinse the beans with cold water. Add to the sauce and heat through. Proceed as above.

- PASTA WITH SPICY TOMATO SAUCE • Add 1 or 2 dried red peppers, crumbled, or ¼ teaspoon red pepper flakes, to the olive oil along with the garlic and proceed as above. This version is particularly good with chickpeas added.

pasta with greens

This traditional southern Italian dish calls for ricotta cheese or ricotta salata, a firmer, saltier ricotta. If you want to lighten it up, you can use a creamy blend of cottage cheese and milk; the dish will lose little in the way of flavor and satisfaction. The "big taste" comes from the greens and pecorino. **MAKES 4 TO 6 SERVINGS**

2 pounds greens, such as Swiss chard leaves,
*   broccoli raab, beet greens, kale, escarole,*
*   dandelion greens, collard greens,*
*   alone or in combination*
Salt to taste
½ cup ricotta or nonfat or low-fat cottage cheese
2 tablespoons low-fat milk (if using the cottage cheese)
1 ounce pecorino, grated (¼ cup)
1 tablespoon extra virgin olive oil
2 large garlic cloves, minced
¼ teaspoon red pepper flakes, or more to taste
¾ to 1 pound bucatini, perciatelli, or spaghetti

1. Begin heating a large pot or pasta pot filled with water for the pasta.

2. Meanwhile, stem the greens and wash them thoroughly. When the water comes to a boil, add 1 tablespoon salt and the greens. Cook for 2 to 5 minutes, until tender (the timing depends on which greens you use). Remove from the water using a slotted spoon, a deep-fry skimmer, or the insert of your pasta pot. Transfer immediately to a bowl of cold water, then drain. Put the top on the pot and reserve the water for cooking the pasta. Gently squeeze most of the water out of the greens and chop them coarsely. Set aside.

3. In a food processor fitted with the steel blade or in a mini-processor, blend the ricotta or cottage cheese until fairly smooth. Scrape down the sides of the bowl and blend again. Add the milk and blend until the mixture is creamy.

4. Heat the oil over medium heat in a large nonstick skillet. Add the garlic and red pepper flakes. Cook, stirring, for about 30 seconds, just until the garlic begins to color. Add the greens.

the best vegetarian recipes

Stir together for 1 minute. Stir in ¾ cup cooking liquid from the greens. Add salt to taste and remove from the heat but keep warm.

5. Bring the pot of water back to a rolling boil and add the pasta. Cook until al dente, firm to the bite, and drain.

6. Transfer the pasta to the pan with the greens. Add the cheeses, toss together, and serve at once.

Advance preparation: The greens can be cleaned and cooked hours ahead of time. The cottage cheese mixture will keep for 3 days in the refrigerator.

pasta with kale and red peppers

This is a colorful version of pasta with greens. If you can find the delicate Russian kale at your farmers' market, use it for this, as the leaves are not as tough as the kale we find at the supermarket. But any type will work. The garlicky, slightly piquant kale and red pepper combination makes a nice vegetable side dish as well as a topping for pasta. **MAKES 4 SERVINGS**

1 large bunch kale (about 1 pound)
Salt to taste
1 tablespoon extra virgin olive oil
1 medium or large red bell pepper,
    cut into thin 2-inch-long slices
¼ teaspoon red pepper flakes (optional)
2 large garlic cloves, minced
¾ pound fettucine, penne, or fusilli
½ cup nonfat or low-fat cottage cheese
¼ cup low-fat milk
Freshly ground black pepper to taste
1 ounce Parmesan, grated (¼ cup)

1. Begin heating a large pot or pasta pot full of water. Meanwhile, stem and wash the kale. When the water comes to a rolling boil, add 1 tablespoon salt and the kale. Cook for about 3 minutes, until the leaves are just tender. Remove the kale from the water with a slotted spoon or deep-fry skimmer and transfer to a bowl of cold water. Drain, squeeze out any water, and chop coarsely.

2. Heat the oil in a large, heavy nonstick skillet over medium heat. Add the red pepper and a pinch of salt. Cook, stirring, until tender, 8 to 10 minutes. Stir in the garlic and red pepper flakes. Stir together for 30 seconds, until the garlic begins to smell fragrant. Stir in the kale and 2 ladles of cooking water from the kale. Stir together for a couple of minutes, until the mixture is heated through. Season to taste with salt and pepper. Keep warm while you cook the pasta.

3. Bring the water in which you cooked the kale back to a boil; add more water if the level seems low. If you add more water, add another 2 teaspoons salt when the water comes to a boil; then add the pasta and cook until al dente, firm to the bite. Drain.

4. While the pasta is cooking, blend together the cottage cheese and milk in a mini-food processor or food processor fitted with the steel blade until completely smooth. Transfer to a large serving bowl.

5. When the pasta is drained, add to the cottage cheese mixture along with the kale, peppers, and Parmesan. Toss to combine. Grind on some pepper and serve at once.

Advance preparation: The kale and pepper mixture can be prepared hours ahead of serving and reheated when you cook the pasta. The blended cottage cheese mixture will keep for 3 days in the refrigerator.

farfalle with asparagus

Delicate asparagus needs little more enhancement than the creamy sauce here. This is a delightful spring and summer pasta. **MAKES 4 SERVINGS**

1 pound asparagus, trimmed and
cut into 1-inch lengths
1 to 2 garlic cloves, peeled (optional)
½ cup nonfat or low-fat cottage cheese
¼ cup low-fat milk
Salt and freshly ground black pepper to taste
¾ pound farfalle
2 tablespoons chopped fresh chives or parsley,
or a combination
1 ounce pecorino or Parmesan, grated (¼ cup)

1. Bring a large pot or pasta pot full of water to a boil, add 1 tablespoon salt, and drop in the asparagus. Boil for 3 to 5 minutes, until just tender, and remove from the water using a slotted spoon or deep-fry skimmer. Refresh with cold water and set aside.

2. Chop the garlic in a mini-processor or a food processor fitted with the steel blade. When it adheres to the sides, stop the machine and scrape down the sides. Add the cottage cheese and blend until fairly smooth. Scrape down the sides. Add the milk and blend again until smooth. Add salt and pepper to taste. Transfer to a wide pasta bowl.

3. Bring the water in the pasta pot back to a boil and add the pasta. Stir to make sure the pasta doesn't stick to the bottom of the pot and cook until al dente, firm to the bite. Reserve ¼ cup of the cooking water and drain.

4. Stir the reserved cooking water into the cottage cheese mixture, and add the pasta, the asparagus, chives, and pecorino. Toss to combine. Serve hot.

Note: Another nice pasta to use for this dish is pappardelle.

Advance preparation: The cottage cheese mixture will keep for 3 days in the refrigerator.

pasta with creamy spinach sauce

I used to get my son to eat spinach when he was a baby by blending it with cottage cheese. I still do, but now I toss the mixture with pasta. This has a mild and comforting flavor, with or without the garlic. **MAKES 6 SERVINGS**

1 large bunch spinach (¾ to 1 pound)
Salt to taste
1 to 2 garlic cloves, peeled (optional)
1 cup nonfat or low-fat cottage cheese
¼ cup low-fat milk
Pinch freshly grated nutmeg
Freshly ground black pepper to taste
1 pound dried pasta (spaghetti or fettuccine are good here)
1 ounce Parmesan, grated (¼ cup)

1. Begin heating a large pot full of water while you wash and stem the spinach. When the water comes to a boil, add about 1 tablespoon salt and the spinach. Cook for 1 minute, remove from the water using a slotted spoon, and transfer to a bowl of cold water. Drain and squeeze dry. Chop coarsely. Retain the spinach cooking water for the pasta.

2. Bring the spinach water back to a boil (turn the heat down to simmer if it reaches a boil before you are ready to cook the pasta). Meanwhile, turn on a mini-food processor or a food processor fitted with the steel blade and drop in the garlic. When it adheres to the sides, stop the machine and scrape down the sides. Add the cottage cheese and blend until fairly smooth. Scrape down the sides. Add the cooked spinach and the milk and blend again until smooth. Add the nutmeg, pepper, and salt to taste. Transfer to a wide pasta bowl.

3. When the water returns to a boil, add 1 tablespoon salt and gradually add the pasta. Stir to make sure the pasta doesn't stick to the bottom of the pot. Then boil until the pasta is cooked al dente, firm to the bite. Drain the pasta.

4. Transfer the pasta to the bowl, toss with the spinach sauce and the Parmesan, and serve.

Advance preparation: The sauce will keep for a couple of days in the refrigerator. Bring to room temperature and reheat by adding a couple of spoonfuls of hot pasta water.

pasta with mushrooms, sage, and rosemary

You can use regular mushrooms for this savory sauce, or you can use more exotic mushrooms, such as oyster mushrooms or shiitakes. No matter which you choose, the sauce will have a meaty texture and gutsy taste. I like using a long pasta like linguine or tagliatelle for this topping. **MAKES 4 SERVINGS**

2 tablespoons extra virgin olive oil
1 small onion or 2 to 3 shallots, minced
1 pound cultivated or wild mushrooms
(such as shiitakes or oyster mushrooms),
or a combination, trimmed and quartered
if small, thickly sliced if large
Salt to taste
4 large garlic cloves, minced
8 large sage leaves, slivered (about 1 tablespoon)
2 teaspoons chopped fresh rosemary or
1 teaspoon crumbled dried
½ cup dry white wine
One 14-ounce can tomatoes, with juice,
chopped
Freshly ground black pepper to taste
¾ pound dried pasta
1 ounce Parmesan, grated (¼ cup)

1. Begin heating a large pot or pasta pot filled with water for the pasta.

2. Heat 1 tablespoon of the oil in a large, heavy nonstick skillet over medium heat. Add the onion. Cook, stirring, until tender, about 5 minutes. Add the mushrooms and a generous pinch of salt. Cook, stirring, until the mushrooms begin to release their juices, about 3 minutes. Add the garlic and continue to cook, stirring, until the liquid has evaporated. Add the sage, rosemary, and the wine. Cook, stirring, until the wine has evaporated and the mushrooms are glazed, 5 to 10 minutes. Add the tomatoes and their juice. Bring to a simmer and cook, stirring often, for 10 to 20 minutes, until the tomatoes have cooked down, and the mixture smells fragrant. Season to taste with salt and pepper and set aside.

3. When the water reaches a boil, add 1 tablespoon salt and gradually add the pasta. Stir to make sure the pasta doesn't stick to the bottom of the pot. Boil until cooked al dente, firm to the bite. Moisten the mushroom topping with 2 to 4 tablespoons of the pasta cooking water. Drain the pasta.

4. Toss the pasta with the mushrooms and remaining 1 tablespoon oil in the pan or in a warm wide pasta bowl. Sprinkle on the cheese and serve, or pass the cheese for people to sprinkle on.

Advance preparation: The mushroom topping will keep for 3 or 4 days in the refrigerator.

pasta with tomatoes, olives, and cauliflower

I developed this as a southern Italian pasta, but the first time I tested it, I had leftover polenta in the refrigerator, so I served the cauliflower topping over grilled polenta. It was great. Either way, this is a delicious dish. **MAKES 4 SERVINGS**

1 head cauliflower, broken into florets,
*   the large florets sliced about ½-inch thick*
1 tablespoon extra virgin olive oil
2 large garlic cloves, minced
¼ to ½ teaspoon red pepper flakes
1½ pounds fresh tomatoes, peeled, seeded, and
*   chopped, or one 28-ounce can chopped tomatoes,*
*   drained*
Salt to taste
2 tablespoons chopped fresh parsley
¾ pound dried pasta,
*   such as fusilli or penne*
1 ounce Parmesan, grated (¼ cup)

1. Begin heating a large pot or pasta pot full of water while you prepare the ingredients. When the water comes to a boil, add the tomatoes, boil for 30 seconds, and transfer to a bowl of cold water. Drain and peel. Add 1 tablespoon salt to the boiling water and add the cauliflower. Boil for 4 minutes, then transfer to a bowl of cold water, and drain.

2. Heat the oil in a large, heavy nonstick skillet over medium heat. Add the garlic and red pepper flakes. Cook, stirring, until the garlic begins to color and smell fragrant, 30 to 60 seconds. Stir in the tomatoes, bring to a simmer, add salt to taste, and cook for 10 to 15 minutes, stirring often, until the tomatoes have cooked down a bit and smell fragrant. Add the cauliflower, stir together, and cook for another 5 minutes or so, until the tomatoes have cooked down a little more. Stir in the parsley and taste. Add salt, if necessary. Keep warm while you cook the pasta.

3. When the water reaches a boil, add 1 tablespoon salt and gradually add the pasta. Stir to make sure the pasta doesn't stick to the bottom of the pot. Boil until cooked al dente, firm to the bite (check the package for time indications; usually 8 to 10 minutes, although very thin pasta cooks more quickly). Drain.

4. Toss the pasta with the cauliflower topping. Serve, passing the Parmesan for sprinkling.

Advance preparation: The topping will keep for several hours on top of the stove, or it can be refrigerated for a day and reheated.

- GRILLED POLENTA WITH TOMATOES, OLIVES, AND CAULIFLOWER • Prepare polenta following the recipe on page 150 and using 1 cup polenta. Cool the polenta while you prepare the cauliflower mixture, as above. Just before serving, prepare a medium-hot fire in a grill or place a nonstick skillet over medium-high heat. Cut the polenta into squares or triangles. Brush each side with olive oil and grill or pan-grill, until lightly browned on each side, 4 to 5 minutes per side. Top the squares with the cauliflower mixture, sprinkle on Parmesan, and serve.

Advance preparation: Polenta will keep for a few days in the refrigerator. Grill it just before serving.

pasta with roasted peppers and favas

Some of the most beautiful and delicious pastas are the color of the Italian flag: red, white, and green. Here's one to make during the short spring fava bean season. **MAKES 4 SERVINGS**

2 large red bell peppers
1 pound fava beans, shelled
Salt and freshly ground black pepper to taste
2 tablespoons extra virgin olive oil
1 garlic clove, minced
12 fresh basil leaves, slivered
¾ pound dried pasta, such as spaghetti, linguine, or fusilli
1 ounce Parmesan, grated (¼ cup), or ricotta salata, cut into small cubes

1. Roast the peppers in the oven. Preheat the oven to 400°F. Cover a baking sheet with foil and place the peppers on it. Roast in the oven for 30 to 40 minutes, turning the peppers every 10 minutes. They should be brown and their skins puffed. Remove from the oven and transfer to a bowl. Cover the bowl with a plate and allow the peppers to cool.

2. Meanwhile, bring a large pot of water to a boil. Drop in the fava beans. Boil for 1 minute, remove with a slotted spoon, and transfer to a bowl of cold water. Drain and peel off the skins. Set aside.

3. When the peppers are cool enough to handle, peel them, holding the peppers over a bowl so that you catch any juices. Remove the stems, seeds, and membranes and cut the peppers into thin 2-inch-long strips. Strain the juices into a pasta bowl. Add the sliced peppers, salt, pepper, olive oil, garlic, and basil. Toss together. Taste and adjust the seasonings.

4. Bring the water in the pot back to a boil. Add 1 tablespoon salt and the pasta. Stir to make sure the pasta doesn't stick to the bottom of the pot. After 5 minutes, add the favas to the pot, and continue to cook until the pasta is cooked al dente, firm to the bite. Stir ¼ cup of the pasta cooking water into the pepper mixture. Drain the pasta and favas.

5. Toss the pasta and favas with the roasted pepper mixture and the cheese. Serve hot or warm.

Advance preparation: The roasted peppers will keep for several days in the refrigerator, tossed with the olive oil. The fava beans will also keep for a few days once blanched and peeled.

pasta with asparagus and gremolata

I love the way the lemon zest, garlic, and parsley team up with the asparagus in this simple pasta. Both long pastas like linguine and shapes work here. The dish is very quickly thrown together. **MAKES 4 SERVINGS**

2 garlic cloves, finely minced
¼ cup chopped flat-leaf parsley
2 teaspoons finely chopped lemon zest
¾ pound fusilli, rigatoni, or linguine
1 pound asparagus, trimmed and cut into 1-inch pieces
Salt and freshly ground black pepper to taste
2 to 3 tablespoons extra virgin olive oil
1 ounce Parmesan, grated (¼ cup)

1. Begin heating a large pot or pasta pot full of water.

2. Mix together the garlic, parsley, and lemon zest. Set aside.

3. When the water reaches a boil, add 1 tablespoon salt and gradually add the pasta. Stir to make sure the pasta doesn't stick to the bottom of the pot. Four to 5 minutes before the end of the pasta cooking time, add the asparagus to the pot. Boil until the pasta is cooked al dente, firm to the bite (check the package for time indications; usually 8 to 10 minutes, although very thin pasta cooks more quickly). Drain the asparagus and pasta.

4. Toss the pasta and asparagus in a warm serving bowl with the garlic/parsley/lemon mixture, salt, pepper, and the olive oil. Serve, passing the Parmesan in a bowl for sprinkling.

Advance preparation: You can prepare the garlic mixture an hour ahead of serving.

shells with zucchini, corn, beans, and tomato

The success of this end-of-summer pasta depends on the quality of your ingredients. The corn must be super-sweet, the tomatoes ripe. If you have a pot of beans with liquid, the dish will be a triumph, but you can also use canned beans with a good result. **MAKES 4 TO 6 SERVINGS**

1 tablespoon extra virgin olive oil

2 medium zucchini (about ½ pound), cut in large dice

Salt to taste

¾ pound tomatoes, peeled, seeded, chopped

2 large garlic cloves, minced

Kernels from 2 ears corn, raw or cooked

2 teaspoons fresh thyme leaves

2 cups cooked beans, preferably pinto, borlotti or cranberry, with ½ cup of
their broth, or 2 cups canned beans, rinsed, plus ½ cup water

Freshly ground black pepper to taste

¾ to 1 pound small or medium shells

1. Begin heating a large pot or pasta pot full of water.

2. Heat the oil over medium-high heat in a large, heavy nonstick skillet. Add the zucchini and cook, stirring, until it begins to brown, 3 to 5 minutes. Add the garlic, stir together for about half a minute, and stir in the tomatoes and salt. Turn the heat down to medium and cook, stirring often, until the tomatoes have cooked down a bit and smell fragrant, about 10 minutes. Stir in the corn, thyme, and beans with their liquid and continue to simmer for another 10 minutes. Taste and add salt and pepper.

3. Meanwhile, cook the pasta. When the water reaches a boil, add 1 tablespoon salt and gradually add the pasta. Stir to make sure the pasta doesn't stick to the bottom of the pot, then boil until cooked al dente, firm to the bite. Drain.

4. Toss the pasta in the pan or a pasta bowl with the vegetables. Serve hot.

Advance preparation: The topping can be made a day ahead of time and refrigerated, or it will hold on top of the stove for a few hours.

quick pasta with tomato sauce, goat cheese, and green beans

When goat cheese is stirred into a tomato sauce, whether you've made the tomato sauce or bought it, the pasta dish takes on a rich, complex dimension. This makes a great last-minute dinner. **MAKES 4 SERVINGS**

1 cup tomato sauce, homemade (page 194) or commercial
¾ pound dried pasta
½ pound green beans, trimmed and cut in half
2 ounces fresh goat cheese, such as Montrachet (about ½ cup)
Salt and freshly ground black pepper to taste

1. Bring a large pot of water to a boil. Meanwhile, heat the tomato sauce in a saucepan or nonstick frying pan.

2. When the water reaches a boil, add 1 tablespoon salt and gradually add the pasta. Stir to make sure the pasta doesn't stick to the bottom of the pot. About 5 minutes before the pasta is done, add the green beans to the pot. Cook until the pasta is al dente, firm to the bite. Drain.

3. Toss the pasta and green beans in a warm pasta bowl with the tomato sauce and goat cheese. Add salt and pepper and serve.

Advance preparation: The tomato sauce can be made days ahead of serving if you're not using a commercial sauce. The beans can be prepared hours ahead of cooking.

Peeling, Seeding, and Chopping Tomatoes

PEELING TOMATOES

Bring a medium or large saucepan of water to a rolling boil. Meanwhile, using a paring knife, cut out the stem and hull of the tomato by cutting a cone out of the top. When the water comes to a boil, carefully drop in the tomatoes; I usually put them on a large spoon and lower them in so that I don't get splashed by the boiling water. Count to 30, then transfer the tomatoes from the boiling water to a bowl of cold water, using a deep-fry skimmer, slotted spoon, or a regular big spoon. Drain and peel away the skins. If the skin doesn't pull away easily, either you didn't leave the tomato in the boiling water long enough, or your tomatoes are too unripe. If you leave the tomatoes in the boiling water for too long, they'll begin to cook and you'll lose some of the pulp with the skins.

SEEDING TOMATOES

If you want to save the juice in the tomatoes, seed them over a strainer set over a bowl. Then you can add the juice to the tomato pulp when you cook the tomatoes. Cut the tomatoes in half, across the equator—i.e., halfway down from the stem end. Hold a tomato half with the rounded side cupped against the inside of your hand. Hold it over the sink or a bowl, and squeeze gently. The seeds will come right out. If the tomato is very mealy it may fall apart in your hand. You can still chop it. If you're working with plum tomatoes, you may find it easier to cut them lengthwise and scoop out the seed pockets with your fingers. I cut canned tomatoes across the equator, even though they are usually plum tomatoes. The seeds slip right out.

CHOPPING TOMATOES

Use a large cutting board with a trough to catch the juice if you have one. Lay a half tomato, cut side down, on your cutting board. Slice the tomato into thin strips, using a chef's knife. Turn a quarter turn and cut across the strips. For finer dice, cut parallel slices first, as you do when you dice an onion, and proceed as above. If you want very finely chopped tomatoes, hold the tip of your knife down and move the knife over the tomatoes in a seesaw motion. They'll spread out over the cutting board; push them back toward the middle with your free hand.

CRUSHING TOMATOES IN A FOOD PROCESSOR

This is a quick way to prepare tomatoes for sauces: Put peeled, seeded tomatoes into a food processor fitted with the steel blade. Pulse 20 to 30 times, until crushed and pulpy but not a smooth puree.

ANOTHER WAY TO PREPARE FRESH TOMATOES

Many Greek, Italian, and Spanish cooks do this. Instead of peeling the tomatoes, cut them in half across the equator and squeeze out the seeds. Place a box grater over a wide bowl. Holding onto the skin side of the tomatoes, grate them on the large holes of the grater. When you get to the skin, stop! Don't grate it or your hand. You will have a coarse puree.

pasta with fresh tomatoes, capers, and olives

During the summer and early fall, when tomatoes are at their height, I rarely cook them—although when I do, the sauces are incredibly sweet. But it's so easy to throw together a truly delicious pasta sauce, just by cutting up the tomatoes and adding seasonings like garlic and fresh basil. From there you can go in many directions; you can keep it simple, or you can add ingredients. The capers and olives here (in Mediterranean Italy anchovies would also be used) make for a wonderful, pungent sauce. **MAKES 4 TO 6 SERVINGS**

2 pounds ripe, sweet tomatoes, peeled, seeded, and chopped
2 garlic cloves, finely minced
8 imported black olives, pitted and coarsely chopped
8 imported brine-cured green olives, pitted and
*   coarsely chopped, or use all black olives*
2 tablespoons capers, rinsed and coarsely chopped
1 teaspoon red wine vinegar or balsamic vinegar (optional)
About 10 good-size basil leaves, slivered
2 tablespoons chopped fresh parsley
2 tablespoons extra virgin olive oil
Salt and freshly ground black pepper to taste
¾ pound to 1 pound spaghettini, spaghetti, or linguine

1. Combine the tomatoes, garlic, olives, capers, vinegar, basil, parsley, olive oil, salt, and pepper in a large bowl; mix together well. Let sit for 1 hour at room temperature.

2. Heat a large pot or pasta pot full of water over high heat. When the water reaches a boil, add 1 tablespoon of salt and gradually add the pasta. Stir to make sure the pasta doesn't stick to the bottom of the pot, then boil until cooked al dente, firm to the bite (check the package for time indications; usually 8 to 10 minutes, although very thin pasta cooks more quickly). Drain.

3. Toss the pasta with the tomato mixture and serve.

Advance preparation: The sauce can be made several hours ahead and kept at room temperature.

summer pasta with corn, tomatoes, and basil

This summer pasta was inspired by a leftover ear of grilled corn. I wouldn't get a charcoal grill going just for two ears of corn, but if you're grilling other foods, it does taste wonderful. But then, so does steamed sweet corn in season. If the tomatoes are less than sweet, the balsamic vinegar will enhance their flavor. **MAKES 4 SERVINGS**

2 ears corn, steamed or grilled (page 154)
1 pound firm ripe tomatoes, peeled if desired,
seeded, and diced
2 garlic cloves, minced
Salt and freshly ground black pepper to taste
1 to 2 tablespoons extra virgin olive oil
2 teaspoons balsamic vinegar (optional)
12 large basil leaves, slivered
¾ pound farfalle, penne, or rigatoni

1. Strip the kernels from the ears of corn and toss with the tomatoes in a pasta bowl. Add the garlic, salt, pepper, olive oil, and basil. Taste and add balsamic vinegar if desired. Let sit at room temperature for 15 minutes or longer.

2. Meanwhile, bring a large pot or pasta pot of water to a boil. Add 1 tablespoon of salt. Gradually add the pasta. Stir to make sure the pasta doesn't stick to the bottom of the pot. Cook until al dente, firm to the bite, and drain.

3. Toss the pasta with the tomato and corn mixture, and serve.

Advance preparation: The tomato and corn mixture, without the basil, can be made hours ahead of serving. Hold it in or out of the refrigerator. Add the basil shortly before serving.

pasta with cherry tomatoes, feta, and herbs

If you have a garden and a surfeit of cherry tomatoes, this is a great way to use them. Although you can get cherry tomatoes most of the year, when they aren't local and in season they can be quite indifferent, so stick to the good seasonal ones for this recipe. The hot pasta will warm the cherry tomatoes just enough when you toss the two together. **MAKES 4 SERVINGS**

1 pound cherry tomatoes,
*   cut into quarters if large, in half if small*
1 to 2 teaspoons balsamic vinegar
1 garlic clove, minced
2 tablespoons extra virgin olive oil
Salt and freshly ground black pepper to taste
2 tablespoons chopped fresh chives
1 tablespoon slivered or chopped fresh basil or mint
2 ounces feta cheese, crumbled (½ cup)
¾ pound fusilli, rigatoni, or penne

1. Combine the tomatoes, balsamic vinegar, garlic, olive oil, salt, pepper, and chives in a large wide pasta bowl. Let sit for 30 minutes or longer at room temperature. Taste and adjust the seasonings.

2. Meanwhile, bring a large pot or pasta pot full of water to a boil. Add 1 tablespoon salt. Gradually add the pasta. Stir to make sure the pasta doesn't stick to the bottom. Cook until al dente, firm to the bite, and drain.

3. Toss the pasta with the tomato mixture, basil, and feta and serve.

Advance preparation: The tomato mixture will hold for several hours at room temperature or in the refrigerator.

pasta gratin

When I am testing recipes I often end up with various pasta dishes in the refrigerator. Not one to throw out food as long as it's edible, I've come up with this all-purpose gratin. This is a kid-pleaser. **MAKES 4 SERVINGS**

3 large eggs, beaten
1 cup low-fat milk
2 tablespoons nonfat dry milk
½ teaspoon salt
Freshly ground black pepper to taste
2 ounces Gruyère cheese or 1 ounce each
      Gruyère and Parmesan, grated (½ cup)
2 to 3 cups leftover pasta, with topping or without

1. Preheat the oven to 375°F. Oil a 2-quart gratin dish with olive oil.

2. In a mixing bowl, beat the eggs and add the milk, dry milk, salt, and pepper. Beat together well to be sure the dry milk is dissolved. Stir in the cheese and the pasta. Turn into the gratin dish.

3. Bake for 35 to 40 minutes, until the custard is set and the top golden brown. Serve hot.

Advance preparation: The gratin can be baked several hours ahead and reheated in a 250° to 300°F oven for 20 minutes.

malaysian noodles with greens and tofu

This is a vegetarian version of mee goreng, a spicy Malaysian noodle dish that always contains tofu but also typically contains shrimp, lamb, or pork. In the authentic dish, the tofu is deep-fried and Chinese noodles are used. Regular egg noodles work very nicely. **MAKES 4 TO 6 SERVINGS**

Salt to taste

½ pound turnip greens or mustard greens,
cleaned, thick stem ends discarded,
and the rest cut into 1-inch lengths,
the leaves coarsely chopped; or
½ pound green cabbage, cut in ¾-inch cubes

½ pound Chinese or regular egg noodles

2 tablespoons canola or peanut oil

2 large eggs, lightly beaten with a little salt

1½ tablespoons soy sauce, or more to taste

½ teaspoon salt

1 teaspoon sugar

2 tablespoons tomato puree or ketchup

1 teaspoon Asian red chili paste or sauce,
such as sambal oelek

1 pound tofu, drained, blotted dry,
and sliced about ¼ inch thick

1 medium red onion, chopped

2 large garlic cloves, minced

¾-inch piece fresh ginger,
peeled and grated or finely chopped

1 large or 2 medium tomatoes (8 to 10 ounces),
seeded and diced

¼ pound bean sprouts (about 2 handfuls)

¼ cup cilantro leaves

1 lime, cut in wedges

1. Bring 3 or 4 quarts water to a boil in a large pot while you prepare the ingredients. When the water reaches a boil, add about 1 tablespoon of salt and the greens. Cook for 30 seconds and immediately transfer to a bowl of cold water, using a slotted spoon or deep-fry skimmer. Drain and set aside.

2. Bring the water back to a boil and add the noodles. If they are Chinese egg noodles, once the water comes to a second boil, cook for 1 minute, drain, and rinse with cold water. For regular egg noodles, cook about 6 minutes, until just tender to the bite; drain and rinse with cold water. Shake off excess water and set aside.

3. Heat 1 teaspoon of the oil in a medium nonstick skillet over medium-high heat until a drop of egg sizzles upon contact. Add the eggs. Tilt the pan to distribute the eggs in an even layer. As soon as they are cooked through, like a thin pancake, remove from the pan by tilting the pan and sliding or rolling out of the pan. Roll up and slice thinly to shred (you can use scissors or a knife for this). Set aside.

4. In a small bowl, mix together 1½ teaspoons of the soy sauce, the salt, sugar, tomato puree, and the chili paste. Stir to dissolve the sugar and salt and set aside.

5. Heat a wok or large nonstick skillet over medium-high heat. Add the remaining 1 tablespoon plus 2 teaspoons oil and the tofu. Cook, stirring, until the tofu is lightly browned, 3 to 5 minutes. Add the onion, garlic, and ginger and cook, stirring constantly, for about 30 seconds, or until the garlic and ginger are lightly browned and fragrant. Add the remaining 1 tablespoon soy sauce and stir to season the tofu. Stir in the tomato and increase heat slightly. Stir until the tomato begins to break down, 2 to 3 minutes. Add the blanched greens or cabbage and cook, stirring, for 2 to 3 minutes, until the vegetables are crisp-tender.

6. Rinse the noodles if they have become sticky after sitting. Add the noodles and soy sauce mixture to the wok and stir together to coat the noodles. Add the shredded egg and the bean sprouts, toss together quickly, and remove from the heat.

7. Transfer to a serving platter or to plates. Sprinkle on the cilantro and serve, with lime wedges on the side.

Advance preparation: The greens or cabbage can be blanched, the noodles cooked, the sauce mixed, and the ingredients prepared hours ahead. Step 5 is a last-minute operation.

asian noodles

The Asian noodles I use most often are Japanese buckwheat noodles (soba), or wheat noodles called udon. Unlike Italian semolina pasta, Asian pasta is usually not cooked in salted water, and the noodles are softer when cooked. They can be cooked ahead and reheated in a little oil, or eaten cold. **MAKES 4 SERVINGS**

½ to ¾ pound udon or soba noodles
1 tablespoon Asian sesame oil

Bring 4 quarts of water (or more) to a boil in a large pot. Gradually add the noodles. When all of the noodles have been added, stir with a long-handled spoon to make sure they don't stick together. When the water comes back to a rolling boil, add a cup of cold water. Bring back to a boil, and add another cup of water. Bring back to a boil again, and add a third cup. By the time the water comes back to a boil after the third cup of water has been added, the noodles should be cooked through. Drain and rinse with cold water. Toss with sesame oil and serve, or store in a tightly covered bowl in the refrigerator.

Note: Salt can be added to the water before adding the noodles if desired.

Advance preparation: The cooked noodles can be stored for 3 days in the refrigerator.

asian noodles with broccoli raab and mushrooms

You can use regular mushrooms, shiitakes, or oyster mushrooms for this pasta. They all have a meaty texture, which lends substance to the dish. **MAKES 4 SERVINGS**

Salt to taste
1 generous bunch broccoli raab (about 1 pound)
  or Chinese broccoli, washed, thick stems trimmed away
8 to 10 ounces soba or udon noodles
½ cup vegetable stock, such as Easy Vegetable Stock (page 63)
  or cooking water from the broccoli raab
1 teaspoon sugar
1 to 2 tablespoons soy sauce
1 pound oyster mushrooms or shiitakes, thickly sliced,
  tough stems cut away if using shiitakes
1 tablespoon peanut oil or canola oil
2 garlic cloves, minced
1 tablespoon chopped fresh ginger
¼ cup dry white wine or sake
1 tablespoon Asian sesame oil

1. Bring a large pot of water to a boil while you prepare the ingredients. Add 1 tablespoon of salt and the broccoli raab. Cook for 2 minutes, or until just tender. Transfer immediately to a bowl of cold water using a slotted spoon or deep-fry skimmer. Drain and squeeze out any water, then coarsely chop. Set aside.

2. Bring the water back to a boil and cook the noodles following the recipe on page 218. Drain, rinse, and set aside.

3. Stir together the stock, sugar, and soy sauce. Set aside.

4. Heat a large, heavy nonstick skillet or wok over medium-high heat. Add the mushrooms and a generous pinch of salt. Stir until they begin to brown and release water, 3 to 5 minutes. Add the peanut oil, garlic, and ginger. Cook, stirring, until the garlic and ginger are fragrant and beginning to color, 30 to 60 seconds. Add the wine. Cook, stirring, until the wine has evaporated,

3 to 5 minutes. Stir in the stock mixture and the broccoli raab. Simmer together, stirring occasionally, for a couple of minutes. Taste and add salt if needed, then stir in the noodles and the sesame oil.

5. Toss together, heat through, and serve.

Advance preparation: The cooked noodles can be kept for up to 3 days in the refrigerator. The greens can be cooked a day ahead and held in the refrigerator. The entire topping will hold for a couple of hours at room temperature. Reheat gently on top of the stove.

soba with hiziki, sesame seeds, and slivered carrots and turnips

Sea vegetables like hiziki go very nicely with Asian noodles. The hiziki threads and carrot and turnip matchsticks make a pretty combination that is perfectly seasoned with the nutty sesame seeds and oil. If you can't get, or don't care for, sea vegetables, make the dish with the soba and vegetables. **MAKES 3 TO 4 SERVINGS**

8 to 10 ounces soba noodles
¼ cup hiziki
2 to 3 tablespoons soy sauce, to taste
1 teaspoon sugar
2 tablespoons peanut oil
½ medium onion, very thinly sliced
1 large garlic clove, minced
1 tablespoon minced fresh ginger
¾ pound carrots, peeled and cut into matchsticks
½ pound tender young turnips,
*   peeled and cut into matchsticks*
¼ teaspoon salt
2 tablespoons sesame seeds, lightly toasted (see page 17)
2 teaspoons Asian sesame oil
3 tablespoons chopped fresh cilantro

1. Cook the soba according to the directions on page 218 and set aside.

2. Cover the hiziki with about ¾ cup water in a small saucepan. Add 2 tablespoons of the soy sauce and the sugar and bring to a simmer. Simmer until soft, about 15 minutes, while you prepare the vegetables.

3. Heat the peanut oil in a wok or large, heavy nonstick skillet over medium-high heat. Add the onion. Cook, stirring, until it softens and colors slightly, about 3 minutes. Add the garlic and ginger. Cook for 30 seconds, stirring. Add the carrots and turnips. Stir-fry for 1 minute. Add the salt and the hiziki with its cooking liquid. Cover the pot and simmer for 1 to 2 minutes, until the carrots and turnips are crisp-tender. Stir in the soba and 1 tablespoon of the sesame seeds and heat through, stirring. Add the sesame oil, stir together, and remove from the heat. Taste and add more soy sauce if desired.

4. Sprinkle on the remaining 1 tablespoon sesame seeds and cilantro and serve.

Advance preparation: The soba and the hiziki can be cooked up to 3 days ahead and refrigerated.

- SOBA WITH TOFU, CARROTS, AND TURNIPS • If you want to boost the protein in this dish, add 4 to 8 ounces firm tofu. Cut the tofu into slivers and add when you add the garlic and ginger.

Pizza

Though it's easy to do, we rarely make pizza at home, which makes it all the more special when we do. Your farmers' markets and supermarkets will provide you with an endless source of toppings, and you can control the amount of cheese and oil that you sprinkle onto your homemade pizzas. Prepared crusts are now available in most supermarkets, but if you like working with dough, I urge you to try your hand at the following recipe.

pizza dough

There are many different types of pizza dough. Those who have baked before might want to try a wetter dough, which makes a slightly crisper crust. But for a beginning cook, wet dough is hard to deal with and can discourage you from making your own dough or any other bread. This dough handles very easily and can be baked either in pizza pans or directly on a hot baking stone. The dough can be refrigerated for a day or two, or frozen for several months, before or after rolling out. If you do not roll it out before refrigerating or freezing, let the dough come to room temperature before rolling out. If you have rolled out the dough, do not thaw, but top and bake directly. **MAKES TWO 12- TO 14-INCH ROUND PIZZA CRUSTS**

> 2 teaspoons active dry yeast
> 1½ cups lukewarm water
> 2 tablespoons extra virgin olive oil
> 2 teaspoons salt
> 1 cup (5 ounces) whole wheat flour
> 3 to 3½ cups unbleached all-purpose flour
> Cornmeal or semolina (optional)

1. Dissolve the yeast in the lukewarm (100° to 110°F) water in a large bowl or in the bowl of your electric mixer, and let it sit for 5 minutes, until the yeast begins to bubble slightly. Stir in the olive oil.

2. TO KNEAD THE DOUGH BY HAND
Mix together the salt and the whole wheat flour, and stir into the water. Fold in 3 cups of the unbleached flour, ½ cup at a time, until the dough can be scraped out of the bowl in one piece. Add ½ cup flour to your kneading surface and knead, adding flour as necessary, for at least 10 minutes. The dough will be sticky at first but will become very elastic. To test if the dough has been kneaded enough, stick a finger into the dough; it should spring back slowly.

TO KNEAD BY USING AN ELECTRIC MIXER
Combine the salt, whole wheat flour, and 2½ cups of the unbleached flour and add all at once to the bowl. Mix together with the paddle, then change to the dough hook. Mix at low speed for 2 minutes, then at medium speed for 8 to 10 minutes. Add unbleached flour as necessary if the

dough seems very wet and sticky. Scrape out the dough onto a lightly floured surface and knead for a minute or so by hand. Shape into a ball.

3. Rinse out your bowl, dry, and brush lightly with olive oil. Place the dough in the bowl, rounded side down first, then rounded side up. Cover with plastic wrap and a dish towel, and set in a warm place to rise for 1½ hours, or until the dough has doubled in size.

4. Preheat the oven, with a baking stone or baking tiles in it if possible, to 450°F. If you are using pizza pans, which I recommend, oil the pans lightly and sprinkle with cornmeal or semolina.

5. Punch down the dough and divide it into 2 or 3 pieces. Cover the portions you aren't working with with plastic or a damp towel and roll out each piece. Rolling out takes a bit of patience, because the dough is springy and elastic and will at first shrink back each time you roll it. But persevere, turning the dough over from time to time, and you'll get it rolled out thin and to the size you desire. Dust your work surface and the dough regularly with flour to prevent sticking. You can use your hands to press out the dough if you prefer this to a rolling pin. The dough should be rolled no thicker than ¼ inch, thinner if possible.

6. Line the prepared pizza pans with the rolled-out dough. Or place smaller crusts on a prepared baking sheet, or if baking directly on the stone, place on a cornmeal- or semolina-dusted baking peel. Whether you are using pizza pans or not, roll the edges of the pizza dough in and pinch an attractive lip all the way around. The dough is now ready for topping and baking.

Advance preparation: The dough can be refrigerated for a couple of days or frozen for 3 to 4 months. I recommend freezing over refrigerating, however, to prevent too much rising. To refrigerate or freeze the dough, punch it down after the dough has risen for 1½ hours. Divide it in half, and shape into balls. Seal the balls in plastic bags and refrigerate or freeze. You can also roll out the dough and refrigerate or freeze directly on the pizza pans.

pizza with sweet onion, red pepper, ricotta, and basil

This beautiful pizza tastes richer than it is. The onion adds a sweet dimension. **MAKES ONE 12- TO 14-INCH PIZZA, 2 TO 4 SERVINGS**

1 to 1½ cups tomato sauce for pasta (page 194),
     or one 14-ounce can tomatoes, drained and chopped
2 garlic cloves, minced (optional)
Salt to taste
½ recipe Pizza Dough (page 223), rolled out to make one
     12- to 14-inch pizza crust
1 sweet red onion, sliced in rings
1 red bell pepper, thinly sliced in strips or rings
½ cup part-skim ricotta
2 tablespoons extra virgin olive oil
Generous handful fresh basil, slivered or torn in pieces

1. Preheat the oven to 450°F for at least 30 minutes, with a baking stone or tiles in it. Soak the onion in a bowl of cold water to cover for 15 to 30 minutes.

2. If you are using canned tomatoes, stir in the garlic and add salt to taste. Spread the tomato sauce or seasoned tomatoes over the crust. Drain the onion, pat dry, and spread over the tomato sauce. Distribute the red pepper slices over the onions. Dollop on the ricotta by the heaped teaspoons. Drizzle on the olive oil.

3. Gently slide the pizza from the peel onto the hot baking stone, or place the pizza pan on top of the baking stone. Bake for 20 to 25 minutes, until the edges of the onions and red peppers are just beginning to brown and the cheese has softened.

4. Remove from the oven, sprinkle the basil over the pizza, and serve.

Advance preparation: The crust will keep for months in the freezer and for a day in the refrigerator after rolling out. The tomato sauce will keep for 3 to 5 days in the refrigerator and for several months in the freezer. The pizza can be made through step 3, reheated for 5 to 10 minutes in a 400°F oven, garnished with the basil and served.

pizza with summer squash, goat cheese, and herbs

The vision of pale yellow and green rounds of squash covering a pizza, dotted with soft white cheese, and finished with mint or oregano inspired this beautiful pizza. **MAKES ONE 12- TO 14-INCH PIZZA, 2 TO 4 SERVINGS**

*½ recipe Pizza Dough (page 223), rolled out to
    make one 12-inch to 14-inch pizza crust
1 to 1½ cups tomato sauce for pasta (page 194) or canned tomatoes, drained
    and chopped
2 garlic cloves, minced (optional)
¾ pound mixed zucchini and yellow summer squash, very thinly sliced
Salt and freshly ground black pepper to taste
Dried thyme or oregano
1 ounce fresh, mild goat cheese, such as Montrachet, crumbled (¼ cup)
2 tablespoons extra virgin olive oil
Generous handful fresh mint or oregano, slivered or torn in pieces*

1. Preheat the oven to 450°F for at least 30 minutes, with a baking stone or tiles in it.

2. Bring a large pot of water to a boil, add a tablespoon of salt and the squash, blanch for 1 minute, drain, and rinse with cold water.

3. If you are using canned tomatoes, toss with the garlic and season to taste with salt. Spread the tomato sauce or tomatoes over the crust. Cover the tomatoes with the sliced squash. Salt and pepper generously. Sprinkle on thyme or oregano and the goat cheese. Drizzle on the olive oil.

4. Gently slide the pizza from the peel onto the hot baking stone, or place the pizza pan on top of the baking stone. Bake for 20 to 25 minutes, until the edges of the squash rounds are just beginning to brown and the cheese has softened.

5. Remove from the oven, sprinkle the fresh herbs over the pizza, and serve.

Advance preparation: The crust will keep for months in the freezer and for a day in the refrigerator after rolling out. The tomato sauce will keep for 3 to 5 days in the refrigerator and several months in the freezer. The squash can be blanched a day ahead.

bruschetta

Bruschetta (pronounced broo-*skeh*-tah) are thick slices of lightly toasted country bread that are rubbed with garlic, brushed or drizzled with olive oil, and often have a topping. They are the Italian answer to the open-faced sandwich, and make an easy, satisfying dinner. Anything that's good with pasta is good on top of thick slices of toasted bread. So are easy combinations like goat cheese and roasted red peppers, tapenade, hummus, or other spreads.

The key to good bruschetta lies in the quality of the bread. Use a crusty, porous country bread for this. The only embellishment here is garlic and olive oil. From there you can go on forever with toppings. I usually toast my bruschetta in a toaster oven, but you can grill or broil the bread as well. **MAKES 4 TO 6 SERVINGS**

8 to 12 thick slices country bread
1 to 2 large garlic cloves, unpeeled and sliced in half
1 to 2 tablespoons extra virgin olive oil (optional)

1. If you are not using a toaster or a toaster oven, prepare a hot fire in a grill or preheat the broiler. Lightly toast the bread, or set the bread over hot coals or under the broiler, 4 to 5 inches from the heat source. The bread should toast on both sides and remain soft inside. This goes very quickly on a grill or under a broiler (a minute or less per side), so watch carefully if you don't want to burn the bread. If using a toaster oven, toast it on medium-high or high.

2. Remove from the heat and immediately rub both sides of the bread with the cut cloves of garlic. Brush with the olive oil if desired. Cut into halves if your slices are wide.

Advance preparation: Bruschetta can be made a few hours ahead. Warm them in a low oven (set on warm) for 15 to 30 minutes.

Vegetable SIDE DISHES, Stews, Stir-Fries, and GRATINS

I was going to call this chapter "Vegetables," but then I realized what a redundant heading that would be; by definition, this is a cookbook full of vegetable recipes. Many of the pasta toppings, the bean and vegetable stews, the gratins, and the stir-fries that appear in other chapters could easily be placed under the heading of "Vegetables." Similarly, the vegetable ragouts, stir-fries, and pan-cooked vegetable dishes in this chapter pair beautifully with pasta or grains. Leftovers of these dishes often find their way into a tart, gratin, pasta, or salad. So if you find that a vegetable you're interested in is absent from the pages of this chapter, look in the index.

Vegetables are the most inspiring aspect of cooking for me. When I go to the market I'm not always sure what I'm going to buy, just that I'm going to buy something green, and whatever else strikes my fancy. If it's July I know that tomatoes and corn will be in my basket when I come home; if it's springtime and the Blue Lake beans and favas have come in, you can be sure that we'll be eating those the following week. In winter, I always come home with beets, broccoli, and other greens (the advantage to buying beets with their tops on is that you get two vegetables in one). I love choosing between different types of potatoes and squash, both winter and summer. I urge you to visit local farmers' markets; talk to the vendors about their produce. Ask them how they cook their vegetables; you'll come away with simple, delicious ways to cook everything.

When I get home I decide what I'm going to do with the produce: Will I make a gratin, a stir-fry or a pasta, a tart, soup, or salad? I hope with this book to impart enough general knowledge of cooking so that you can let the market be your guide to what vegetables you are going to cook, knowing that you have many choices for ways of enjoying them.

Many of the dishes in this chapter would qualify as "side dishes," although just by serving grains alongside or pasta underneath, they can become the focus of the meal. When so many vegetables are in season at the height of summer, I often make a meal around more than one of these. I might serve Yellow Squash with Kale (page 257) and the Summer Tomato Gratin (page 255) with rice, then follow with a salad. A big globe artichoke with tofu mayonnaise, followed by a Potato Gratin (page 250) and a salad makes a fine dinner for me. You can also make a meal of grilled vegetables with polenta (see page 154). Vegetables can be blanched, steamed, roasted, braised or stewed, and grilled.

steamed artichokes

A steamed artichoke, hot or cold, can make a light lunch, supper, or starter. Sometimes they're so large that one will be sufficient for two people. I love the slow, deliberate, and sensuous activity of eating an artichoke, leaf by leaf, each leaf dipped into a savory, tangy sauce. When no more leaves are edible they're cut away to reveal the treasured heart. As for dips, I use a vinaigrette, or a garlicky yogurt dip, or a tofu mayonnaise. **SERVES 4**

2 large or 4 medium artichokes
½ lemon

1. Prepare the artichoke: Break off the small tough leaves at the stem end. Lay the artichoke on a cutting board, and using a sharp chef's knife, cut away the entire top quarter in one slice. Now, using scissors, cut away the thorny ends of the leaves. This goes faster than you think. Cut the stems flush with the bottom of the artichoke so that the artichoke will stand upright, and rinse thoroughly under cold water. Rub the cut surfaces with the cut side of your lemon.

2. Bring about 1 inch of water to boil in the bottom of a saucepan, wok, or steamer. Place the artichokes on a steaming rack, or if the rack is too high and the lid won't fit over the artichokes, place them right in the water. Cover, turn the heat down to medium, and steam 30 to 40 minutes, depending on the size of the artichokes. Bring a kettle or small pot of water to a boil, in case you need to add more water. From time to time, check the artichokes to make sure the water hasn't all evaporated, and add simmering water if necessary. Test for doneness by pulling a leaf away; it should not resist. Remove from the heat and serve, or rinse with cold water, allow to cool and serve cold or at room temperature.

Dipping Sauces
Lemon Yogurt or Buttermilk Vinaigrette (page 29)
Classic Vinaigrette (page 25)
Tofu Green Goddess Dressing (page 18)
Tofu Mayonnaise (page 15)

yogurt dip with mint or dill

¾ cup nonfat yogurt or Yogurt Cheese (page 8, for a thicker dip)
1 garlic clove, peeled and halved
¼ teaspoon salt
¼ cup chopped fresh mint or dill
Fresh lemon juice to taste

1. Place the yogurt in a bowl.

2. Pound together the garlic and salt to a paste in a mortar and pestle. Stir into the yogurt along with the mint or dill and the lemon juice.

creamy garlic dip

1 to 2 garlic cloves, to taste, peeled and halved
¼ teaspoon salt (or more to taste)
½ cup nonfat cottage cheese
3 tablespoons plain nonfat yogurt
2 tablespoons mayonnaise, preferably Hellman's or Best Foods

1. Pound together the garlic and salt to a paste in a mortar and pestle.

2. Blend the cottage cheese in a food processor fitted with the steel blade until fairly smooth. Add the yogurt and mayonnaise and continue to blend until very smooth. Add the garlic and combine well. Taste and adjust salt.

broccoli with garlic and lemon

Fresh lemon juice is one of my favorite seasonings for broccoli. I love the way it catches in all the little folds of the broccoli flowers. This dish is a take on a classic greens preparation.
MAKES 4 SERVINGS

1 large bunch broccoli (about 1½ pounds)
1 tablespoon extra virgin olive oil
2 garlic cloves, minced
¼ teaspoon red pepper flakes,
      or more to taste (optional)
Salt and freshly ground black pepper to taste
1 to 3 tablespoons fresh lemon juice

1. Break or cut off the broccoli florets. Peel the stems, cut them in half lengthwise, or if very thick into quarters, and slice about ½ inch thick. Bring about 1 inch of water to a boil in a saucepan or pot fitted with a steamer that will accommodate all of the broccoli florets. Place the broccoli in the steamer, cover, and steam for 5 to 7 minutes, until tender and bright. Remove from the heat and refresh with cold water. Drain.

2. Heat the oil over medium heat in a large, heavy nonstick skillet. Add the garlic and red pepper flakes and cook, stirring, until the garlic just begins to color, 30 to 60 seconds. Add the broccoli. Stir to heat through, and add salt, pepper, and some of the lemon juice. Taste. Add more lemon juice, if desired, and remove from the heat. Serve hot or warm.

Advance preparation: This can be made hours ahead and reheated, but don't add the lemon juice until just before serving. If you do, the broccoli will discolor, and the flavors will not be as vivid.

cabbage gratin with red pepper and tomato

When you cook cabbage for a long time, as you do here, it caramelizes and the result is an incredibly sweet dish with a melt-in-your-mouth texture. The tomatoes add a hint of acidity.
MAKES 4 SERVINGS

2 tablespoons extra virgin olive oil
1 small or medium onion, finely chopped
1 medium red bell pepper, diced
1¼ pounds green cabbage, cored and finely chopped
    (1 small cabbage; about 8 cups)
Salt to taste
1 tomato, or ½ a 14-ounce can, peeled, seeded, and chopped
    (heaped ½ cup)
1 teaspoon paprika
Freshly ground black pepper to taste
2 to 3 plum (Roma) tomatoes, thinly sliced

1. Preheat the oven to 350°F. Oil a 2-quart baking dish or gratin dish.

2. Heat 1 tablespoon of the olive oil in a large nonstick skillet over medium heat. Add the onion and red pepper. Cook, stirring, until the vegetables begin to soften, about 3 minutes. Add the cabbage and about ½ teaspoon salt, stir together, cover, and turn the heat to low. Cook, stirring occasionally, for 10 to 15 minutes, until the cabbage is tender and limp. Add 3 tablespoons water, cover, and cook for another 15 minutes. The cabbage will be tender and its bright green color will have faded. Stir in the chopped tomatoes, paprika, and pepper, and remove from the heat.

3. Transfer the mixture to the baking dish. Arrange the sliced tomatoes over the top, sprinkle them with salt and pepper, and drizzle on the remaining 1 tablespoon oil.

4. Bake in the upper part of the oven for 40 to 50 minutes, until the vegetables are charred around the edges and the tomato slices are shriveled. Serve hot or at room temperature.

Advance preparation: This can be made several hours or even a day ahead of time and reheated for 15 to 20 minutes in a 250° to 300°F oven.

stir-fried eggplant and green beans

One of the reasons why eggplant works so well in stir-fries is that it absorbs flavors—ginger, soy sauce, garlic—so well. Japanese eggplant, the smaller long type, is ideal for this recipe, but regular big eggplants work just fine as well. The eggplants are roasted for a short time before being stir-fried; that way they don't require too much oil in the pan. Serve with rice. **MAKES 4 SERVINGS**

1½ pounds eggplant,
    preferably Japanese eggplant
2 teaspoons salt
½ pound green beans, trimmed
½ cup vegetable stock or water
2 tablespoons soy sauce, or more to taste
2 tablespoons rice wine or dry sherry
1 tablespoon rice wine vinegar or
    cider vinegar
2 teaspoons sugar
2 tablespoons peanut or canola oil
1 onion, chopped, or 1 bunch scallions,
    white and green parts separated, chopped
2 garlic cloves, minced
1 tablespoon minced or grated fresh ginger
1 dried hot chile, crumbled
2 teaspoons arrowroot or cornstarch
    mixed with 2 tablespoons water
2 tablespoons chopped fresh cilantro

1. Preheat the oven to 450°F.

2. Pierce Japanese eggplants in several places and place on a baking sheet. If using a large eggplant, cut in half lengthwise and score the cut side down to the skin, being careful not to pierce the skin. Place on an oiled baking sheet, cut side down. Bake for 15 to 30 minutes, until softened. Remove from the heat and when cool enough to handle, peel if desired and dice.

3. Bring a large pot of water to a boil. Add the salt and the green beans. Cook for 5 minutes, drain, and transfer the beans to a bowl of ice water to cool. Drain.

4. In a small bowl, combine the stock, soy sauce, wine, vinegar, and sugar. Set aside.

5. Heat the oil in a wok or a large, heavy nonstick skillet over medium-high heat. Add the onion or the white part of the scallions. Stir for a couple of minutes, until it begins to soften. Add the garlic and ginger. Stir for 30 to 60 seconds, until the garlic and ginger smell fragrant. Add the eggplant, green beans, and chile. Stir together for a minute, then add the soy sauce mixture. Cook, stirring, until the eggplant is cooked through and fragrant, about 3 minutes. Taste and add soy sauce as desired. Add the arrowroot mixture and stir together until glazed.

6. Remove from the heat, sprinkle on the cilantro and, if using scallions, the green part of the scallions. Serve at once.

Advance preparation: The eggplant can be baked and the green beans blanched hours ahead of making this.

- STIR-FRIED EGGPLANT, GREEN BEANS, AND TOFU • Drain ½ pound tofu, blot dry, and cut into 1- by ½-inch pieces. Before adding the ginger and garlic to the oil, brown the tofu: Heat 1 tablespoon of the oil, add the tofu and cook, stirring, until lightly browned, about 5 minutes. Remove from the heat and drain on a paper towel. Proceed with the recipe as written, adding the second 2 tablespoons of oil and the onion, then the garlic and ginger to the pan. Return the tofu to the pan when you add the eggplant and beans.

spicy cauliflower with chutney

This is inspired by a delicious cauliflower "franky," a sort of Indian burrito. It is adapted from the franky filling recipe in *The Bombay Cafe Cookbook* by Neela Paniz with Helen Newton Hartung. This is excellent with Rice Pilaf with Chickpeas (page 164) and Bulgur Pilaf with Cumin and Chickpeas (page 141). **MAKES 4 SERVINGS**

1 large cauliflower, cut into 1-inch pieces
2 tablespoons canola or peanut oil
½ to 1 teaspoon cumin seeds
2 serrano chiles, cut in half lengthwise, seeded (optional), and thinly sliced
1-inch piece ginger, peeled, thinly sliced, then cut into slivers (julienne)
2 small or medium tomatoes, chopped
1 tablespoon ground coriander
¼ teaspoon cayenne pepper
¼ teaspoon turmeric
Salt to taste
¼ cup chopped fresh cilantro
¼ cup mango or tamarind chutney, mashed if the chutney is chunky
1 lime, cut in wedges

1. Place the cauliflower in a steaming basket above 1 inch of boiling water. Cover and steam for 1 minute. Lift the cover for 15 seconds, then cover and steam for 5 minutes. Remove from the heat, refresh with cold water, and set aside.

2. Heat the oil in a large nonstick skillet over medium-high heat. Add the cumin seeds, chiles, and ginger. Stir-fry for 1 minute, until fragrant. Add the cauliflower and turn down the heat to medium-low. Cook, stirring, for a couple of minutes. Then stir in the tomatoes, coriander, cayenne, turmeric, and salt (½ to ¾ teaspoon). Cook, stirring, for another 5 minutes, or until the tomatoes are cooked down and the mixture is fragrant. Taste and adjust the salt.

3. Stir in the cilantro and chutney and serve with lime wedges for squeezing.

Advance preparation: Serve this soon after it is made.

green beans with tomatoes and garlic

This Mediterranean dish can be made with any type of green bean, such as Blue Lake, Kentucky Wonder, or the flat Romano beans. Serve as a side dish, toss with pasta, or pile over grains.
MAKES 4 SERVINGS

1 pound green beans, trimmed
Salt
1 tablespoon plus 1 teaspoon extra virgin olive oil
1 medium onion, chopped
2 large garlic cloves, minced
1 pound fresh ripe tomatoes, or one 14-ounce can, peeled, seeded, and chopped
Freshly ground black pepper to taste
2 teaspoons chopped fresh marjoram (optional)
2 tablespoons chopped fresh parsley or basil, or a combination

1. Bring a large pot of water to a boil, add a couple teaspoons of salt and the green beans. When the water comes back to a boil, cook for 3 minutes. Transfer to a bowl of cold water, then drain. Save ½ cup of cooking water for moistening the bean mixture.

2. Heat 1 tablespoon of the olive oil in a large, heavy nonstick skillet over medium heat. Add the onion. Cook, stirring, until the onion is tender, about 5 minutes. Add the garlic. Cook for about 30 seconds, until the garlic begins to color. Stir in the tomatoes. Add salt, pepper, and the marjoram, if using. When the tomatoes begin to sizzle, add the beans and stir together. Cook, stirring occasionally, for about 20 minutes, until the beans are tender but bright green and the tomatoes are fragrant. If the mixture seems dry, stir in some of the cooking water from the beans.

3. Stir in the parsley and the remaining 1 teaspoon olive oil, taste, and adjust the seasoning. Serve hot or at room temperature.

Advance preparation: This can be made a day ahead and reheated.

- GREEN BEANS WITH TOMATOES AND GARLIC OVER PASTA • This makes enough for ¾ pound pasta. Cook the pasta until al dente, firm to the bite, in the water you used for the beans. Add a spoonful or two of the boiling water to the beans. When the pasta is done, drain and add to the beans, along with ¼ cup freshly grated pecorino cheese.

mediterranean greens

Not surprisingly, garlic and olive oil are used throughout the Mediterranean to season greens. Lemon juice is widely used as well, and in southern Italy, hot red pepper flakes might be added. I've made that ingredient optional here. **MAKES 4 SERVINGS**

2 large bunches greens (about 2 pounds), such as Swiss chard, beet greens,
  turnip greens, or kale
Salt
1 to 2 tablespoons extra virgin olive oil
2 large garlic cloves, minced
1 dried hot chile, seeded and crumbled, or ¼ teaspoon red pepper flakes
  (optional)
Freshly ground black pepper to taste
1 lemon, cut in wedges

1. Begin heating a large pot of water while you stem and wash the greens. Pull the leaves away from the stems and discard the stems. Place the leaves in a large bowl of cold water or the bottom of a salad spinner, and swish around to remove sand. Lift the greens from the water, change the water, and repeat. When the water comes to a boil, add 1 tablespoon salt and the greens. Meanwhile, fill the bowl you used for cleaning the greens with cold water and place it next to the pot with the greens. Cook the greens for 2 to 5 minutes (depending on the type of greens), until tender. Transfer with a slotted spoon or deep-fry skimmer to the bowl of cold water. Drain and gently squeeze out excess water (you don't have to squeeze them completely dry). Chop coarsely with a chef's knife or kitchen scissors.

2. Heat the oil in a large, heavy nonstick skillet over medium heat. Add the garlic and red pepper flakes if using. Cook for 30 to 60 seconds, just until the garlic begins to color. Stir in the greens. Stir for a couple of minutes, until the greens are nicely seasoned with the oil and garlic. Add salt and pepper to taste and remove from the heat.

3. Serve, passing the lemon wedges for people to squeeze over their greens.

Advance preparation: The greens can be blanched up to a day ahead and held in the refrigerator in a bowl or plastic bag, then cooked in the oil with the flavorings just before serving.

asian greens

Ginger, garlic, and soy sauce give these pungent greens an unmistakable Asian character.
MAKES 4 SERVINGS

2 large bunches greens (about 2 pounds),
*   such as Swiss chard, beet greens,*
*   turnip greens, or kale*
Salt
1 to 2 tablespoons canola or peanut oil
2 large garlic cloves, minced or pressed
1 tablespoon minced or grated fresh ginger
1 tablespoon soy sauce

1. Begin heating a large pot of water while you stem and wash the greens. Pull the leaves away from the stems and discard the stems. Place the leaves in a large bowl of cold water or the bottom of a salad spinner, and swish around to remove sand. Lift the greens from the water, change the water, and repeat. When the water comes to a boil, add 1 tablespoon salt and the greens. Meanwhile, fill the bowl you used for cleaning the greens with cold water and place it next to the pot with the greens. Cook the greens for 2 to 5 minutes (depending on the type of greens), until tender. Transfer with a slotted spoon or deep-fry skimmer to the bowl of cold water. Drain and gently squeeze out excess water (you don't have to squeeze them completely dry). Chop coarsely with a chef's knife or kitchen scissors.

2. Heat the oil in a large, heavy nonstick skillet over medium-high heat. Add the garlic and ginger. Cook, stirring, until they begin to color, 30 to 60 seconds. Stir in the greens, add the soy sauce and salt to taste.

3. Heat through, remove from the heat, and serve.

Advance preparation: The greens can be blanched up to a day ahead and held in the refrigerator in a bowl or plastic bag, then cooked in the oil with the flavorings just before serving.

chopped grilled vegetables with chickpeas

This smoky mixture can be served as a salad, a starter on a bed of lettuce or arugula, a side dish, or a main dish over rice, couscous, bulgur, polenta, or pasta. The vegetables are grilled until charred and softened, and the peppers and eggplant then steam for a time in a covered bowl before being chopped or sliced. When all of the vegetables are tossed together, the eggplant and tomato tend to fall apart, spreading through the mixture and seasoning it with smoke while adding their individual flavors and textures. The dish is inspired by roasted pepper and tomato salads I've eaten in North Africa. **MAKES 6 SERVINGS**

*1 large or 2 medium eggplant (about 1½ pounds),
   cut in half lengthwise
2 large or 3 small red bell peppers (about 1 pound)
3 medium tomatoes, cut in half across the equator
1 large sweet onion, sliced in rings
One 15-ounce can chickpeas, drained and rinsed
¼ cup chopped fresh parsley
2 to 4 tablespoons slivered basil
¼ cup extra virgin olive oil
2 tablespoons sherry vinegar
1 tablespoon balsamic vinegar
Salt and freshly ground black pepper to taste
1 to 2 garlic cloves, minced*

1. Salt the eggplant on the cut sides and let sit for 30 minutes, while you light the grill and prepare the remaining vegetables. Meanwhile, prepare a medium-hot fire in a charcoal grill or preheat a gas grill on medium-high for 15 minutes.

2. Grill the peppers on all sides until blackened. Transfer to a bowl and place a plate over the top. Allow the peppers to cool (they will also steam and soften) until you can handle them.

3. Pat the eggplant dry with paper towels. Brush the cut side of the eggplant lightly with olive oil. Lay each half on the grill rack and grill until the eggplant is charred and softened. This may take 8 to 10 minutes, or more if the eggplant is large. Turn the eggplant halves over and grill the other side until charred and softened. Transfer to the bowl with the peppers. Cover with the plate, so that the eggplant steams and softens a bit more.

4. Lightly oil a vegetable grill rack, if using one, and heat it on the grill for at least 5 minutes. Brush the cut side of the tomatoes lightly with olive oil and place cut side down on the grill or vegetable grill rack. Grill until they begin to brown and lose their shape, 4 to 5 minutes. Turn the tomato halves over and grill on the skin side until browned and beginning to collapse, 4 to 5 minutes. Transfer to a bowl and allow to cool until you can handle them.

5. Grill the onions, turning often, until charred and softened, 5 to 10 minutes. Some of the pieces may blacken to a crisp before most of the onion is done; discard the hard blackened bits. Transfer to the bowl with the tomatoes.

6. Remove all of the blackened skin from the peppers. Clean off the surfaces with paper towels. Cut the peppers in half lengthwise; remove the seeds, cores, and membranes; and cut into thin strips. Transfer to a large attractive bowl. Gently squeeze the eggplant halves to extract any bitter juices. Peel away the blackened skin and hard blackened bits from the cut sides and discard. Dice the eggplant; don't worry if the pieces don't hold their shape. Transfer to the bowl with the peppers. Pour any juice that has accumulated in the bowl with the tomatoes over the peppers and eggplant. Remove the skin and cores from the tomatoes and discard. Dice the tomatoes and add to the peppers and eggplant. Don't worry if they don't hold their shape but become pulpy. Just scrape the pulp into the bowl. Add the onions, chickpeas, parsley, and basil to the bowl.

7. Mix together the olive oil, vinegars, salt, pepper, and garlic and toss with the vegetables. Taste and make sure there is enough salt (it can take a lot). Serve at room temperature or warm, or refrigerate overnight, and remove from the refrigerator to allow to come to room temperature before serving.

Advance preparation: The dish will keep for a few days in the refrigerator and is even better if you give it a day for the flavors to mature.

roasted vegetable stew with bulgur or rice

This is an amazing stew, partly because it tastes so good, partly because it requires so little work. Basically you just throw everything into the pot, put it in the oven, and an hour and a half later, you have dinner. The long cooking of the vegetables does away with bright green colors, but it brings out their sweetness.

I like to serve this over bulgur, topped with a sprinkle of feta cheese. It's also good with rice. Serve crusty bread for soaking up the juice. **MAKES 4 TO 6 SERVINGS**

1 medium eggplant, cut in half lengthwise
¼ pound small okra, stems cut off but pod intact
One 10-ounce package frozen peas, thawed (about 2 cups),
    or 2 cups fresh shelled peas
¼ pound green beans, trimmed and cut into 1-inch pieces
1 pound zucchini, sliced
1 large onion, finely chopped
3 large garlic cloves, minced
1 pound potatoes, peeled and diced
One 14-ounce can tomatoes, drained and chopped
    (you can use recipe-ready tomatoes)
1 large red bell pepper,
    seeded and cut into ½-inch squares
Leaves from 1 large bunch parsley,
    washed and chopped (about 1 cup)
2 teaspoons paprika
2 tablespoons extra virgin olive oil
2 to 3 teaspoons salt
3 ripe tomatoes, sliced (optional)
1 to 2 ounces feta cheese, crumbled (¼ to ½ cup)
Cooked medium or coarse bulgur or rice

1. Preheat the oven to 450°F.

2. Score the eggplant halves once down the middle, without cutting through the skin. Oil a baking sheet with olive oil and place the eggplant on it, cut side down. Bake for 20 minutes.

Remove from the oven and place in a colander. Let sit for 20 to 30 minutes, during which time some of the liquid should drain out. Peel and dice.

3. Turn the oven down to 375°F. Combine the eggplant, okra, peas, green beans, zucchini, onion, garlic, potatoes, canned tomatoes, bell pepper, parsley, paprika, and olive oil in a large ovenproof Dutch oven or earthenware casserole. Add 2 teaspoons salt to begin with (you can adjust later). Cover and place in the oven. Bake for 1 hour, stirring from time to time, until the vegetables are tender.

4. Remove the lid from the casserole. If using the tomatoes, place in an even layer over the top and return the casserole uncovered to the oven (do this whether you are using the tomatoes or not). Bake for another 30 minutes, to let the juices in the pan reduce and concentrate. The sliced tomatoes should be just beginning to brown.

5. Remove from the oven, taste, and adjust the salt. Serve hot or at room temperature, sprinkled with feta and over warm bulgur or rice.

Advance preparation: This is great the day after you make it and will keep for about 5 days in the refrigerator. You can also use leftovers for an omelet, frittata, or tart (see page 117).

leeks cooked in white wine

In this heavenly dish, leeks sweeten and soften in a savory mixture of wine, olive oil, and garlic. Serve it warm or cold, as a starter or side dish. You could follow the dish or accompany it with a gratin, omelet, tart, or risotto, and a green salad. **MAKES 4 TO 6 SERVINGS**

*6 medium leeks (about 2½ pounds), white and light green parts only,
   washed well and cut into 2-inch pieces*
Salt to taste
2 tablespoons extra virgin olive oil
1 cup dry white wine
Freshly ground black pepper to taste
4 large garlic cloves, minced
6 lemon wedges (optional)
Chopped fresh parsley (optional)
Black olives (optional)

1. Bring a 3- or 4-quart pot of water to a boil. Add the leeks and 1 teaspoon salt. Blanch for 2 minutes and drain.

2. Place the leeks in a heavy nonstick skillet or wide saucepan in one layer. Add the oil, wine, about ½ teaspoon salt, pepper, and garlic. Bring to a boil, cover, and reduce the heat to low. Simmer for 30 to 60 minutes, until the leeks are very tender but still intact, and most of the liquid has evaporated.

3. Remove from the heat and serve, or allow to cool in the juices remaining in the pan. Garnish with the lemon wedges, olives, and chopped parsley.

Advance preparation: These will keep for a day or two in the refrigerator.

pan-cooked mushrooms
with gremolata

This zesty mushroom dish makes a nice meal, on toast or bruschetta or tossed with pasta; or it can be served as a side dish or starter. **MAKES 2 GENEROUS MAIN-COURSE SERVINGS, OR 4 FIRST-COURSE OR SIDE-DISH SERVINGS; OR ENOUGH FOR 1 PIZZA OR ¾ POUND PASTA**

2 tablespoons extra virgin olive oil
1 pound cultivated or wild mushrooms
    (such as shiitakes or oyster mushrooms),
    or a combination, trimmed and quartered if small,
    thickly sliced if large
Salt to taste
½ cup dry white wine, such as Sauvignon Blanc or Pinot Grigio
Freshly ground black pepper to taste
1 to 2 large garlic cloves, finely minced
¼ cup chopped flat-leaf parsley
2 teaspoons finely chopped or grated lemon zest

1. Heat 1 tablespoon of the olive oil in a large, heavy nonstick skillet over medium heat. Add the mushrooms and a generous pinch of salt. Cook, stirring, until the mushrooms begin to release water. Continue to cook, stirring, until the liquid has just about cooked off. Add the wine. Cook, stirring, until the wine has just about evaporated and the mushrooms are glazed, 5 to 10 minutes. Stir in the remaining 1 tablespoon oil, garlic, parsley, and lemon zest, and cook, stirring, for 1 minute.

2. Remove from the heat, taste, and adjust the seasonings. Serve hot.

Advance preparation: These can be made several hours before serving and reheated, but it is best if the parsley and lemon zest are added close to serving time.

mashed potatoes with kale

This is one of many recipes for colcannon, one of Ireland's signature potato dishes. The most common version pairs cabbage with potatoes, but the dish is also made with kale and with parsnips (see page 247). Again we find greens and potatoes together, a beautiful combination. Try this at Thanksgiving for a change. **MAKES 6 SERVINGS**

2 pounds baking potatoes,
*   scrubbed and peeled*
Salt to taste
1 large bunch kale (1 pound),
*   ribs removed, leaves washed*
1¼ cups low-fat milk
2 heaped tablespoons chopped scallions
*   (about 3 scallions), white part only*
2 tablespoons butter
Freshly ground black pepper to taste

1. Cover the potatoes with water in a saucepan, add about ½ teaspoon salt, and bring to a boil. Reduce the heat to medium, cover partially, and cook until tender all the way through when pierced with a knife, 30 to 45 minutes. Drain off the water, return the potatoes to the pan, cover tightly, and let steam over very low heat for another 2 to 3 minutes. Remove from the heat and mash with a potato masher or a fork while still hot.

2. While the potatoes are cooking, bring a large pot of water to a boil. Add 1 tablespoon salt and the kale. Cook for 4 to 5 minutes, until the leaves are tender but still bright green. Drain, squeeze out excess water, and chop fine. You can do this in a food processor fitted with the steel blade.

3. When the potatoes are almost done, combine the milk and the scallions in a saucepan and bring to a simmer. Remove from the heat.

4. Stir the chopped kale into the hot mashed potatoes and beat in the milk and butter. The mixture should be fluffy (you can do this in an electric mixer fitted with the paddle). Add salt to taste (you will need more than you think), and freshly ground pepper.

5. Serve hot, right away, or transfer to a buttered baking dish, cover with foil, and hold for 20 minutes in a 350°F oven before serving.

Advance preparation: The dish can be prepared several hours ahead of serving and reheated in a buttered baking dish, covered with foil, for 20 to 30 minutes at 250°F.

- MASHED POTATOES AND PARSNIPS WITH KALE • Substitute 1 pound parsnips for 1 pound of the potatoes. Reduce the milk to 1 cup (or use more as needed). Peel, quarter, and core the parsnips, and cook and mash with the potatoes as above. You will need less milk because the parsnips don't absorb as much as the potatoes.

potato and greens galette

This savory galette, based on an Italian recipe, is like a garlicky mashed potato pie. The potatoes are flecked with greens, and it's lovely to behold as well as to eat. The most delicate crust to use is the Yeasted Butter Pastry, but the yeasted olive oil crust works well, too, and would probably be used in the Mediterranean. **MAKES 6 TO 8 SERVINGS**

½ recipe Yeasted Butter Pastry (page 110) or
Yeasted Olive Oil Pastry (page 108)
4 medium baking potatoes (2 to 2½ pounds),
peeled
Salt to taste
1 small bunch greens or spinach (½ pound),
washed and stemmed
¼ cup nonfat or low-fat cottage cheese or
low-fat ricotta
2 large garlic cloves, minced
½ cup low-fat milk, or more as needed
1 large egg
2 ounces Parmesan, grated (½ cup)
Freshly ground black pepper to taste
1 tablespoon extra virgin olive oil

1. Mix the dough and let it rise while you prepare the filling.

2. Place the potatoes in a large saucepan, cover with water, add about 1 teaspoon salt, and bring to a boil. Reduce the heat to medium, cover partially, and cook until the potatoes are soft all the way through when pierced with a knife, about 30 minutes. Remove the potatoes from the pot, add water if it is low, and bring back to a boil. Add the greens and cook for 1 to 3 minutes, depending on the type of greens, until just wilted but still bright green. Transfer to a bowl of cold water, then drain. Squeeze out any water and chop coarsely. Drain the water from the pot, turn off heat, and return the potatoes to the pot. Cover tightly and let steam for 5 minutes.

3. Preheat the oven to 375°F.

4. Mash the potatoes in a bowl. Blend together the cottage cheese or ricotta and garlic until smooth in a mini food processor or press the cottage cheese through a sieve and mix in the garlic with a fork. Add 2 tablespoons of the milk and blend until smooth. Beat in the egg. Stir into the potatoes, along with the Parmesan, salt, and pepper. Stir in the greens and the remaining 6 tablespoons milk, and stir until you have a smooth mixture. Add a few more tablespoons milk as needed. Taste and adjust the seasonings.

5. Lightly oil and flour a 14-inch pizza pan. Roll out the dough on a large lightly floured surface to about 15 inches in diameter, and place on the pizza pan so the dough hangs over the sides. Spread the filling over the crust, leaving a 3-inch border of crust all the way around. Gently pull and stretch the dough up over the filling, twisting each fold and leaving a small open space in the middle. Drizzle the olive oil over the crust and exposed potatoes, and rub the olive oil over the crust.

6. Bake for 35 minutes, or until golden.

7. Remove from the heat and serve hot or warm.

Advance preparation: This can be made a day ahead and reheated in a 325°F oven for 20 minutes. It can also be served at room temperature.

potato gratin

A potato gratin is one of the most pleasing and satisfying of dishes. The classic version is rich, with lots of cream and butter. But what I love about potato gratins isn't the rich ingredients, but the potatoes themselves, and the delicious crust that forms on the top and sides after long baking. Don't slice the potatoes too thinly or they'll fall apart. **MAKES 6 SERVINGS**

2 large garlic cloves, cut in half lengthwise
3 pounds baking potatoes or Yukon Golds,
*   scrubbed and sliced about ¼ inch thick*
2 large eggs
3½ cups low-fat milk
About 1 teaspoon salt
Freshly ground black pepper to taste
2 ounces Gruyère, grated (½ cup)

1. Preheat the oven to 375°F. Rub the inside of a 3-quart gratin dish all over with the cut side of the garlic.

2. Slice up the garlic that remains and toss with the potatoes. Place in an even layer in the gratin dish.

3. Beat the eggs and add the milk, salt, pepper, and cheese. Pour over the potatoes.

4. Bake for 1 to 1½ hours. During the first hour, every 15 minutes, remove the gratin from the oven and break up the top layer with a large spoon or knife, then stir and fold into the rest of the gratin. Bake until the top is golden and crusty.

5. Serve hot or warm.

Advance preparation: This should be baked as soon as it is assembled, but it can be made ahead and reheated in a 325°F oven for 20 minutes.

steamed potatoes with sage

Potatoes and sage make a delicious pair, and this recipe is reason enough to have a pot of sage in your window or garden. I like to use small potatoes, such as new potatoes, fingerlings, or baby Yukon Golds, which I can steam whole for this. **MAKES 4 SERVINGS**

1½ pounds small waxy potatoes,
    scrubbed, or larger waxy potatoes,
    scrubbed and quartered
Coarse sea salt and freshly ground black pepper to taste
1 tablespoon extra virgin olive oil
6 to 12 sage leaves, slivered

1. Steam the potatoes for 15 to 20 minutes, or until tender.

2. Drain and toss in the pan, or in a warm serving bowl, with the salt, pepper, olive oil, and sage. Serve hot.

Advance preparation: You can steam the potatoes hours ahead of time. Reheat by steaming for another couple of minutes or by plunging into a pot of simmering water and draining. Then proceed with the recipe.

spring/summer vegetable stew

This is a beautiful mixture of delicate spring and summer vegetables—sweet red or white onions, yellow and green squash, carrots, and green beans. The onions and tarragon give it a sweet flavor. Serve it in a wide bowl over pasta, such as penne or fusilli, or grains, or on thick bruschetta (page 227). **MAKES 4 GENEROUS SERVINGS**

2 medium leeks, white and light green parts only,
    cleaned and sliced (dark green leaves washed and set aside)
1 pound baby carrots, peeled and halved, or small carrots,
    peeled, quartered, and cut into 2-inch lengths (peels set aside)
Salt to taste
½ pound green beans, trimmed and broken into halves or thirds,
    or sugar snap peas, ends trimmed
1 tablespoon extra virgin olive oil
1 large or 2 small to medium sweet red or white onions
1 small head green garlic, minced,
    or 4 garlic cloves, minced
1 pound small waxy potatoes, such as fingerlings
    or new potatoes, diced
1 pound mixed yellow summer and zucchini squash,
    quartered lengthwise if thick, and sliced
1 tablespoon chopped fresh tarragon
¼ cup chopped fresh parsley
Freshly ground black pepper to taste
1 tablespoon unsalted butter

1. Place the leek greens and carrot trimmings in a pot and add 8 cups water. Bring to a boil and simmer for 30 minutes while you prepare the remaining vegetables. Strain and return to the pot, discarding the solids.

2. Bring the leek stock back up to a rolling boil and add 2 teaspoons salt, the carrots, and green beans. Blanch for 3 minutes and remove from the water with a slotted spoon. Transfer to a bowl of cold water, drain, and set aside.

3. Heat the oil in a large heavy nonstick skillet or a Dutch oven over medium heat. Add the onions and sliced leeks. Cook, stirring often, until tender, about 5 minutes. Add the garlic. Cook, stirring, until fragrant, about 1 minute. Add the potatoes, 3 cups stock, and salt to taste. Bring to a simmer, cover, and simmer for 10 minutes. Add the squash, stir together, cover, and simmer for 5 minutes, or until the squash and potatoes are tender.

4. Stir in the carrots and beans. Taste and adjust the salt. Stir in the tarragon, parsley, pepper, and butter. Stir until the butter melts and serve.

Note: If serving with pasta, turn off the heat when you add the beans and carrots to the stew. Add water as necessary to the remaining leek stock. Bring to a boil, add salt if necessary, and the pasta. Cook the pasta, drain, and place in wide bowls. Top with the stew and serve.

Advance preparation: You can prepare the stew up until the point that you add the blanched carrots and beans hours ahead of serving. Do not add the carrots and beans until you heat the stew, then stir them in, heat through, and proceed with the recipe.

roasted asparagus
with parmesan

The color, texture, and flavor of roasted asparagus is incredibly vivid. This must be served right away or the appearance will suffer. **MAKES 4 SERVINGS**

1 pound asparagus, ends trimmed
1 tablespoon extra virgin olive oil
Salt and freshly ground black pepper to taste
1 ounce Parmesan, grated (¼ cup)

1. Preheat the oven to 350°F.

2. Tightly wrap the asparagus, in one or two bunches, in aluminum foil. Roast for 15 to 25 minutes. It is done when it is tender but still has some texture.

3. Put the olive oil in a baking dish in which the asparagus will fit in one layer. Remove the asparagus from the foil packet and roll in the olive oil. Sprinkle with salt and pepper, and with the Parmesan. Roll the asparagus around to coat evenly with the Parmesan.

4. Return to the oven for 5 minutes, until the Parmesan is just beginning to melt, or longer if you'd like it to brown. Remove from the heat and serve at once.

Advance preparation: This should be served at once, but the asparagus can be prepped and wrapped in foil hours ahead of roasting.

summer tomato gratin

I have eaten this dish all over Provence, where there are many variations. Sometimes the tomatoes are cooked for a very long time, until they are quite dry and caramelized. In other versions the tomatoes are baked only until the topping browns. But they all highlight the rich, sweet dimension of tomatoes in season. I've even enjoyed the dish when I've made it with less-than-exciting tomatoes, because the long cooking time brings out whatever sugars there are. **MAKES 4 SERVINGS**

2 pounds ripe but firm tomatoes, sliced
Salt to taste
1 teaspoon sugar
1 cup fresh or dry bread crumbs
2 tablespoons chopped fresh parsley or basil
2 tablespoons extra virgin olive oil

1. Preheat the oven to 400°F. Oil a 2-quart baking dish.

2. Layer the tomatoes in the dish, sprinkling each layer with salt and sugar. Toss together the bread crumbs, parsley, and olive oil. Spread over the top of the tomatoes in an even layer.

3. Bake for about 1½ hours, until the top is golden brown and the juices that are left in the pan are quite thick. Serve warm, at room temperature, or cold.

Advance preparation: Since this is best served at room temperature, you can make it hours ahead.

baby turnip and turnip greens ragout

The onions and leeks create a sweet broth for the bitter turnip greens and the pungent turnips. Couscous is the perfect accompaniment for this dish. **MAKES 2 TO 3 MAIN-COURSE SERVINGS, 4 SIDE-DISH SERVINGS**

2 medium leeks, white and light green parts only, cleaned and sliced
(dark green leaves washed and set aside)
1 tablespoon extra virgin olive oil
1 large or 2 small-to-medium sweet red or white onions, chopped
1 small head green garlic, minced, or 2 to 4 garlic cloves, minced or pressed
1 bunch baby turnips, with greens (about 1 pound), turnips peeled and
cut in wedges, greens stemmed, washed well, and chopped
Salt to taste
Freshly ground black pepper to taste
3 tablespoons chopped fresh herbs, such as tarragon, parsley, chives, or chervil
1 tablespoon unsalted butter

1. Place the leek greens in a pot and add 8 cups water. Bring to a boil and simmer for 30 minutes while you prepare the remaining vegetables. Strain and return to the pot, discarding the solids.

2. Heat the oil in a large nonstick skillet. Add the onions and sliced leeks. Cook, stirring often, until tender, about 5 minutes. Add the garlic. Cook, stirring, until fragrant, about 1 minute. Add the turnips, 2½ cups of the leek stock, and salt to taste. Bring to a simmer, partially cover, reduce the heat to medium-low, and simmer for 10 minutes, or until the turnips are tender. Stir in the greens and simmer for another 5 minutes. If the greens are quite tough, simmer a few minutes longer; however, their color will not be as bright.

3. Add pepper, taste, and adjust the salt. Stir in the fresh herbs and butter. When the butter has melted, serve in wide bowls over couscous.

Note: If serving with couscous, use the remaining stock with water to make 1¼ cups, to reconstitute the couscous. See directions on pages 142–143.

Advance preparation: This can be made, up to the addition of the greens, hours ahead of serving. Reheat, add the greens, and proceed with the recipe close to serving time.

yellow squash with kale

The color alone makes this dish pleasing. Kale isn't the only type of green that works here—beet greens, chard, and spinach all go well with the delicate yellow summer squash (though beet greens will turn the dish pink). You can serve this as a side dish, or with pasta or rice.
MAKES 4 SERVINGS

*¾ pound kale or other greens, stemmed, washed,
    and coarsely chopped
1 tablespoon extra virgin olive oil
1 pound yellow summer squash, sliced
2 large garlic cloves, minced
Salt to taste
1 teaspoon fresh thyme leaves or
    ½ teaspoon dried (optional)
¼ to ½ cup water or Easy Vegetable Stock (page 63)
Freshly ground black pepper to taste*

1. If the greens are dry, rinse them again and do not shake dry. Heat the oil in a large, heavy skillet over medium heat. Add the squash. Cook, stirring often, for about 5 minutes, until the squash is lightly browned and slightly translucent. Add the garlic, stir together for about 30 seconds, until fragrant, then add the greens, which should still be wet from washing. Continue to cook, stirring, until the greens wilt, about 3 to 4 minutes. Add the salt and thyme and ¼ cup water and continue to cook, stirring, for another 5 minutes, until the squash and the greens are tender. Add more water if the mixture seems dry or begins to stick to the pan.

2. Add pepper, taste, and adjust the seasonings. Serve hot or at room temperature.

Advance preparation: Everything can be prepped and ready to go hours ahead of time, but the cooking should be done close to serving time.

Tofu

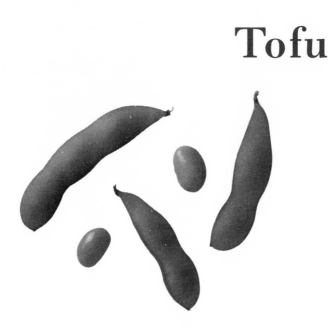

For millions of people in Asia, soy foods are a vital source of plant protein. And for Americans, these foods, particularly tofu (or bean curd), have become increasingly familiar over the years. Tofu is a curd made from soy "milk," the liquid extracted from soaked, ground raw soybeans, to which a coagulating agent is added. The curds are pressed and molded into blocks that are then stored in water. The tofu comes in several consistencies: soft, medium, and firm. It is sold in the refrigerated dairy sections of most supermarkets and whole foods stores, usually in sealed plastic tubs. Silken tofu, often vacuum-packed in cartons that can be stored at room temperature until opened, has a particularly smooth texture. This type of tofu is best for blended tofu preparations like the mayonnaise and the dressing in the dips and spreads chapter and is also good in broths and miso soup. For stir-fries and other tofu dishes—most of the dishes in this chapter—I prefer regular firm tofu. I have tasted some of the seasoned tofus that are being made and distributed mostly in whole foods stores; I find them too salty, and I think you could do better by using the marinades in this chapter.

A nutritional powerhouse, tofu is very high in perfect protein and low in calories (about 130 per 3½ ounces). The fat content is fairly high—about 9 grams per 3½ ounces—but this is unsaturated fat.

Not everybody likes tofu, because of its blandness and spongelike texture. But I have always been a tofu lover. I enjoy the texture, the way that it soaks up flavors, and its satisfying, almost meaty bulk. I don't think of tofu as an acquired taste: You either like it or you don't. Following a vegetarian diet, whether full-time or part-time, doesn't require you to like it or any other soy product. I think the reason many don't like bean curd is that it has been misused as a "substitute" for meat and cheese, which it really doesn't resemble at all, despite its high protein content. Because it absorbs flavors so nicely, it works well in savory stir-fries and Asian hot-pots. Soy sauce is the perfect seasoning for it. If it is going to be used in Western dishes, its best application is as a blended sauce-like mayonnaise or béchamel.

Tofu Basics

- Buy firm tofu for pan-cooked tofu and stir-fries, broiled and grilled tofu, and hot pots.
- Buy silken tofu for blended tofu dishes and some soups.
- Buy packaged tofu unless your source of bulk tofu has a fast turnover, and check the sell-by date on the package. Chinese markets are a good source of very fresh tofu, which is sold in bulk. Whether buying packaged or bulk tofu, rinse it and place it in a bowl or tub of fresh water when you get it home. Change water daily or every other day. It will keep for a week if properly stored. It is no longer good when it begins to smell sour. If the tofu is vacuum-packed or packed in a carton, like Japanese silken tofu often is, do not open it until you are ready to use it, and try to use it up quickly. Silken tofu doesn't keep as well as the firmer tofus.
- Before you cook or marinate tofu, drain and blot dry with kitchen towels. For extra-firm tofu, wrap slices or a block in a clean kitchen towel and weight by placing under a heavy cutting board with cans or a pot on top. Let sit for 30 to 60 minutes.
- Tofu benefits from being marinated. It should be drained, blotted dry, and sliced first. It can stay in the marinade for several days in the refrigerator. It can also be marinated after it has been cooked.

- For excellent firm texture, fry plain or marinated tofu in a small amount of oil in a nonstick pan until lightly browned. Do not overcook, or the tofu will become hard and dry. Fried tofu can be kept in the refrigerator for a few days, plain or in a marinade, covered with plastic, and used in stir-fry recipes and salads.
- To achieve a firm texture without frying the tofu, cut into cubes and add to simmering water. Cook for 5 minutes, then drain.

Tofu Marinades

Tofu soaks up flavors like a sponge and always benefits from being marinated, the longer the better. Use the marinades to flavor tofu before pan-frying, roasting, broiling, or grilling. Any length of a soak, from 15 minutes to a day, will heighten a dish. All of these have Asian flavors and are great to have on hand for quick tofu meals. The recipes yield enough marinade for 1 pound of tofu.

spicy tofu marinade

Based on a recipe by Andrea Chesman from her book *The Vegetarian Grill*, this is one of my favorites. **MAKES ABOUT ½ CUP**

1 to 2 tablespoons Asian sesame oil
¼ cup soy sauce
2 tablespoons mirin (sweet Japanese rice wine)
1 tablespoon rice wine vinegar
2 garlic cloves, minced (optional)
1 tablespoon minced or grated fresh ginger
1 teaspoon sugar
1 teaspoon Asian chili paste,
     such as sambal oelek

Combine all the ingredients in a small bowl, using a whisk or fork. If you are not using it right away, transfer the marinade to a jar and refrigerate.

Advance preparation: The marinade will keep for a couple of weeks in the refrigerator, making tofu meals a snap.

soy-sherry marinade

MAKES ABOUT ⅓ CUP

¼ cup soy sauce
1 tablespoon white or light brown sugar
1 tablespoon dry sherry

Combine all the ingredients in a small bowl, using a whisk or fork. If you are not using it right away, transfer the marinade to a jar and refrigerate.

Advance preparation: The marinade will keep for a couple of weeks in the refrigerator, making tofu meals a snap.

soy-ginger marinade

MAKES ABOUT ½ CUP

1 to 2 tablespoons Asian sesame oil
¼ cup soy sauce
2 tablespoons mirin (sweet Japanese rice wine)
1 tablespoon rice wine vinegar
1 tablespoon minced or grated fresh ginger
1 teaspoon sugar

Combine all the ingredients in a small bowl, using a whisk or fork. If you are not using it right away, transfer the marinade to a jar and refrigerate.

Advance preparation: The marinade will keep for a couple of weeks in the refrigerator, making tofu meals a snap.

hoisin marinade

Hoisin sauce is sold in most supermarkets, in the Asian section. **MAKES ABOUT ⅔ CUP**

¼ cup hoisin sauce
¼ cup mirin (sweet Japanese rice wine)
2 tablespoons soy sauce
2 teaspoons sugar

Combine all the ingredients in a small bowl, using a whisk or fork. If you are not using it right away, transfer the marinade to a jar and refrigerate.

Advance preparation: The marinade will keep for a couple of weeks in the refrigerator, making tofu meals a snap.

Toppings and Glazes for Tofu

These sauces are great as spreads, glazes, or dipping sauces for tofu. They are particularly good with pan-cooked or broiled or grilled tofu (pages 268 to 269).

peanut sauce

This can also be used as a topping for rice or other grains, and it makes a great dip for vegetables. It should be used as a topping for cooked tofu, not as a marinade. **MAKES ABOUT ½ CUP**

3 tablespoons natural unsalted,
 unsweetened peanut butter
1 tablespoon rice wine vinegar
2 teaspoons soy sauce
2 tablespoons plain nonfat yogurt
1 to 2 teaspoons light brown sugar
1 to 2 teaspoons grated or finely chopped fresh ginger (optional)
Pinch of cayenne, or more to taste

Blend together the peanut butter, rice vinegar, soy sauce, yogurt, sugar, ginger, cayenne, and 2 tablespoons hot water. Thin with additional water as desired. Brush or spread on cooked or uncooked tofu.

ketchup and mustard sauce

This topping for pan-cooked or broiled or grilled tofu (pages 268 to 269) has a distinctly American taste. You can marinate the tofu in it before you cook it as well. **MAKES ¼ CUP**

¼ cup ketchup
1 teaspoon Dijon mustard, or more to taste
¼ teaspoon ground dry mustard
1 teaspoon soy sauce

Blend together all the ingredients. Marinate the tofu in the sauce before cooking, and/or brush it on the tofu as soon as it comes off the heat.

hot chipotle barbecue sauce

I've always thought it was sort of a waste to throw away the adobo sauce that chipotle chiles are canned in. Now I have a good use for it, in this very spicy sauce. The addition of the chile makes for a fiery sauce. **MAKES ABOUT ⅓ CUP**

1 tablespoon adobo sauce from canned chipotles
1 tablespoon light or dark brown sugar
½ teaspoon salt
¼ cup ketchup
1 tablespoon extra virgin olive oil
1 teaspoon soy sauce
1 canned chipotle,
*   seeded and mashed (optional)*

Mix together all of the ingredients. Marinate the tofu in the sauce before cooking, and/or brush it on the tofu as soon as it comes off the heat.

Advance preparation: This will keep for a couple of weeks in the refrigerator.

pan-cooked tofu

Tofu browns very nicely in a nonstick skillet, taking on a firm, almost meaty texture. You can marinate it first, or season it with a marinade, pages 261 to 264, sauce, or just with soy sauce after browning. Use this chewy tofu in other stir-fried dishes or add to salads. It's great to have on hand in the refrigerator. **MAKES 4 SERVINGS**

1 pound firm tofu
1 to 2 tablespoons canola or peanut oil

Cut the tofu into ¼-inch-thick slices, or thicker slices if desired, or dice it. Heat 1 tablespoon of the oil in a nonstick skillet over medium-high heat. Add the tofu in one layer and cook for 2 to 4 minutes, until lightly browned. Turn the tofu and brown on the other side. Alternately, stir-fry the tofu, moving it around and flipping it constantly for 3 to 8 minutes, or until lightly browned on all sides. Add the other tablespoon of oil, if necessary. Don't overcook or the tofu will be too hard. Serve with any of the toppings on pages 265 to 267, or with plain soy sauce. Or use in another recipe. Or keep in a covered bowl in the refrigerator. Makes a great snack.

Advance preparation: Browned tofu can be kept in the refrigerator for a day or two, or it can be marinated for several days.

broiled or grilled tofu

The trick to success here is not to overcook the tofu. It should brown, but you need to remove it from the heat before the edges become blackened and hard, after 3 to 4 minutes per side. The tofu will definitely benefit from a marinade, and it can be served with a topping or sauce.
MAKES 4 SERVINGS

> *1 pound firm tofu*
> *Marinade (pages 261 to 264) or*
>   *1 tablespoon canola or peanut oil*
> *Glaze or sauce (pages 265 to 267)*

1. Preheat the broiler or prepare a medium-hot grill. Oil a baking sheet or grill pan, if using.

2. Drain the tofu and pat dry with paper towels. Slice into ½-inch-thick slabs and blot each slab with paper towels. Marinate the tofu for as little as 15 minutes or as long as a day or two, or simply brush with oil.

3. Grill or broil until just beginning to brown, about 2 to 4 minutes per side. Serve, passing additional marinade or one or more of the glazes or sauces for dipping.

Advance preparation: The tofu can be marinated for a day or two in the refrigerator.

stir-fried tofu with broccoli

This is about as simple a tofu stir-fry as you can make, yet it is deeply satisfying. Since both broccoli and tofu keep well in the refrigerator for a week, this can be a standby dish. The sugars in the marinade caramelize when you fry the tofu, adding a complex, sweet dimension. The marinade keeps for a week in the refrigerator and is good to have on hand. If you like, you can marinate the tofu and even steam the broccoli before you go to work; then when you get home you can cook this dish very quickly. Serve with hot cooked rice or noodles. **MAKES 4 SERVINGS**

MARINADE

1 tablespoon Asian sesame oil

¼ cup soy sauce

2 tablespoons mirin (sweet Japanese rice wine)

1 tablespoon rice wine vinegar

2 garlic cloves, minced

1 teaspoon Asian chili paste

1 teaspoon sugar

TOFU AND BROCCOLI

1 pound firm tofu, cut in strips about ¼-inch-thick
    and 1½ to 2 inches long

1 generous bunch broccoli (about 1½ pounds)

½ cup Easy Vegetable Stock (page 63),
    Soy Sauce Bouillon (page 68), or water

2 tablespoons peanut or canola oil

1 tablespoon finely chopped or grated fresh ginger

1 bunch scallions (about 6), trimmed and sliced,
    white and green parts separated

Salt to taste

2 teaspoons arrowroot or
    cornstarch dissolved in 3 tablespoons water

1. Mix together the ingredients for the marinade. Toss with the tofu. Cover and refrigerate for 15 to 60 minutes, or even for several days. Toss the tofu from time to time to distribute the marinade evenly.

2. Trim the stems away from the broccoli and break the tops into small pieces (florets). Peel the stems, quarter lengthwise, then slice. Steam the broccoli for 3 to 4 minutes, until crisp-tender. Remove from the heat and rinse abundantly with cold water, or transfer to a bowl of ice-cold water, then drain. Set aside.

3. Transfer the tofu from the marinade to a small bowl. Mix 2 tablespoons of the marinade with the stock or water, and set aside.

4. Heat a wok or large, heavy nonstick skillet over high heat until a drop of water evaporates immediately upon contact. Add the oil, swirl it around, and turn the heat down to medium-high. Add the tofu. Cook, stirring and tossing, until the tofu is lightly browned, 3 to 8 minutes. Stir in the ginger and white part of the scallions, add a pinch of salt, and cook, stirring, for about 1 minute, until the ginger colors slightly and the scallions are just tender. Add the broccoli and the marinade/stock mixture, bring to a simmer, and stir together for a minute or two, until the broccoli is heated through and the stock simmering.

5. Give the arrowroot and water a stir and add to the pan. Cook, stirring, until the sauce glazes the tofu and broccoli, which will happen very quickly. Sprinkle on the green part of the scallions. Remove from the heat and serve at once, with rice or noodles. Pass soy sauce at the table for those who want extra.

Advance preparation: The marinade will keep for a week in the refrigerator, and the tofu can marinate in the marinade for a few days in the refrigerator. The broccoli, once steamed, will keep for 2 or 3 days in the refrigerator.

Reusing Marinades

Tofu marinades can be kept in the refrigerator for a week and reused with more tofu. Never reuse marinade if you have marinated poultry, fish, or meat in it.

stir-fried tofu with asparagus and mushrooms

This stir-fry is nice with noodles or rice. If you are serving it with noodles, cook the noodles ahead of time and stir them in with the vegetables and tofu just before serving. **MAKES 4 SERVINGS**

2 tablespoons soy sauce
1 teaspoon sugar
1 teaspoon dry sherry
12 ounces firm tofu, blotted dry and
    cut into 1- by ½-inch pieces
Salt to taste
1 pound asparagus,
    trimmed and cut into 1-inch pieces
½ pound mushrooms,
    trimmed and sliced
2 tablespoons canola or peanut oil
4 scallions, thinly sliced, white and green parts separated
1 tablespoon plus 1 teaspoon finely minced or grated fresh ginger
2 large garlic cloves, minced
2 teaspoons arrowroot or cornstarch dissolved in 2 tablespoons water
1 dried red chile, crumbled (optional)
2 tablespoons chopped cilantro

1. Combine the soy sauce, sugar, and sherry in a medium bowl and stir to dissolve the sugar. Toss with the tofu, cover, and refrigerate for anywhere from 15 minutes to several hours or overnight. Remove the tofu from the marinade and reserve the marinade.

2. Bring a large pot of water to a boil, add a tablespoon of salt and the asparagus. Cook for 2 minutes, drain, and rinse with cold water or transfer to a bowl of ice water, then drain. Set aside. If you are serving the dish with noodles, cook the noodles in the asparagus water, following the directions on page 200.

3. Heat a large, heavy nonstick skillet or wok over medium-high heat and add the mushrooms and a bit of salt. Stir until the mushrooms begin to release liquid. Add the oil, white part of the scallions, ginger, garlic, and chile. Stir together for about 30 seconds, until the aromatics are fragrant, then add the tofu. Cook, stirring, for about 3 minutes, until the tofu just begins to brown. Stir in the asparagus and the tofu marinade. Stir together for a minute or two, until the asparagus is crisp-tender. Give the dissolved arrowroot a stir and add to the pan, stirring, until the tofu and vegetables are glazed. Stir in the green part of the scallions and the cilantro. Remove from the heat and serve with rice or noodles.

Advance preparation: The tofu can marinate for a day. The marinade will keep for several days, even weeks, in the refrigerator. The asparagus can be blanched hours ahead of time.

stir-fried tofu and bok choy with chili sauce

Bok choy, a typical Asian green, has thick stems that add crunch and a clear, clean flavor to this spicy dish. Serve it with rice or other grains, or with noodles. **MAKES 4 TO 6 SERVINGS**

1 pound firm tofu
2 tablespoons peanut or canola oil
2 to 4 garlic cloves, minced
1 tablespoon finely chopped or grated fresh ginger
2 scallions, white and green parts separated, chopped
1 teaspoon Asian chili paste, such as sambal oelek
2 tablespoons soy sauce
2 pounds bok choy, stems sliced, leaves left whole
¼ teaspoon salt, or more to taste
½ cup Easy Vegetable Stock (page 63) or water
1 tablespoon arrowroot or cornstarch dissolved in 3 tablespoons water or stock

1. Drain the tofu and pat dry with paper towels. Cut into pieces ½ inch thick and 1 inch long.

2. Heat 1 tablespoon of the oil in a large, heavy nonstick skillet or wok over medium-high heat. Add the tofu in one layer. Cook until just colored, 2 to 4 minutes. Turn over and cook until the other side colors, 2 to 4 minutes, or stir-fry, tossing constantly for 3 to 8 minutes, until lightly colored. Carefully remove from the heat with a spatula and drain on paper towels.

3. Add the remaining 1 tablespoon oil to the pan, turn the heat to medium-high, and add the garlic, ginger, the white part of the scallions, and chili paste. Cook for 30 to 60 seconds, until the garlic and ginger begin to color. Add the browned tofu and soy sauce. Stir together for 1 minute. Add the bok choy and salt. Cook, stirring, for about 1 minute to coat the bok choy with the seasonings, and add the stock or water. Turn the heat to high and cook, stirring, for 2 to 3 minutes, until the bok choy stems are crisp-tender and the leaves are wilted. Give the dissolved arrowroot or cornstarch a stir and add to the pan. Stir until the sauce thickens and glazes the mixture.

4. Remove from the heat, sprinkle on the green part of the scallions, and serve.

stir-fried greens with tofu

Both tofu and greens have a particularly nice way of soaking up Asian flavors. Kale, Swiss chard (red or green), broccoli raab, spinach, and any Asian greens all work well here. Serve with rice, noodles, or other grains. **MAKES 4 SERVINGS**

2 tablespoons soy sauce
2 tablespoons chopped or
	grated fresh ginger
2 teaspoons sugar
½ pound firm tofu,
	cut into 1- by ½-inch pieces
Salt to taste
2 bunches greens (1½ to 2 pounds),
	stemmed and thoroughly cleaned
1 tablespoon canola oil
2 large garlic cloves, minced

1. Drain the tofu and pat dry with paper towels. Mix together the soy sauce, 1 tablespoon of the ginger, and the sugar. Stir to dissolve the sugar. Toss with the tofu in a bowl and set aside. Marinate for 15 minutes or longer. Refrigerate if you are not using it right away.

2. Bring a large pot of water to a boil, add 1 tablespoon of salt, and the greens. Blanch for 2 to 4 minutes, until tender to the bite. Transfer immediately to a bowl of ice water, then drain and squeeze out some of the water. Chop coarsely.

3. Heat the oil in a large, heavy nonstick skillet or wok over medium-high heat. Add the tofu, reserving the marinade, and cook, stirring, until lightly browned, 3 to 8 minutes. Add the garlic and remaining ginger and stir together for 30 seconds to 1 minute. Stir in the greens and stir-fry for another minute or two, until heated through and fragrant. Serve hot.

Advance preparation: The greens can be blanched and chopped a day ahead of time and refrigerated. The tofu can marinate for several hours in the refrigerator.

sweet-and-sour tofu and cabbage

Sweet-and-sour cabbage has been a favorite of mine ever since my first days of vegetarian cooking, before I knew anything about tofu. Tofu works itself into this recipe beautifully, providing enough protein for a substantial main dish. Serve with grains; consider millet or bulgur, as well as rice. **MAKES 4 SERVINGS**

1 pound firm tofu
Salt to taste
2 tablespoons peanut or canola oil
1 bunch scallions, white and green parts
    separated and thinly sliced
2 garlic cloves, minced
1 tablespoon chopped fresh ginger
1 tablespoon soy sauce, or more to taste
½ medium Napa cabbage,
    cored and coarsely chopped (about 10 cups)
1 cup chopped peeled fresh or canned tomatoes
¼ cup unseasoned rice wine vinegar
2 tablespoons light brown sugar
Pinch of cayenne (optional)
1 tablespoon cornstarch or
    arrowroot dissolved in ¼ cup water

1. Drain the tofu and cut into slabs about ½ inch thick. Bring 8 cups water to a simmer in a large saucepan, add about ¼ teaspoon salt, and the tofu. Simmer for 3 to 4 minutes, drain, and transfer to a bowl of cold water. Drain and blot the tofu dry, then cut the slabs into slices, ¼ to ½ inch thick. Blot dry again.

2. Heat the oil in a large heavy nonstick skillet or wok over medium-high heat. Add the tofu in one layer, if possible. When it begins to color, after a minute or two, flip it over and cook on the other side until it begins to color; or stir-fry, stirring constantly, for 3 to 8 minutes. Add the white part of the scallions, the garlic, and ginger. Cook, stirring, for 1 minute, until the aromatics are fragrant and slightly colored. Add the soy sauce. Stir together well so that the soy sauce seasons the tofu.

3. Add the cabbage and stir-fry for a couple of minutes, until the cabbage begins to wilt. Add the tomatoes, vinegar, and sugar and cook, stirring often, for 5 to 10 minutes, until the tomatoes have cooked down a bit and the cabbage has wilted. Taste and add salt and cayenne, if desired. Give the cornstarch or arrowroot a stir, and add it to the pan. Cook, stirring, until the sauce thickens and glazes the mixture (this should happen quickly).

4. Remove from the heat, sprinkle on the green part of the scallions, and serve.

Advance preparation: The tofu can be simmered days ahead of time and kept in water in the refrigerator.

tofu and red chard hot pot

Red chard was the inspiration for this wonderful spicy stew. It adds a red hue to the broth, and the stems contribute texture and crunch to the mixture. The hot pot makes a hearty meal when served over buckwheat noodles or somen; it can also be served with rice or other grains. **MAKES 4 SERVINGS**

1 ounce dried shiitake mushrooms (about 7)
3 tablespoons soy sauce
Salt to taste
2 teaspoons sugar
2 tablespoons dry sherry or rice wine
2 tablespoons canola or peanut oil
1 pound firm, regular, or silken tofu, sliced
1 red or yellow onion, thinly sliced
1 large red bell pepper,
    cut into thin 2-inch-long strips
2 to 4 garlic cloves, minced
1 tablespoon chopped fresh ginger
2 teaspoons Asian chili paste,
    or more to taste
1 large bunch red chard or 2 smaller bunches
    (about 1½ pounds; more is fine),
    stems trimmed and chopped,
    leaves washed and chopped

1. Put the mushrooms in a bowl and pour in 3 cups boiling water. Let the mushrooms sit for 15 to 30 minutes, until softened, while you prepare the other ingredients.

2. Remove the mushrooms and squeeze out any liquid over the bowl. Strain the liquid and add water to measure 3 cups. Add 1 tablespoon of the soy sauce and salt to taste. Remove and discard the stems from the mushrooms, and slice the caps about ¼ inch thick. Set the mushrooms and stock aside.

3. Stir together the remaining 2 tablespoons soy sauce, sugar, and sherry. Make sure all the sugar has dissolved; set aside.

4. Heat 1 tablespoon of the oil in a large heavy nonstick skillet or wok over medium-high heat. Add the tofu and cook, shaking the pan or flipping the tofu with a spatula, until golden on both sides, 2 to 4 minutes per side. Or stir-fry, stirring for 3 to 8 minutes. Remove from the heat and drain on paper towels. Add the remaining 1 tablespoon oil and cook the onion and red pepper until tender, stirring, about 5 minutes. Add the garlic, ginger, and chili paste and stir together for a minute, until fragrant. Add the sliced mushrooms and chard stalks and stir-fry for about 3 minutes. Stir the soy sauce/sherry mixture and add, along with the tofu. Cook, stirring, for another minute. Add the soaking liquid from the mushrooms. Bring to a simmer and simmer for 10 minutes.

5. Add the chard and simmer for 3 to 5 minutes, until the chard is wilted and tender, but still bright. Taste and adjust the seasoning, adding salt as desired. Serve in wide soup bowls over Asian noodles or white or brown rice.

Advance preparation: The hot pot can be prepared through step 2 hours ahead of serving. Bring back to a simmer and add the chard shortly before serving (otherwise it loses its bright color). Cook the grains or noodles before adding the chard.

tempeh and shredded vegetable salad

Tempeh has an almost meaty texture and a strong flavor. This is like a vegetarian version of a chicken salad, though tempeh has a more pronounced flavor than chicken. The technique of simmering the tempeh in a strong soy-sauce broth is adapted from a recipe in Deborah Madison's *Vegetarian Cooking for Everyone*. **MAKES 4 MAIN-COURSE SERVINGS, 6 TO 8 STARTER SERVINGS OR SIDE-DISH SERVINGS**

TEMPEH

¼ cup soy sauce
2 garlic cloves, minced
2 slices fresh ginger
½ pound tempeh, cut into 4 pieces
1 tablespoon canola oil

SALAD

1 large carrot, peeled and grated
1 small cucumber or ½ European cucumber,
*   cut into matchsticks*
1 small red or yellow bell pepper,
*   cut into thin slivers*
1 Romaine lettuce heart (the inner leaves),
*   cut into chiffonade (see page 37; about 4 cups)*
⅓ cup chopped fresh cilantro
1 tablespoon toasted sesame seeds (see page 17)

DRESSING

1 tablespoon fresh lime juice
2 tablespoons rice wine vinegar (plain or seasoned)
1 tablespoon soy sauce
½ teaspoon sugar
1 small garlic clove, minced
½ teaspoon Asian chili paste
¼ cup plain nonfat yogurt
2 tablespoons Asian sesame oil

1. To make the tempeh, combine the soy sauce, ¼ cup water, garlic, and ginger in a small skillet just large enough to accommodate the tempeh. Cut the tempeh into 1-inch squares and place in the pan in a single layer. Bring the liquid to a boil, reduce the heat to low, cover, and simmer for 8 minutes. Turn the tempeh over (tongs are easiest for this), cover the pan, and simmer for another 8 minutes, or until all of the liquid in the pan is absorbed. Transfer the tempeh to a plate and rinse and dry the pan.

2. Heat the canola oil in the pan over medium-high heat and add the tempeh in one layer. Cook until brown on one side, about 2 minutes, and turn over. Brown on the other side for 2 minutes and remove from the heat.

3. Combine the salad ingredients. Slice the tempeh squares ¼ inch thick and add to the salad.

4. Mix together the ingredients for the dressing, toss with the salad, and serve.

Advance preparation: All of the ingredients for this salad can be prepared hours ahead of time. The simmered or simmered and fried tempeh will keep for a few days in the refrigerator.

Desserts

Desserts are special, not just because they're sweet, but because we usually make them only when we're having company to dinner, or when we have a surfeit of a particular fresh fruit. With the exception of the occasional chocolate cake (page 310), my desserts are fruit-based treats—crumbles and cobblers, tarts and galettes, clafoutis, sorbets, compotes—inspired by in-season fruit from local farmers' markets.

The farmers' market movement, which has become so widespread in the United States, allows me to experience the same kind of excitement I used to feel when I lived in France and shopped at open-air markets. What a thrill when the peaches and apricots arrive in July, the figs in August, and the pears in the fall. No matter where you live in the United States, you will find farmers' markets and roadside stands that sell in-season fruit that is ready, or near ready, to eat.

Local fruit has its time; cherries come in June in California, July in Washington and

Michigan. Peaches are a midsummer fruit on the East Coast, but they are still available in late September where I live. Almost everywhere, apples mean fall with the exception of a few specific varieties, like the Northern California Gravenstein, which is ready in July and August.

In my home, for daily dining we eat unadorned fresh fruit in season after a meal if we want something sweet. And sometimes, when the melons or strawberries are so luscious, the pears so juicy that they couldn't be improved upon, I pass a platter of fruit to guests for dessert. I might offer a plate of cookies to accompany the fruit.

But you don't have to cook to make dessert. A bowl of cut-up fruits in their own juices, tossed with mint, spices, or liqueur, can be as welcome and beautiful as a tart. Here are some combinations that I like:

Oranges and pomegranate • Oranges or blood oranges and strawberries (quarter the strawberries) • Mixed citrus and dates • Oranges and mint • Strawberries in fresh orange juice, with mint • Strawberries doused with lemon or lime and a little sugar, garnished with mint • Pineapple and mint; pineapple, strawberries, and mint • Mangoes and berries (strawberries, blueberries, or raspberries) • Stone fruit (apricots, peaches, nectarines, plums) and berries (strawberries, raspberries, blackberries, blueberries) • Papayas and blueberries • Pears and currants • Melon and berries • Watermelon and mint • Mixed melon balls and mint

Ripe, in-season fruit can stand on its own, or it can be further enhanced by the addition of flavorful ingredients. A little lime or lemon juice and sugar will bring out and further sweeten the juices of strawberries, melons, mangoes, peaches, and papayas, to name just a few. Mint will perk up a bowl of melon balls or pineapple wedges, orange slices, or kiwi. Other ingredients that add a dimension to fruit are liqueurs like Grand Marnier, Cointreau, Triple Sec, and Kirsch, and vanilla and almond extracts.

ENHANCERS AND THE FRUIT THEY COMPLEMENT

Fresh lime juice and a small amount of sugar: With strawberries, melons, mangoes, papayas • Fresh lemon juice and a small amount of sugar: With peaches, nectarines, strawberries, apricots, pears, apples • MINT: With berries, melons, oranges, tangerines, pineapple, mangoes, kiwis • ORANGE LIQUEUR (Grand Marnier, Cointreau, Triple Sec): With citrus fruits, strawberries • KIRSCH: With cherries, pears, plums • VANILLA EXTRACT: With plums, peaches, apricots, apples, pears • ALMOND EXTRACT: With apricots, peaches • ALMOND ESSENCE: With apricots, peaches

apple clafouti

A clafouti is a cross between a fruit-filled flan and a pancake. When made in a fluted ceramic tart pan, it looks like a fancy dessert, with the panache of a tart, but without the hassle of making a crust. This batter, which includes plain nonfat yogurt, is not the traditional batter used in France, which would be made with cream or, at least, whole milk. You need to use slightly tart apples that don't fall apart when cooked; Braeburns, Galas, and Granny Smiths work well. I urge you to use vanilla beans for this; it's a splurge, but the little flecks look and taste delicious. **MAKES 8 SERVINGS**

Juice of ½ lemon
2 pounds apples, such as Braeburn,
*   Granny Smith, or Gala*
2 tablespoons unsalted butter
2 tablespoons light brown sugar
½ teaspoon ground cinnamon
3 tablespoons Calvados
3 large eggs
1 vanilla bean or
*   ½ teaspoon pure vanilla extract*
6 tablespoons granulated sugar
Pinch of salt
⅔ cup sifted unbleached all-purpose flour
½ cup plain nonfat yogurt
¾ cup low-fat milk
About 2 teaspoons confectioners' sugar

1. Preheat the oven to 375°F. Butter a 10- or 10½-inch ceramic tart pan or clafouti dish.

2. Fill a bowl with water and add the lemon juice. Drop the apples into the water as you peel, core, and slice them, to prevent them from discoloring.

3. Heat the butter in a large heavy nonstick skillet over medium heat. Drain the apples and add to the skillet. Cook, stirring, until they begin to look translucent, about 5 minutes. Add the brown sugar, cinnamon, and 2 tablespoons of the Calvados. Stir together for another couple of minutes, until the apples have softened slightly. Remove from the heat and transfer to the buttered baking dish. Spread over the dish in an even layer.

4. Beat the eggs with the seeds from the vanilla bean or the vanilla extract in the bowl of an electric mixer, or with a whisk, until smooth. Add the granulated sugar and the salt and beat together. Slowly beat in the flour. Add the remaining 1 tablespoon Calvados, the yogurt, and the milk. Mix together well. (You can also blend all the ingredients at high speed in a blender.) Pour over the apples in the baking dish.

5. Bake for 30 to 45 minutes, until the top is browned and the clafouti is firm and slightly puffed. Press gently on the top in the middle to see if it's firm. If it isn't, return to the oven for 2 to 5 minutes.

6. Remove from the oven and cool on a rack. Put the confectioners' sugar in a strainer and tap over the clafouti to dust. Serve warm or at room temperature.

Advance preparation: The dish will hold for several hours at room temperature. Leftovers are good.

dessert galette pastry

This yeasted pastry rolls out easily and is perfect for free-form tarts, also called galettes. These are much easier than tarts—no fiddling with pans, edges, and prebaking. The dough is rolled out like a pizza, topped with bread crumbs (sometimes) and fruit (the bread crumbs absorb liquid as the fruit cooks), then the edges are folded over the fruit. **MAKES ENOUGH FOR TWO 10-INCH GALETTES**

1½ teaspoons active dry yeast
2 tablespoons plus ¼ teaspoon sugar
1 large egg, at room temperature
2 to 2½ cups unbleached all-purpose flour
½ teaspoon salt
4 tablespoons unsalted butter, softened

1. Dissolve the yeast in ½ cup lukewarm water, add ¼ teaspoon of the sugar, and let sit for 5 to 10 minutes, until creamy. Beat in the egg.

2. Combine 2 cups of the flour, the remaining 2 tablespoons sugar, and the salt. Stir 1 cup into the yeast mixture. Add the butter and stir in. (This can be done in an electric mixer; combine the ingredients using the paddle, then switch to the kneading hook; or mix in the food processor fitted with the steel blade, using the pulse action.) Add the remaining 1 cup of the flour mixture. Work the dough until it comes together in a coherent mass, adding flour as necessary if it is very moist and sticky. Then turn out onto a lightly floured surface. Knead, adding flour as necessary, just until the dough is smooth, and shape the dough into a ball. Do not overwork. Place in a lightly oiled or buttered bowl, rounded side down first, then rounded side up, cover the bowl tightly with plastic wrap, and let it rise in a warm spot for 1 hour or until doubled.

3. When the pastry has risen and softened, punch it down gently and shape into a ball. Cut into two equal pieces and shape each piece into a ball. Cover loosely with plastic wrap and let rest for 10 minutes.

4. Butter two baking sheets. Roll out each piece of dough on a lightly floured surface to a thin circle (about ⅛ inch thick), 14 to 15 inches in diameter, dusting each side of the dough with flour so that it doesn't stick to your rolling pin or the table. Transfer to the baking sheets.

the best vegetarian recipes

5. Top as instructed with fruit, leaving a 2-inch lip all the way around. Fold the edge over the fruit, draping it in folds all the way around. Bake as directed.

Advance preparation: This dough will keep for several months in the freezer. You can freeze the dough before rolling; allow to thaw, then roll out. You can also keep the dough, before rolling out, in the refrigerator for a day. You will need to dust it generously with flour when you roll it out at room temperature.

free-form apple tart
(apple galette)

This marvelous apple galette reminds me somewhat of the rustic—and richer—apple tarts from the Poilâne bakery that I used to enjoy when I lived in Paris. **MAKES 8 SERVINGS**

½ recipe Dessert Galette Pastry (page 286)
Juice of ½ lemon
2 pounds slightly tart apples, such as Pink Ladies or Galas
2 tablespoons unsalted butter
½ teaspoon ground cinnamon
¼ teaspoon freshly grated nutmeg
¼ cup dark brown sugar

1. Preheat the oven to 425°F. Lightly butter a pizza pan or baking sheet.

2. Fill a bowl with water and add the lemon juice. Drop the apples into the bowl as you peel, core, and slice them, to prevent them from turning brown. When they are all sliced, drain.

3. Heat the butter over medium heat in a large, heavy nonstick skillet. Add the apples and cook, stirring, until they are slightly softened, 5 to 10 minutes. Add the cinnamon, nutmeg, and brown sugar and stir together, then remove from the heat.

4. Roll out the dough to a large, thin circle, about 14 to 15 inches in diameter. Transfer it to the baking sheet or pizza pan. Spread the apples over the dough, leaving a 2-inch border. Fold the edges of the dough in over the apples, pleating as you go around, to make a free-form tart. The apples will be enclosed by the dough at the edges of the tart but not in the middle.

5. Bake for 15 minutes. Turn the heat down to 375°F and continue to bake for another 15 minutes, or until the crust is nicely browned. Remove from the oven and allow to cool slightly or completely before serving.

Advance preparation: The crust can be made in advance and frozen, either before or after rolling out. The apple mixture can be prepared hours ahead of time. The baked tart will hold for several hours, but eventually the crust will become soggy on the bottom.

baked apples with ginger and raisins

Ginger, lemon, and a little brown sugar provide a sweet and pungent background for these baked apples. The apple juice in the pan reduces as the apples bake, providing a luscious syrup to spoon over the apples. I like to use slightly tart apples that begin to fall apart at the end of baking; Gravensteins fit that description perfectly. Braeburns and Granny Smiths are also good.

MAKES 4 SERVINGS

4 tart, firm apples
½ lemon
4 teaspoons golden raisins or currants
1 tablespoon dark or light brown sugar
½ teaspoon ground ginger
Zest of 1 lemon, half of it finely chopped, the rest in strips
½ cup apple juice
Plain nonfat yogurt, cream, or vanilla ice cream (optional)

1. Preheat the oven to 350°F.

2. Peel the top quarter of the apples. Core by cutting a cone out of the stem end, using either a paring knife or the tip of your peeler. Rub the peeled parts with the cut lemon half. Place the apples in a small baking dish, and fill the cones with the raisins. Mix together the brown sugar, ginger, and the finely chopped lemon zest. Sprinkle over the top of each apple. Pour the apple juice over the apples and into the dish, and add the remaining lemon zest to the apple juice in the dish. Cover with aluminum foil or a lid.

3. Bake for 30 to 40 minutes, until the apples are tender. Remove the foil or lid, spoon some of the juice over the apples, and continue to bake for another 5 to 10 minutes, until the sugar has dissolved.

4. Serve warm or at room temperature, with some of the juice spooned over the apples. Top with yogurt or ice cream or drizzle with cream, if desired.

Advance preparation: These can be baked several hours ahead and served at room temperature, or reheated for 15 minutes in a medium (325° to 350°F) oven.

apricot clafouti

This is a beautiful summer clafouti. Make sure your apricots are not overripe, or they'll fall apart during baking and all the batter will end up on the top. **MAKES 8 SERVINGS**

1½ pounds firm but ripe apricots, cut in half if small,
  quartered if large, and pitted
2 tablespoons peach or apricot brandy
1 tablespoon fresh lemon juice
6 tablespoons granulated sugar
3 large eggs
1 vanilla bean or ½ teaspoon pure vanilla extract
Pinch of salt
⅔ cup sifted unbleached all-purpose flour
¾ cup low-fat milk
½ cup plain nonfat yogurt
About 2 teaspoons confectioners' sugar

1. Toss the apricots with the brandy, lemon juice, and 2 tablespoons of the sugar in a bowl. Let sit for 30 minutes.

2. Preheat the oven to 375°F. Butter a 10- or 10½-inch ceramic tart pan or clafouti dish.

3. Beat the eggs with the seeds from the vanilla bean or the vanilla extract in the bowl of an electric mixer, or with a whisk, until smooth. Drain the liquid from the apricots into the eggs, and add the remaining 4 tablespoons granulated sugar and the salt. Beat together. Slowly beat in the flour, then the milk and yogurt. Mix together well.

4. Arrange the apricots in the tart pan, rounded side up. Pour in the batter.

5. Bake for 30 to 45 minutes, or until the top is browned and the clafouti is firm and puffed. Press gently on the top in the middle to see if it's firm. If it isn't, return to the oven for 2 to 5 minutes.

6. Remove from the oven and cool on a rack. Put the confectioners' sugar in a strainer and tap over the clafouti to dust. Serve warm or at room temperature.

Advance preparation: The dish will hold for several hours at room temperature.

cherry cobbler with cornmeal topping

Cobblers—fruit baked under a sweet biscuit crust—are very comforting American desserts. Cornmeal contributes crunch, a rich flavor, and golden hue to the topping here. This is a terrific way to use up a batch of cherries that are a little less than sweet (though of course, the sweeter the better); they'll sweeten up as they bake. **MAKES 6 TO 8 SERVINGS**

FRUIT

6 cups cherries (about 2½ pounds),
*   stemmed and pitted*
2 tablespoons Kirsch (cherry eau-de-vie)
3 tablespoons sugar
1 tablespoon fresh lemon juice
2 tablespoons sifted unbleached all-purpose flour

TOPPING

½ cup stone-ground cornmeal
1 cup unbleached all-purpose flour
2 teaspoons baking powder
½ teaspoon baking soda
1 tablespoon sugar
½ teaspoon salt
5 tablespoons cold unsalted butter,
*   cut into pieces*
⅔ cup plain nonfat yogurt
2 tablespoons mild honey,
*   such as clover or acacia*
Plain low-fat yogurt, whipped cream,
*   or vanilla ice cream (optional)*

1. Preheat the oven to 375°F. Butter a 2-quart gratin or baking dish.

2. To prepare the fruit, toss the cherries with the Kirsch, sugar, lemon juice, and flour in a bowl.

3. To prepare the topping, sift together the cornmeal, flour, baking powder, baking soda, sugar, and salt. Transfer to the bowl of a food processor, if using, and pulse a few times to amalgamate the ingredients. Cut in the butter, pulsing with the food processor or mixing with forks, until the mixture has a coarse mealy texture. Add the yogurt and honey and process or stir just until the mixture is homogeneous.

4. Stir the cherries and transfer them to the buttered baking dish. Scrape all the liquid in the bowl in with the cherries. Spoon heaped tablespoons of the topping mixture over the cherries. They should be just about covered, although there may be some small spaces between the dollops of batter; lightly moisten your fingertips and spread the topping if there are big spots where the fruit isn't covered. Place the baking dish on a baking sheet so that if the fruit bubbles over, the juices won't run over onto your stove.

5. Bake for 30 to 35 minutes, or until the fruit is bubbling and the top is golden brown.

6. Remove from the heat and cool on a rack until warm. Serve warm, with yogurt, whipped cream, or vanilla ice cream, if you wish.

Advance preparation: This can be made a few hours ahead, but it is best served warm. You can warm it for 15 to 20 minutes in a 250° to 300°F oven.

citrus and date gratin

This amazing winter gratin is based on a recipe in my book *Feasts & Fêtes*. It is a lightened version with a couple of other changes. I hadn't made it in a long time when I began testing it for this book, and now it is a standard dinner party dessert in my home, particularly during the winter. **MAKES 6 TO 8 SERVINGS**

> 6 navel oranges
> 3 pink grapefruit
> 1 vanilla bean, cut in half,
>   or 1 teaspoon pure vanilla extract
> 2 tablespoons mild honey,
>   such as clover or acacia
> 12 dates, the fresher the better,
>   pitted and quartered lengthwise
> 4 egg yolks
> ⅓ cup sugar
> 2 tablespoons rum or Grand Marnier
> ⅓ cup regular or lowfat sour cream

1. Squeeze the juice from one of the oranges and one of the grapefruit. Scrape in the seeds from the vanilla bean, if using, and set aside.

2. Peel the remaining oranges and grapefruit and cut away the white pith. Cut the ends off, then hold the fruit above a bowl, and cut wide strips from top to bottom, cutting away the pith as you go. Divide the fruit into sections and toss together in the bowl with the honey and the dates. Transfer to a 2-quart gratin dish or baking dish.

3. Combine the vanilla bean pod, if using, with the juice in a heavy 2-quart saucepan and bring to a simmer. Remove the pod.

4. Meanwhile, beat together the eggs yolks and sugar until thick and lemon colored. You can do this in a food processor fitted with the steel blade. Make sure that the juice isn't boiling, and slowly whisk into the egg yolks or, if using a food processor, slowly pour in the juice with the machine running. Return the mixture to the saucepan and place over medium heat. Heat through, stirring constantly with a wooden spoon, until the custard thickens and coats the spoon like thick cream. Make sure that it does not boil, or the mixture will curdle. It will begin to thicken when you see wisps of steam coming off the surface. When the custard is thick, remove from the heat and stir in the rum and the vanilla extract, if using. Stir for a minute and set aside.

5. About 15 minutes before serving, preheat the broiler with the rack at the highest setting. Whisk the sour cream into the custard sauce. Give the citrus mixture a stir and pour on the sauce. Place under the broiler for 3 to 6 minutes, until the top begins to brown. Remove from the heat and serve.

Advance preparation: The custard sauce will hold for a day in the refrigerator in a covered bowl. The fruit can be prepared several hours ahead of time. Assemble just before broiling.

in half, then lift it onto the pan and unfold it. Ease it into the corners of the pan, without stretching the dough or working it, as this causes shrinkage during baking. Pinch an attractive lip around the edge of the dough. Cover with plastic wrap and refrigerate for 2 hours, or for up to 3 days, or freeze for up to 3 months.

4. FOR A PARTIALLY BAKED CRUST

Preheat the oven to 375°F. Line the dough with foil, shiny side up. Ease the foil into the corners to prevent the pastry from shrinking and cover the edges. Put about ¼ cup dried beans or rice on top of the foil to weight the dough and bake for 20 minutes. Remove from the heat and remove the foil.

FOR A FULLY BAKED CRUST

Partially bake the crust as above. Cut the foil that was covering the edges so that you now have just a collar, and re-cover the edges of the dough loosely. Return to the oven for another 10 minutes, until golden.

peach cobbler with raspberries

This cobbler is delicious even when the peaches are less than excellent. They get sweeter as they bake, and the raspberries add a nice acidic touch and beautiful color. **MAKES 6 GENEROUS SERVINGS**

FRUIT

2½ pounds peaches, pitted and sliced (6 cups)
2 tablespoons mild-flavored honey,
    such as clover or acacia
2 tablespoons fresh lemon juice
½ teaspoon ground cinnamon
1 to 2 tablespoons peach brandy
2 tablespoons sifted unbleached all-purpose flour
1 cup raspberries

TOPPING

½ cup stone-ground cornmeal
1 cup unbleached all-purpose flour
2 teaspoons baking powder
½ teaspoon baking soda
1 tablespoon sugar
½ teaspoon salt
4 tablespoons cold unsalted butter,
    cut into pieces
⅔ cup plain nonfat yogurt
2 tablespoons mild-flavored honey,
    such as clover or acacia

1. Preheat the oven to 375 °F. Butter a 2-quart gratin or baking dish.

2. To prepare the fruit, toss the peaches in a bowl with the honey, lemon juice, cinnamon, brandy, and the 2 tablespoons flour.

3. To make the topping, sift together the cornmeal, flour, baking powder, baking soda, sugar, and salt. Transfer to the bowl of your food processor fitted with the steel blade, if using, and pulse a few times to amalgamate the ingredients. Cut in the butter, pulsing with the food processor or mixing with forks, until the mixture has a coarse mealy texture. Add the yogurt and honey and process or stir just until the mixture is homogeneous.

4. Stir the raspberries into the peaches and transfer the fruit to the buttered baking dish. Scrape all the liquid in the bowl in with the peaches. Spoon heaped tablespoons of the topping mixture over the peaches. They should be just about covered, although there may be some small spaces between the dollops of batter; lightly moisten your fingertips and spread the topping if there are big spots where the fruit isn't covered. Place the baking dish on a baking sheet so that if the fruit bubbles over the juices won't run over onto your stove.

5. Bake for 30 to 35 minutes, until the fruit is bubbling and the top is golden brown.

6. Remove from the oven and cool until warm on a rack. Serve warm.

Advance preparation: This can be made a few hours ahead, but it is best served warm. You can warm it for 15 to 20 minutes in a 250° to 300°F oven.

lemon tart

I happen to have a Meyer lemon tree, so I make this tart a lot in the spring (to my husband's utter delight), when my lemons come in. It's great made with regular lemons as well. The filling isn't too sweet and not at all rich; it contrasts beautifully with the pastry. The recipe is incredibly easy. The only fuss is prebaking the pastry. **MAKES 8 SERVINGS**

1 recipe Dessert Pastry, fully baked and cooled (page 296)
⅔ cup fresh lemon juice, strained
½ cup sugar
2 tablespoons yogurt, Yogurt Cheese (page 8), or crème fraîche
4 large eggs

1. Preheat the oven to 375°F.

2. Whisk together the lemon juice and sugar. When the sugar has dissolved, whisk in the yogurt or crème fraîche. Whisk in the eggs, one at a time. Pour into the crust. Place a foil collar on the crust.

3. Bake for 25 to 30 minutes, until set and shiny. Remove from the oven and cool on a rack. Serve at room temperature.

Advance preparation: This can be made several hours ahead of serving.

free-form peach tart (peach galette)

This luscious summer tart is as easy as, well, pie. Easier in fact, because the yeasted galette pastry is so easy to handle. The peaches will release a lot of juice. I always fear that it will make the dough completely soggy, but somehow the dough stands up. However, if you have some plain fresh bread crumbs on hand, spread them underneath the peaches to absorb some of the liquid (this hint comes from Deborah Madison's *Vegetarian Cooking for Everyone*). One guest who ate this tart commented that it was like a "peach calzone." **MAKES 8 SERVINGS**

½ recipe Dessert Galette Pastry (page 286)
2 pounds ripe but firm peaches,
    pitted and sliced (peeling is optional)
2 tablespoons plain fresh bread crumbs (optional)
2 tablespoons sugar

1. Preheat the oven to 425°F. Lightly butter a pizza pan or baking sheet.

2. Roll out the dough to a thin circle, 14 to 15 inches in diameter. Transfer it to the pan. If you are using the bread crumbs, sprinkle them over the dough, leaving a border about 2 inches wide. Spread the peaches over the dough, leaving the same border. I usually just pile them on and spread them out, not worrying about a pattern. Fold the edges of the dough in over the peaches, pleating as you go around. The peaches will be enclosed by the dough at the edges of the tart but not in the middle. Sprinkle the sugar over the peaches and the dough.

3. Bake for 15 minutes. Turn the heat down to 375°F and continue to bake for another 15 to 25 minutes, until the crust is nicely browned.

4. Remove from the oven and allow to cool slightly or completely before serving.

Advance preparation: The crust can be made in advance and frozen, either before or after rolling out. The peaches can be prepared hours ahead of time. The baked tart will hold for several hours but eventually the crust will become soggy.

summer stone fruit crumble

Crumbles are definitely my weakness. They're such an easy dessert to assemble, and they're universally popular. **MAKES 6 TO 8 SERVINGS**

FILLING
3 pounds mixed peaches, plums,
*   and nectarines, pitted and sliced*
¼ cup granulated sugar or
*   3 tablespoons mild-flavored honey,*
*   such as clover or acacia*
2 tablespoons fresh lemon juice
1 teaspoon finely chopped orange zest
½ teaspoon pure vanilla extract

TOPPING
¼ cup shelled pecans
¾ cup rolled oats
½ cup unbleached all-purpose flour
¼ cup firmly packed light brown sugar or
*   unrefined turbinado sugar*
¼ teaspoon salt
¼ teaspoon freshly grated nutmeg
1 teaspoon finely minced orange zest
6 tablespoons cold unsalted butter,
*   cut into small pieces*
Sweetened plain yogurt, vanilla ice cream,
*   or whipped cream*

1. Preheat the oven to 375°F. Butter a 2½- or 3-quart baking dish or gratin dish.

2. Toss together all the ingredients for the filling and turn into the prepared dish.

3. Make the topping. Heat the pecans in a dry skillet over medium heat, shaking it or stirring the pecans constantly, until they begin to smell toasty after a few minutes. Remove from the skillet at once and chop coarsely. Mix together the oats, flour, brown sugar, salt, nutmeg, and orange zest, in a bowl or in a food processor fitted with the steel blade. Cut in the butter using the pulse action of the food processor, or by taking up the mixture in handfuls and rubbing it briskly between your fingers and thumbs. The mixture should have a crumbly consistency. Stir in the pecans. Spoon the crumble topping over the fruit in an even layer.

4. Bake until browned, 40 to 45 minutes. If you wish, finish very briefly under the broiler, being careful not to burn it.

5. Serve warm or at room temperature, with sweetened yogurt, vanilla ice cream, or whipped cream, if desired.

Advance preparation: This can be baked a few hours ahead, but it's best if not baked too far in advance, to ensure a crisp topping.

peach sorbet with raspberry garnish

This is a beautiful, easy sorbet. If you have an ice-cream scoop, pile scoops into a big bowl or individual bowls and add the raspberries, for a lovely presentation. **MAKES 8 SERVINGS**

2 pounds fresh ripe peaches
¼ teaspoon pure almond extract
¼ cup fresh lemon juice
½ cup plus 2 teaspoons sugar
1 pint raspberries

1. Peel the peaches by dropping them into a pot of boiling water for 30 seconds, then transferring to a bowl of ice-cold water. Pull away the skin. It should come away easily unless the peaches are unripe. Pit and transfer to a food processor fitted with the steel blade. Add the almond extract and lemon juice. Process to a smooth puree and transfer to a bowl.

2. Combine ½ cup of the sugar with 1 cup water in a saucepan and bring to a boil. Reduce the heat and simmer until the sugar melts. Remove from the heat and allow to cool slightly. Whisk into the peach puree. Transfer to a baking dish or ice-cube trays, cover, and freeze the mixture, or freeze in an ice-cream maker following the manufacturer's instructions.

3. When the mixture is frozen solid, remove from the freezer and blend the mixture, in batches, in a food processor fitted with the steel blade, until smooth. This will take a lot of starting and stopping, and scraping the sides of the bowl. Puree until the mixture looks creamy. Transfer each batch to clean serving dishes or a freezer container and place them immediately in the freezer to prevent melting. Cover each dish with plastic wrap, then foil, or secure the plastic wrap with rubber bands, and freeze until shortly before serving.

4. About 15 minutes before serving, place the sorbet in the refrigerator. Meanwhile, toss together the raspberries with the remaining 2 teaspoons superfine sugar.

5. Serve the sorbet, topping each bowl with a spoonful of raspberries. Another way to present this is to scoop balls into a bowl with an ice-cream scoop, and toss the raspberries on top. Bring to the table and serve two or three balls per serving.

pear-vanilla compote

The syrup is reason alone to make this delicious compote of poached pears. I use very little sugar, but the vanilla bean sweetens and perfumes the liquid, making it a perfect medium for the pears. The poached pears give up some of their flavor into the syrup, so spoon plenty of it over the pears with each serving. **MAKES 4 SERVINGS**

1 cup dry or fruity white wine
⅓ cup sugar
1 cup water
1 vanilla bean, split in half
4 ripe but firm pears
Vanilla ice cream, sweetened plain nonfat yogurt, or Yogurt Cheese
(page 8) (optional)

1. Combine the wine, sugar, 1 cup water, and vanilla bean and bring to a boil. Reduce the heat to low and simmer until slightly reduced, 5 to 10 minutes.

2. Working with one piece of fruit at a time, peel the pears, quarter, and core them. Cut each quarter lengthwise into two slices and add then directly to the syrup. Simmer for 10 minutes.

3. Remove from the heat. Remove the vanilla bean. Serve warm or cold, with ice cream or yogurt, if desired.

Advance preparation: This keeps well in the refrigerator for a couple of days. The syrup will keep for months in the refrigerator.

plum and nectarine compote

This is inspired by a recipe in *Classic Home Desserts* by the late Richard Sax. It's a simple compote of summer stone fruits in a vanilla-flavored wine syrup. You can add a bit of color to the compote by garnishing each serving with raspberries. **MAKES 4 TO 6 SERVINGS**

1½ pounds firm but ripe plums,
pitted and quartered
1½ pounds firm but ripe nectarines,
pitted and sliced into six wedges
2 tablespoons mild-flavored honey,
such as clover or acacia
1 tablespoon fresh lemon juice
⅔ cup dry or fruity white wine
⅓ cup sugar
½ vanilla bean, split in half
½ to 1 cup raspberries (optional)
Vanilla ice cream, plain nonfat yogurt, or
Yogurt Cheese (page 8), if desired

1. Toss the plums and nectarines with the honey and lemon juice and let it sit while you make the syrup.

2. Combine the wine, sugar, ⅔ cup water, and vanilla bean and bring to a boil. Reduce the heat to low and simmer until slightly reduced, 5 to 10 minutes.

3. Pour the syrup over the fruit, stir gently a few times, and let it stand for at least 30 minutes.

4. Remove the vanilla bean and stir in the raspberries, if using. Serve warm or cold, with ice cream or yogurt, if desired.

Advance preparation: This keeps well in the refrigerator for a couple of days.

free-form plum tart (plum galette)

Plums make another great filling for galette pastry. I've always been particularly fond of plum tarts, and this is a twist on that theme. **MAKES 8 SERVINGS**

½ recipe Dessert Galette Pastry (page 286)
2 pounds plums, pitted and sliced
2 tablespoons mild-flavored honey,
   such as clover or acacia
2 teaspoons finely minced orange zest
2 tablespoons plain fresh bread crumbs
1 tablespoon sugar

1. Preheat the oven to 425°F. Lightly butter a pizza pan or baking sheet.

2. Toss the plums with the honey and orange zest in a bowl.

3. Roll out the dough to a thin circle, 14 to 15 inches in diameter. Transfer it to the pan. If you are using the bread crumbs, sprinkle them over the dough, leaving a border about 2 inches wide. Spread the plums over the dough, leaving the same border. Fold the edges of the dough in over the plums, pleating as you go around. The plums will be enclosed by the dough at the edges of the tart but not in the middle. Sprinkle the sugar over the plums and the dough.

4. Bake for 15 minutes at 425°F. Turn the heat down to 375°F and continue to bake for another 15 to 25 minutes, until the crust is nicely browned.

5. Remove from the oven and allow to cool slightly or completely before serving.

Advance preparation: The crust can be made in advance and frozen, either before or after rolling out. The plums can be prepared hours ahead of time. The baked tart will hold for several hours but eventually the crust will become soggy.

- PLUM TART IN PHYLLO PASTRY • Instead of the galette pastry, use commercial phyllo pastry. You will need 8 to 9 sheets, plus 3 tablespoons melted unsalted butter.

Layer the first six sheets in a 10- or 12-inch tart pan, overlapping the layers so that there is an overhang of phyllo all the way around the pan. Brush each layer lightly with butter before laying the next sheet of phyllo on top. Top with the bread crumbs, then the plums. Fold the overhanging layers in over the plums, and top with the remaining two or three sheets, brushing each sheet with butter. Push the edges of the dough into the sides of the pan. Prick in a couple of places with the tip of a knife so steam can escape. Bake for 30 minutes, or until crisp and browned. Allow to cool slightly or completely, and serve. If the phyllo dough loses its crispness, return to a 250° to 300°F oven for 20 to 30 minutes to crisp.

Frozen Yogurt

Frozen yogurt is extremely easy to make. It's best if you flavor it with a tart fruit such as strawberries, apricots, or plums, fruits whose acidity complements the acidity in the yogurt. If you routinely thicken your yogurt, you can make this in a flash. And it keeps very well in the freezer.

strawberry frozen yogurt

This is great to have on hand. The pureed strawberries must be strained to remove the little seeds, or the frozen yogurt won't have a smooth texture. **MAKES 3 CUPS, 6 SERVINGS**

1 pound strawberries, hulled
2 cups Yogurt Cheese (page 8)
⅔ cup superfine sugar

1. Puree the strawberries in a food processor fitted with the steel blade and push through a medium strainer into a bowl. Use the back of a spoon to force the puree through, and knock the strainer against the edge of the bowl to get out all the puree.

2. Combine the yogurt and sugar in the food processor or blender and blend together. Add the strawberry puree and blend well. Transfer to a container and freeze. For a smoother texture, blend once more in a food processor once the mixture is frozen.

3. Transfer to individual serving dishes or to a container, cover well, and freeze.

4. Let soften in the refrigerator for 15 minutes before serving.

Advance preparation: This will keep for 2 to 3 weeks in the freezer.

austrian chocolate cake (sacher torte)

Every cook needs a great chocolate cake in his or her repertoire. This one is a classic Austrian Sacher torte, a one-layer, intensely chocolate cake with a chocolate glaze poured over a thin coating of apricot jam. Use the best-quality chocolate you can get for this. **MAKES ONE 9- TO 10-INCH TORTE, 10 TO 12 SERVINGS**

6 large or extra-large eggs
1 cup unbleached all-purpose flour
5 ounces high-quality bittersweet chocolate
5 ounces (10 tablespoons) unsalted butter
1¼ cups confectioners' sugar
¼ teaspoon cream of tartar
½ cup apricot jam

GLAZE
4 ounces high-quality bittersweet chocolate
2 ounces (½ stick) unsalted butter
½ cup confectioners' sugar

1. Preheat the oven to 350°F. Butter and flour a 9- to 10-inch cake pan or springform pan.

2. Separate the eggs and let them come to room temperature. Sift the flour twice.

3. Break the chocolate into small pieces and cut the butter into small pieces. Combine in a heat-proof or microwave-safe bowl. Melt above simmering water, or in a microwave at 50 percent power for about 2 minutes. Stir to combine the chocolate and butter and set aside.

4. Beat together the egg yolks and 1 cup of the sugar until thick and lemon colored. Stir in the melted chocolate and butter. Gradually stir in the flour and combine well.

5. Beat the egg whites until they begin to foam. Add the cream of tartar and continue to beat until stiff but not dry. Beat in the remaining ¼ cup sugar. Stir one-fourth of the beaten egg whites into the batter to lighten it, then carefully fold in the rest. Turn into the prepared cake pan.

6. Bake for about 50 minutes, until firm, and a cake tester comes out clean.

7. Remove from the oven and allow to cool completely on a rack in the pan. When completely cool, level the cake by pushing down on the sides that have risen above the middle. Then unmold onto a large plate, platter, or cake round.

8. Spread the apricot jam in an even layer over the top.

9. Make the glaze. Melt the chocolate and butter together in a bowl over simmering water, or in a microwave at 50 percent power for about 2 minutes. Stir together well, then stir in 3 tablespoons water. Combine well, and stir in the confectioners' sugar. Strain and allow to cool to 90° to 92°F. Glaze the cake by pouring the icing over the top and quickly spreading it with an icing palette. It helps to place your plate on a larger platter or pan, which you can turn (and the pan will catch the drips). Keep at room temperature and do not cover.

Advance preparation: You can make this the day before you serve it. Keep it at room temperature. It will keep for a few days, and you can refrigerate it. But if you do, the icing won't remain shiny.

apricot frozen yogurt

The intense, slightly acidic flavor of apricots lends itself to frozen yogurt. A drop of almond extract adds a delicious dimension to this. **MAKES 4 CUPS, 8 SERVINGS**

2 pounds apricots,
   peeled and pitted
¼ teaspoon almond extract
2 tablespoons mild-flavored honey,
   such as clover or acacia
2 tablespoons fresh lemon juice
½ cup fresh orange juice
2 cups Yogurt Cheese (page 8)
½ cup superfine sugar

1. Peel the apricots by dropping them into a pot of boiling water for 30 seconds, then transferring to a bowl of ice-cold water and draining. Peel away the loosened skins. Cut in half and remove the pits.

2. Puree the apricots with the almond extract, honey, lemon juice, and orange juice in a food processor fitted with the steel blade or a blender; you should have about 2 cups puree. Add the yogurt and sugar to the food processor or blender and blend together. Transfer to a container and freeze. Blend once more in the food processor once the mixture is frozen.

3. Transfer to individual serving dishes or to a plastic container. Cover well and freeze.

4. Transfer to the refrigerator 15 minutes before serving.

Advance preparation: This will keep for 2 to 3 weeks in the freezer.

fruit tart in a meringue shell (pavlova)

Australians and New Zealanders both claim this as their invention. Whoever did invent it was brilliant. A huge meringue serves as a pastry shell here for whatever fruits strike your fancy. Tropical fruits like passion fruit are often found in Pavlovas down under. And, of course, kiwis. Choose whatever fruits you like, such as berries, sliced peaches, passion fruit; just make sure they're nice and sweet. **MAKES 6 TO 8 SERVINGS**

4 egg whites
1 teaspoon pure vanilla extract
1 teaspoon fresh lemon juice or ¼ teaspoon cream of tartar
¼ teaspoon salt
¾ cup sugar
1 cup heavy cream, whipped
3 kiwifruit, sliced
1 pint strawberries, sliced
¼ ripe pineapple, cored and thinly sliced

1. Preheat the oven to 250°F. Cover a baking sheet with foil and lightly spray the foil with oil.

2. Beat the egg whites until frothy and add the vanilla, lemon juice, and salt. Beat at high speed until soft peaks form. Gradually add the sugar and continue to beat until the egg whites are stiff and glossy.

3. Spoon the meringue mixture onto the foil-covered baking sheet. Make a circle about 9 inches in diameter, with a depression in the middle and sides about 1½ inches thick.

4. Bake for about 90 minutes, or until the meringue is crisp on the outside and firm to the touch. Turn off the heat and allow it to cool with the oven door propped open.

5. Place the meringue on an attractive serving platter. Fill the center with the whipped cream and top the cream with the fruit. Serve at once.

Advance preparation: If your climate is at all humid, the meringue will get soggy if made too far ahead. If it's dry in your home, then you can make the meringue a day or two ahead. Wrap in foil and keep at room temperature.

summer berry compote with vanilla ice cream

It's worth having a rose geranium plant just so you can perfume the syrup for these berries. The berries—raspberries and blueberries in this recipe, but you could also include red or black currants, blackberries, and strawberries—macerate in the warm syrup. I don't cook them because I want them to maintain their shape. Spooned over vanilla ice cream, this makes a heavenly dessert. **MAKES 4 SERVINGS**

1¼ cups sugar
2 sprigs rose geranium,
     with or without flowers
2 cups mixed fresh blueberries and raspberries
Vanilla ice cream

1. Combine the sugar and 1½ cups water in a saucepan and bring to a boil over medium heat. Drop in the sprigs of rose geranium, reduce the heat, and simmer for 2 minutes. Turn off the heat and allow the syrup to sit, undisturbed, for 2 hours. Remove the rose geranium.

2. Pour the syrup over the berries, cover, and let sit for 2 hours or longer, in or out of the refrigerator.

3. Serve over vanilla ice cream.

Advance preparation: The syrup will keep for several weeks in the refrigerator. The marinated berries will keep for a day or two, longer if you don't mind them losing their shape.

Index

noodles:

Asian, 218

Asian, with broccoli raab and mushrooms, 219–20

Malaysian, with greens and tofu, 216–17

see also pasta; soba

nuts, toasting of, 17

Olive(s):

grilled polenta with tomatoes, cauliflower and, 205

hearts of romaine with preserved lemon and, 54

orange, and onion salad, 58

pasta with fresh tomatoes, capers and, 212

pasta with tomatoes, cauliflower and, 204–5

olive oil pastry, yeasted, 108–9

omelet(s), 92

egg white, with beet greens or Swiss chard, 96

filled with leftovers, 95

fines herbes, 95

mushroom, 95

quick individual, flat or folded, 94–95

steamed broccoli or asparagus, 95

Swiss chard or spinach, 95

tomato, 95

onion(s):

frittata with red peppers, peas and, 99

orange, and olive salad, 58

and parsley frittata, 100

raw, soaking and rinsing of, 47

sweet, pizza with red pepper, ricotta, basil and, 225

and tomato frittata, 102

orange, onion, and olive salad, 58

oyster mushrooms, polenta with chipotles and, 152–53

Paprika, baked beans with mint and, 183–84

Parmesan, roasted asparagus with, 254

parsley, 34

and onion frittata, 100

parsnips:

kasha with, 147

and potatoes, mashed, with kale, 247

pasta:

with asparagus and gremolata, 207

with cherry tomatoes, feta, and herbs, 214

with creamy spinach sauce, 201

with fresh tomatoes, capers, and olives, 212

garlic soup with, 87

gratin, 215

green beans with tomatoes and garlic over, 237

with greens, 196–97

Italian, cooking of, 192–93

with kale and red peppers, 198–99

with mushrooms, sage, and rosemary, 202–3

quick, with tomato sauce, goat cheese, and green beans, 209

with roasted peppers and favas, 206

shells with zucchini, corn, beans, and tomato, 208

with spicy tomato sauce, 195

summer, with corn, tomatoes, and basil, 213

with tomatoes, olives, and cauliflower, 204–5

with tomato sauce, 194–95

with tomato sauce and a green vegetable, 195

with tomato sauce and chick-peas, 195

pastry:

dessert, 296–97

dessert galette, 286–87

phyllo, plum tart in, 307

yeasted butter, 110–11

yeasted olive oil, 108–9

pâté, white bean, 10–11

pâte sucrée, 296–97

pavlova, 313

pea(s):

basmati rice pilaf with Indian spices and, 162–63

black-eyed, *see* black-eyed peas

frittata with onions, red peppers and, 99

garlic soup with, 87

risotto with, 167

risotto with corn and, 170–71

soup, cream of, with mint, 88

sugar snap, garlic soup with, 87

peach:

cobbler with raspberries, 298–99

sorbet with raspberry garnish, 304

tart, free-form, 301

peanut sauce, 265

pear:

arugula, and walnut salad, 39

-vanilla compote, 305

pepper(s):

grilled, 4

grilled, and tomato salad, 48

roasted, 4

roasted, pasta with favas and, 206

see also red pepper(s)

phyllo pastry, plum tart in, 307

piecrust, Mediterranean, 106–7

pilaf:

basmati rice, with Indian spices and peas, 162–63

bulgur, with cumin and chick-peas, 141

rice, with chickpeas, 164

pizza, 222

dough, 223–24

with summer squash, goat cheese, and herbs, 226

with sweet onion, red pepper, ricotta, and basil, 225